THE SACRED IDENTITY
OF
EPHESOS

THE SACRED IDENTITY OF EPHESOS

Foundation Myths of a Roman City

Guy MacLean Rogers

London and New York

First published in 1991
by Routledge
11 New Fetter Lane, London EC4P 4EE

Simultaneously published in the USA and Canada
by Routledge
a division of Routledge, Chapman and Hall, Inc.
29 West 35th Street, New York, NY 10001

Typset in 10/12pt Bembo by
Columns Ltd, Reading
Printed in Great Britain by
T J Press (Padstow) Ltd, Padstow, Cornwall

British Library Cataloguing in Publication Data
Rogers, Guy MacLean
The sacred identity of Ephesos: foundation myths of a
Roman city.
1. Classical world. Cities
I. Title
307. 7640938

Library of Congress Cataloging in Publication Data
Rogers, Guy MacLean.
The sacred identity of Ephesos: foundation myths of a
Roman city
Guy MacLean Rogers.
p.   cm.
Includes bibliographical references and index.
1. Ephesus (Ancient city) – Religion. 2. Rome – Religion.
I. Title.
BL813.E64R64 1991
939'.23—dc20   90–46822

ISBN 0 415 05530 X

To the memory of my mother

Εἰς τοὺς αἰῶνας αὔξι, ἡ μεγάλη Ἐφεσίων πόλις

CONTENTS

FIGURES

ix

PREFACE

Dressed up in round felt hats, frilled shirts, and black corduroy trousers, my older brothers, Mark and Christopher, and I played the parts of pilgrim children in the 'Pageant of Ancient Woodbury' on 4 July 1959, at the Tercentenary Celebration of Woodbury Connecticut. In this Pageant, we showed how settlers from nearby Stratford, where the Puritan Church had split over issues of church membership, baptism, and discipline, bought land from the Pagasset Indians of Derby on 20 April 1659, and, under the leadership of the Reverend Zechariah Walker, established a plantation along the Pomperaug River at a place called Good Hill.

The message of the Pageant was simple, eloquent, and explicit: the descendants of the founders of Woodbury could look upon their landed possessions as having come to them by fair, honest, and legitimate titles. No violence, no conquest, no stain of blood 'attached to the hem of the garments of the town's forefathers'.

The children of Woodbury who took part in such plays during the late 1950s and early 1960s came away from these experiences with a special feeling for the topography and history of their town. In an isolated village of barely 4,000 souls, the festivals of Woodbury not only provided entertainment for everyone in the middle of hot, humid summers, but also gave the people of the town a firm sense of who we were, and where we came from, during a time of great change in the whole area of north-western Connecticut.

Beginning in the late 1950s, weekenders, summer people, and finally year-rounders built condominiums, then houses, and finally whole retirement villages in the woods and fields of Woodbury. This building brought in new money, transformed the map of the town, and finally required a larger government. In less than a decade, Woodbury changed from a sleepy farming town into a bedroom community for executives in Waterbury, Hartford, and even New York.

And yet, the celebrations of the town continued. The actors changed, but the festival script remained the same. The new residents of Woodbury took pride in the beautiful greens of the town, in the shining white churches along Main Street, and especially in the story of Woodbury's peaceful foundation. Meanwhile, the descendants of the founders learned how to live with and profit from their new neighbors. How and why a classical city could use *its* foundation myths as a source of inspiration, power, and compromise during a period of equally rapid change will be the abiding theme of this book. Before we turn to that classical foundation story, however, we should remember that a book, just like a foundation, usually needs the support of friends, colleagues, and institutions before it is ready for a wider audience. This study, which presents an interpretation of the foundation of C. Vibius Salutaris from Ephesos in AD 104, is no exception – except perhaps in the quality of the support I have been privileged to receive.

Fergus Millar, Camden Professor of Ancient History at Oxford University, suggested the general topic of research upon imperial Ephesos during a memorable undergraduate seminar at University College London in 1979. He also read the first draft of the text as a Princeton University doctoral dissertation on short notice in 1986, and made his usual incisive suggestions for improvement. I can never repay him for his support over the past decade, for his pointed Scottish humor, and for his company from the Ashmolean to the fields of Fenway. Most of all, however, I, and many others who attempt to approach his daunting standards of learning and production, owe him for the courage he quietly inspires – the courage to follow one's own ideas, to swim against the tides if necessary, to do the best work possible. His generosity of spirit is matched only by his enormous contribution to the field of Roman History.

Mary Lefkowitz, Mellon Professor in Humanities at Wellesley College, has read the entire book at least twice, and subjected it to her very sharp critical powers. Again and again Professor Lefkowitz has urged me to sacrifice to the Muses of clarity, precision, and grace. Under her exacting tutelage, I hope I have become at least an initiate, if not a full priest, of these demanding arts. If I am able to imitate Professor Lefkowitz's polished prose at all, the gain will be all my readers'.

Professor C. P. Jones of the University of Toronto read the penultimate version of the manuscript, and saved me from a number of embarrassing errors. I would like to thank him for his detailed comments, which rest upon a profound knowledge of Ephesian history, archaeology, and epigraphy. I should also like to express my gratitude to E. Varinlioğlu in Ankara, E. Champlin in Princeton, W. R. Connor in North Carolina, W. Eck in Köln, R. van Bremen, T. Cornell, A. Kuhrt, J. North, and the other members of the Ancient History Seminar at the Institute of Classical Studies in London, for their reactions to various versions of this work. I alone remain responsible for the ideas expressed within this book.

The American Philosophical Society, the oldest learned society in America, provided a grant which allowed me to visit the site of Ephesos during 1987–8. At the site, I was able to check over my translations of many inscriptions, to walk the sacred processional route of the city, and to reassess my interpretation of the Salutaris foundation. A Fellowship from the National Endowment for the Humanities for 1989–90 enabled me to spend a sabbatical year at Wolfson College Oxford, where I revised the manuscript into its final form, using the superb research resources of the Ashmolean Library. Without the generous support of these institutions, I would not have been able to complete my work on the Salutaris foundation.

Richard Stoneman, a Senior Editor at Routledge in London, offered wise advice and encouragement at every stage during the final revisions of the work, and patiently helped to turn a difficult manuscript into a book. Jayne Lewin, the cartographer for Routledge, expertly drew the fine maps of the site in AD 104 from my rough drawings.

My mother, however, who died on 2 August 1987, made by far the greatest contribution to this book. The example of her indomitable spirit in the face of death has inspired me to finish the work I began, not despite, but precisely because of those whose deeds, as Churchill once said, 'fell beneath the level of events'. I affirm her spirit with the completion of this book.

G. M. R.
Wolfson College Oxford
May 1990

ABBREVIATIONS OF FREQUENTLY CITED ARTICLES AND BOOKS

AJP	*American Journal of Philology* (Baltimore 1880–).
Alzinger (1962)	Alzinger, W. *Die Stadt des Siebenten Weltwunders* (Wien).
Alzinger (1974)	Alzinger, W. *Augusteische Architektur in Ephesos* (Wien).
ANRW	*Aufstieg und Niedergang der römischen Welt* (Berlin 1972–).
Anz.	*Anzeiger der Österreichischen Akademie der Wissenschaften* (Wien 1863–).
Arch. Anz.	*Archäologischer Anzeiger* (Berlin 1886–).
AS	*Anatolian Studies* (London 1960–).
Atkinson (1962)	Atkinson, K. 'The Constitutio of Vedius Pollio and its analogies', *Revue Internationale des Droits de l'Antiquité*, 3,9: 261–89.
Bammer (1984)	Bammer, A. *Das Heiligtum der Artemis von Ephesos* (Graz).
BCH	*Bulletin de Correspondance Hellénique* (Paris 1877–).
BE	*Bulletin Épigraphique*, published annually in *Revue des Études Grecques* (Paris 1888–).
Berger (1969)	Berger, P. *The Sacred Canopy* (New York).
CIG	Boeckh, A. *Corpus Inscriptionum Graecarum*, I–IV (Berlin 1828–77).
Davis (1981)	Davis, N. 'The Sacred and the Body Social in Sixteenth–Century Lyon', *Past and Present*, 90: 40–70.

Dörner (1978)	Şahin, S., Schwertheim, E. and Wagner, J. (eds.) *Studien zur Religion und Kultur Kleinasiens. Festschrift für Friedrich Karl Dörner zum 65. Geburtstag am 28. Februar 1976,* I and II (Leiden).
FiE	*Forschungen in Ephesos,* I–XI/1 (Wien 1906–89).
Geertz (1973)	Geertz, C. *The Interpretation of Cultures* (New York).
GRBS	*Greek, Roman and Byzantine Studies* (San Antonio 1958–).
Head (1964)	Head, B.V. *Catalogue of Greek Coins in the British Museum* (London).
Hicks (1890)	Hicks, E.L. *Ancient Greek Inscriptions in the British Museum,* III, 2 (Oxford).
Iasos	Blümel, W. *Die Inschriften von Iasos,* I and II (Bonn 1985).
IE	*Die Inschriften von Ephesos,* Ia–VIII,2 (Bonn 1979–84).
IGR	Cagnat, R. *Inscriptiones Graecae ad Res Romanas Pertinentes,* I (Paris 1911), III (1906), IV (1927).
Ilion	Frisch, P. *Die Inschriften von Ilion* (Bonn 1975).
ILS	Dessau, H. *Inscriptiones Latinae Selectae,* I–III,2 (Berlin 1892–1916).
Ist. Mitt.	*Mitteilungen des Deutschen Archäologischen Instituts, Abteilung Istanbul,* (Tübingen 1966–).
JÖAI	*Jahreshefte des Österreichischen Archäologischen Instituts* (Wien 1898–).
Jones (1983)	Jones, C.P. 'A Deed of Foundation from the Territory of Ephesos', *JRS,* 73: 116–25.
JRS	*Journal of Roman Studies* (London 1911–).
Keil (1955)	Keil, J. *Ephesos; ein Führer durch die Ruinenstätte und ihre Geschichte* (Wien).
Kenner (1985)	*Pro Arte Antiqua: Festschrift für Hedwig Kenner,* ed. W. Alzinger, I and II (Wien–Berlin 1982–5).

Laum, I, II (1914)   Laum, B. *Stiftungen in der griechischen und römischen Antike*, I and II (Leipzig).

Magie, I, II (1950)   Magie, D. *Roman Rule in Asia Minor*, I and II (Princeton).

Magnesia   Ihnken, T. *Die Inschriften von Magnesia am Sipylos* (Bonn 1978).

Melville Jones (1971)   Melville Jones, J. 'Denarii, Asses and Assaria in the Early Roman Empire', *Bulletin of the Institute of Classical Studies*, 18: 99–105.

Merkelbach (1979)   Merkelbach, R. 'Die ephesischen Monate in der Kaiserzeit', *ZPE*, 36: 157–62.

Muir (1981)   Muir, E. *Civic Ritual in Renaissance Venice* (Princeton).

OGIS   Dittenberger, W. *Orientis Graeci Inscriptiones Selectae*, I and II (Leipzig 1903–5).

Oliver (1941)   Oliver, J. *The Sacred Gerusia* (Baltimore).

Oliver (1953)   Oliver, J. *The Ruling Power: A Study of the Roman Empire in the Second Century After Christ Through the Roman Oration of Aelius Aristides* (Philadelphia): 963–5.

Oster (1987)   Oster, R. *A Bibliography of Ancient Ephesus* (Metuchen).

Picard (1922)   Picard, C. *Éphèse et Claros* (Paris).

Pleket (1970)   Pleket, H. 'Nine Greek Inscriptions from the Cayster valley in Lydia: A republication', *Talanta*, II: 55–82.

Price (1985)   Price, S. *Rituals and Power: The Roman Imperial Cult in Asia Minor* (Cambridge).

RAGW (1987)   *Roman Architecture in the Greek World* (London).

RE   *Real–Encyclopädie der classischen Altertumswissenschaft. Supplementband*, XII (Stuttgart 1970).

REA   *Revue des Études Anciennes* (Bordeaux 1899–).

Rev. Phil.	*Revue de Philologie* (Paris 1877–).
Rice (1983)	Rice, E. *The Grand Procession of Ptolemy Philadelphus* (Oxford).
Rossner (1974)	Rossner, M. 'Asiarchen und Archiereis Asias', *Studii Clasice*, XVI: 101–42.
SEG	*Supplementum epigraphicum graecum* (Leiden 1923–).
Sherwin-White (1984)	Sherwin-White, A. *Roman Foreign Policy in the East* (London).
Sylloge	Dittenberger, W. *Sylloge Inscriptionum Graecarum*, I–IV (Leipzig 1915–24).
TAPA	*Transactions of the American Philological Association* (Hartford 1869–).
Tralleis	Poljakov, F. *Die Inschriften von Tralleis und Nysa*, I (Bonn 1989).
Trexler (1974)	Trexler, R. 'Ritual in Florence: Adolescence and Salvation in the Renaissance', in *The Pursuit of Holiness in Late Medieval and Renaissance Religion*, eds. C. Trinkaus and H. Oberman (Leiden) 200–64.
Trexler (1983)	Trexler, R. 'Ritual Behavior in Renaissance Florence: The Setting', *Medievalia et Humanistica*, 34: 125–44.
Vermeule (1968)	Vermeule, C. *Roman Imperial Art in Greece and Asia Minor* (Cambridge).
Wood (1877)	Wood, J. *Discoveries at Ephesus* (London).
Wörrle (1988)	*Stadt und Fest im kaiserzeitlichen Kleinasien* (Munich).
ZPE	*Zeitschrift für Papyrologie und Epigraphik* (Bonn 1967–).

1

THE DISPLAY OF WRITING

At the ancient site of Ephesos, amidst the well-tended tombstones of Jews, Christians, and Muslims, a pile of grey marble slabs lies abandoned in a tangle of russet-colored weeds. Although trampled upon by barefooted pilgrims of three religions, the fragmentary lines inscribed on the slabs still speak to us faintly of a bequest made to the boule and demos of Ephesos in AD 104 by a wealthy Roman equestrian, C. Vibius Salutaris.

The stones tell us first about a yearly scheme of lotteries and distributions in the city, cash donations doled out to crowds of beneficiaries within the temple of Artemis, one of the seven wonders of the Hellenistic world. We see the beneficiaries mix in the temple with other Ephesians, their Ionian brothers and Greeks from around the Mediterranean world, who have come to celebrate the mysteries of Artemis, the annual re-enactment of the birth of the goddess Artemis at Ephesos. Citizens of Ephesos, dressed as Kuretes, priests originally attached to the Artemision, protect Leto from Hera, who jealously spies upon Leto giving birth to Artemis in the sacred grove of Ortygia. Some of Salutaris' lot-winners pray, others buy incense and animals for bloody sacrifices. The majority, however, clutch their bronze coins and watch the birthday party of Artemis unfold before their eyes.

The mute stones then bear testimony to a long procession of gold and silver statues carried through the streets of Ephesos by a train of young men. Artemis, the Roman emperor, Lysimachos, and Androklos march through the bustling marble streets of the city, beneath the windows of the wealthy along the street known as the Embolos. They pass in front of the shops of the merchants on their way into the Great Theatre, along a circular route,

1

repeated once every few weeks, which begins and ends at the temple of Artemis.

From these broken lines, this bequest, and these slices of public culture, this book reconstructs part of the conceptual world of Ephesos[1] during the early Roman empire. Such a reconstruction, based upon a series of fragmentary inscriptions, may raise the eyebrows of more than one ancient historian accustomed to building worlds upon literary texts. This response would be premature, if not surprising. For although the Salutaris foundation comprises one of the longest, most complex, and important foundation-deeds to have survived from the Roman world,[2] no historian has yet tried to study the content, purpose, and significance of the Salutaris foundation framed against the background of the city life of Ephesos at the beginning of the second century AD. Recent topographical studies and publication of the epigraphical corpus of the city now help provide this background for the first time.[3] When set within the context of the city life of Ephesos, as I shall try to show, the Salutaris foundation, essentially one monumental display of writing,[4] reveals that the past of Ephesos, most importantly, the story of the birth of Artemis at Ortygia, but also the Ionian foundation of Androklos, was very much alive in AD 104, and provided the members of the boule and the demos with a tangible source of power, to be wielded over the youth of the city, over new founders, and, at last, over new gods. At Ephesos in AD 104, the boule and demos did not merely pretend that the past was the present. The past, in certain ways, *was* the present.

EPHESOS IN ASIA FROM 133 BC UNTIL AD 104

The following narrative sketch of the history of the city within the Roman province is intended to provide only an immediate political background for beginning to understand how, and perhaps even why, the Hellenistic, Ionian, and sacred past of the city became the present at Ephesos in AD 104, at precisely the time when the imperial government at Rome had provided the necessary generations of peace and stability within the province of Asia which made the Ephesians' assertion of the Greek identity of their city in AD 104 possible.

The province of Asia was born the child of an heirless monarch. After the death of the last king of Pergamon, Attalos III, perhaps in September of 134 BC, the inhabitants of his kingdom discovered that the king, who lacked a legitimate heir, had named the Roman people as heir to all of his possessions in his last will.[5] These possessions included not only his private fortune, but all royal lands and subject cities. Not included were lands belonging to temples of gods and goddesses within the boundaries of the kingdom, and the city of Pergamon itself.

This royal will was brought to Rome by the spring of 133 BC, but the Senate did little more than appoint a commission of five senators to lay the foundation for the formation of the province during the rest of 133, and, quite possibly, most of 132 as well. During this time, the will became a source of political, and even armed contention both in Rome and Asia Minor.

At Rome, the tribune Tiberius Gracchus brought a bill before the assembly of the people which proposed to use the treasure of the Pergamene kings for the benefit of those to whom he had allotted land. He also planned to submit the question of the ultimate status of the cities included in the will before the assembly of the people. His violent death prevented these measures from being implemented, and it devolved upon the Senate to settle all questions relating to the will and the formation of the new Roman province.

Before the province could be formed, however, a certain Aristonikos, the illegitimate son of Eumenes, led a revolt against the terms of the bequest. During the war against Aristonikos, the Ephesians defeated the fleet of the pretender in a sea battle off Kyme,[6] but Manius Aquilius only crushed the last vestiges of the revolt before the end of 129/8 BC. Aquilius then set about organizing the new Roman province.

By 126 BC, Aquilius had divided up the land of the new province, which comprised a territory largely restricted to the western districts of the former kingdom,[7] into a series of conventus or assize districts, each with a city center where the governor would hold court days and listen to petitions.[8] Ephesos, while technically a free city,[9] as it had been under Pergamene rule probably since 167 BC, was one of the original assize centers of the province designated by Aquilius, and remained a conventus center of the province from the late Republic (c. 56–50 BC) well into the third century AD. Along with the occasional presence of the governor (perhaps more frequently at Ephesos than elsewhere), assize status over these centuries brought with it various legal privileges in the form of exemptions and, perhaps more importantly, inherent economic benefits derived from the arrival of large numbers of litigants with their advisors, friends, and followers into the designated cities.[10]

At the end of the second century BC, the report of a dispute over revenues claimed by the tax-collectors, known as the publicani, and officials of the temple of Artemis at Ephesos, perhaps sheds some light on the evolving relationship between Ephesos and the imperial government twenty years or so after the formation of the province. In 104 BC the Ephesians sent the famous geographer Artemidoros to the Senate in Rome to protest about the publicani forcibly converting revenues from lakes designated as sacred (at the mouth of the Kaystros River which flowed into the harbor of the city) for their own use.[11] The success of the embassy in this instance – the publicani were ordered to keep their hands off the sacred lakes of Artemis – may be attributed either to the persuasive speech of Artemidoros, or perhaps to the influence of sympathetic listeners at Rome, including the powerful Q. Mucius Scaevola, who knew Asia well. In either case, the Ephesians' success demonstrates the critical importance of personal ability and contacts for the Greek cities of Asia within a Roman administrative system which succeeded in the long run largely because it attempted to do so little – maintain law and order and collect taxes – and depended so much upon local initiative.

The episode also neatly symbolizes the attempt of agents of the publicani throughout the province of Asia to tax all the land to which they might conceivably assert any claim whatsoever; particularly during the last years of the Roman Republic, the publicani tried to impose taxes upon the lands of the free cities and the estates of temples. Only the more settled political conditions of the principate, when political rivalries at Rome no longer were fueled by fortunes acquired during oppressive governorships abroad, and the severe scrutiny of the emperor often acted as a kind of pre-emptive guarantee of fair dealing on the part of the tax-collectors, would bring relief from such attempts by the publicani.

Indeed, the record of the performance of the Republican governors of the province of Asia was decidedly mixed. Quintus Mucius Scaevola, who probably governed the province of Asia in 94/3 BC, perhaps made the greatest impact upon the office itself, and certainly created a very positive impression among some provincials. When Scaevola entered upon his office, he issued an edict, or statement of principles, to be followed while he was in office, which served as a blueprint for future governors beginning their offices.[12]

From the point of view of the Greeks of Asia, the most important clause of the edict related to their freedom. According to Cicero, Scaevola stipulated that Greek cases were to be settled according to Greek law.[13] That Scaevola followed the spirit of his own edict in this area of administration can be seen through the agreement he negotiated between the cities of Sardeis and Ephesos.[14] By the terms of this agreement, the cities compacted that wrongs suffered by a citizen of one of the two cities should be tried in the court of the defendant, that they should refrain from making war upon each other, or giving aid to each other's enemies, and that they should submit all matters of dispute to a neutral city.

Although to some historians Scaevola's negotiation between Sardeis and Ephesos has seemed to constitute interference in the inter-city affairs of free cities, the cities themselves have left no record of such an objection; indeed, in gratitude for Scaevola's performance as governor of the province, 'the peoples and tribes, as well as persons individually received in friendship with Rome', established a festival in honor of Scaevola to be celebrated every four years.[15] Some scholars have seen the organization founded to celebrate this festival as the basis for the subsequently well-attested koinon of Asia, which later would serve as an official intermediary for communications between the cities of Asia and Rome and, perhaps most importantly, would undertake supervision of the cult of Roma and Augustus, the foundation of the imperial cult.[16]

Not all of the Republican governors after Mucius Scaevola and his legate Publius Rutilius Rufus, however, successfully balanced the interests of the provincials and the Roman businessmen. In fact, only five years after the governorship of Scaevola, the greed of the publicani, Roman bankers, and merchants in Asia furnished at least the mob in Ephesos with a very good reason, or excuse, for welcoming Mithridates VI of Pontos into their city as a deliverer. We can measure the intensity of Ephesian, if not provincial, hostility to the Romans living among them, by recalling that the Ephesians first overthrew the Roman statues in their city, and in 88 BC took full, and even exuberant, part in the massacre of all Romans and Italians in Asia, including freedmen, women, and children.[17] The Ephesians went so far as to tear Italian fugitives away from images of Artemis and slaughter them on the spot.[18] Mithridates, in fact, issued the massacre order from Ephesos and, during his stay in the city, gained the support of the priests of the Artemision at least, by shooting an arrow from the roof of the temple of Artemis, and then granting to the sanctuary the right of inviolability as far as the arrow fell.[19]

By 86 BC, Mithridates had left the city, and placed it under the rule of Philopoemen of Stratonikeia, who was the father of Mithridates' latest wife, Monime. Mithridates' actions against other cities, such as Chios, during this time, alarmed the Ephesians, who eventually executed Zenobios, another one of Mithridates' commanders. Having broken with the king by this act, the Ephesians quickly passed a decree declaring war on Mithridates on behalf of Roman rule and common freedom.[20]

Although the Ephesians (as well as dwellers of other cities in Asia) maintained that they had submitted to Mithridates only out of fear, Sulla, the general sent out from Rome to drive Mithridates out of Asia, did not accept their excuses. Along with the rest of the cities which had received enemies of Rome, and massacred Roman citizens in 88 BC, Ephesos was deprived of its freedom in 84 BC, and shared fully in the fine of 20,000 talents, which probably covered taxes for the previous five years as well as the costs of the war.[21] Appian also informs us that Sulla punished the Ephesians especially severely because they had treated the Roman offerings in their temples with indignity.

The results of these measures for Ephesos and the province were disastrous: Ephesos would not recover its freedom until c. 47 BC, and Sulla's exactions ruined both formerly free cities and subject cities. The political weakness of the cities of Asia in Sulla's wake left them prey to the depredations of the publicani, whose opportunities for exploitation increased vastly with the loss of independence suffered by many cities after the first Mithridatic war. At the same time, the pirates in the eastern Mediterranean disrupted trade along the entire coast of Asia Minor. Nor did Sulla's successors in the province, including Murena, Marcus Minucius Thermus, and Caius Claudius Nero, the last especially through his acquiescence in the execution of Philodamos of Lampsakos and his son, held responsible for the death of the notorious Verres' lictor, assist the impoverished province.

Partial recovery came to the western edges of the province only after Pompey's victory over the pirates at Korakesion off Kilikia in 67 BC cleared the eastern Aegean of that particular menace, and allowed Ephesos and the other ports of Asia Minor to pursue their trading interests across the Mediterranean without fear. Six years after Pompey left Asia Minor, or by 57/56 BC at any rate, perhaps in order to lighten the responsibilities of the governor, the three dioceses of which Phrygia consisted, Kibyra-Laodiceia, Apameia, and Synnada, were taken from Asia and transferred to Kilikia – only to be returned to Asia during the governorship of Gaius Fannius in 49 BC.

When Caesar and Pompey embarked upon the civil war in 49 BC which would eventually destroy the Roman Republic, the city of Ephesos and most of Asia Minor remained at peace. After the decisive defeat of Pompey at Pharsalus, Caesar came to Ephesos in the late summer of 48 BC, and received the ambassadors of the Ionians, Aeolians, and other peoples of lower Asia.[22] During his few weeks in the city, perhaps to the surprise of many provincials, Caesar remitted one-third of the tax Asia had previously paid, abolished the old method of collecting direct taxes in the province through contracts let out to corporations of publicani, and replaced it with a system by which amounts raised by the communities themselves were paid to a quaestor or financial official of the province. The cities, peoples, and tribes of Asia subsequently honored Caesar with a statue at Ephesos, which praised him as 'the descendant of Ares and Aphrodite, a god made manifest and the common saviour of human life'.[23] It was probably also at this time that Pamphylia, along with a portion of the mountain region of Milyas and Pisidia, was added to the province of Asia.

After the defeat of Brutus and Cassius, the assassins of Caesar, at Philippi, Antony in turn came to Ephesos in 41 BC, greeted by women dressed as Bacchants, and men and boys as Satyrs and Pans.[24] At Ephesos, Antony assembled the Greeks and other tribes around Pergamon, and settled upon nine years' taxes payable in two years as the punishment for their support of Brutus and Cassius.[25] Exceeding the demands even of his greedy predecessors, Antony demanded payments not only from the free and subject cities, but also from client kings and minor rulers as well. As partial compensation for the co-operation of the priests of the Artemision, Antony doubled the area of asylum surrounding the temple, which therefore included a section of the city itself.[26] This was an invitation to civil discord which the Roman emperors would find necessary to rectify.

During the final stages of the struggle between Antony and Octavian, Antony and Kleopatra spent the winter of 33/32 BC in the city, joined there by 300 Roman senators and a huge fleet of over 500 warships.[27] After the crucial defeat of Antony at Actium in 31 BC, according to the historian Cassius Dio, Octavian punished the cities in Asia which had aided his opponent by levying payments of money and suspending their governmental assemblies.[28] The inscriptional record indicates, however, that many cities also had benefits conferred upon them in the aftermath of Actium, and Ephesos itself apparently remained at least nominally free. We can see further evidence of Octavian's concern for the welfare of the Greek cities in his order that an issue of gold and silver coins commence at Ephesos and Pergamon in 29 BC, a measure undertaken, no doubt, to help improve the economic situation in Asia, which had suffered from exactions of Roman tax-collectors, governors, and generals since at least the time of Sulla.

Two years later, in January 27 BC, when Octavian 'restored' the *Res Publica* to the Roman people, the province of Asia reverted to being one of the *provinciae populi Romani*, governed by proconsuls appointed by lot.[29] The governorship of this wealthy, if troubled, province thereafter became the apex of the senatorial career under the empire, and many able and later famous men, including the father of the future emperor Trajan, were to hold the post during the first and second centuries AD.

The symbolic importance of Octavian in the eyes of the inhabitants of Bithynia and Asia, even before the division of the senatorial and imperial provinces, can be seen in the development of the imperial cult. Besides attending to the other administrative business at hand in 29 BC, Octavian gave permission for the dedication of sacred precincts in Ephesos and Nikaia to Rome and Caesar, and commanded that the Romans resident in the cities should pay honor to these two deities. He also permitted the Greeks to consecrate precincts to himself, the Asians to have theirs at Pergamon and the Bithynians at Nikomedeia.[30]

Responsibility for maintenance of the cult of the emperor fell upon the koinon of the Hellenes, which had already conferred honors upon Scaevola, and had served as an intermediary between the cities of Asia and the Roman government. Indeed, from the foundation of the imperial cult, the koinon held annual meetings for the worship of the new deities and for the transaction of business by its deputies. Member cities chose representatives up to three, according to the size of the city. The koinon also celebrated a festival with a sacred contest each year in honor of the deities called the Romaia Sebasta. The principal official of the cult was known as the chief priest of Asia, and was chosen annually at the meeting of the assembly for a one-year term. The primary function of this office was to conduct the worship of the divinities, although the chief priest also brought proposals before the assembly, arranged for the execution of its enactments, and might also serve as agonothete or supervisor of the koinon's festivals.

The activities of the koinon, however, were not confined to management of the imperial cult. In 9 BC, the koinon enacted a decree by which member cities adopted a new calendar proposed by the proconsul, although Ephesos chose to retain its old Ionian calendar well into the second century. Later, the koinon sent embassies to Rome to watch over the interests of Asia in the capital, and in AD 22, the koinon presented charges against Roman officials who had abused their power in the province.

Thus the koinon gradually assumed a position of dealing with the Roman government in a corporate capacity on behalf of the province. This assumption of responsibility in turn led to the creation of a new provincial nobility, since the city representatives developed many contacts with the imperial administration. Furthermore, the sons of the chief priests were admitted to the equestrian order, and their sons sometimes became members of the Senate. By such methods were Asian aristocrats integrated into the ruling class of the empire.

An Augusteum was probably already in place within the temenos, or sacred precinct of the Artemision by 6/5 BC, and Ephesos gradually supplanted Pergamon as the focus of religious, economic, and political activity in the province.[31] Augustus, in fact, seems to have devoted special care to the cult of Artemis, first by nullifying Antony's extension of the area of asylum of the temple,[32] and then by at least allowing the transfer of the college of priests known as the Kuretes, whose responsibility it was to celebrate the mysteries of Artemis, from the Artemision to the new prytaneion in the Upper City.

During the summer of 20 BC, while on an inspection tour of the eastern provinces, Augustus restored some revenues to Artemis which were generated from lands in the plain of the Kaystros River just north-east of the city.[33] The concern of the imperial family was not, however, limited to a single cult in the city, especially if the activities of cult members were potentially divisive. We can see this most clearly in the case of the treatment of the Jewish community at Ephesos. In 14 BC, Agrippa wrote to the boule and demos of Ephesos, perhaps at the instigation of Herod of Judaea, and ordered that the care of the money contributed by Jews to the temple in Jerusalem should be left in Jewish hands, and that no Jew should be required to appear in court on the Sabbath.[34] The sensitivity of the Roman government to the problems of the Jewish community at Ephesos, especially attempts by the Greeks at Ephesos to lay their hands upon the temple tax or question Jewish exemptions, stands in marked contrast to the activities of some of the governors in Judaea itself during the first century. Nevertheless, the conflict between the Jewish and Greek communities over questions of citizenship at Ephesos, which dated back into the Hellenistic period, continued well into the second century AD.

When Augustus died on 19 August AD 14 his reign had provided exactly the peace and administrative stability which Ephesos required to assume that position of prominence in the eastern Mediterranean which its fine geographical position had always promised.

The great earthquake of AD 17, which leveled many cities in Asia, apparently did not substantially damage the city of Ephesos, although the city does appear in a list of cities of Asia which thanked the emperor Tiberius after the catastrophe.[35] Following this incident, in AD 23 Ephesos competed, along with eleven other cities in the province, for the privilege of erecting a temple dedicated to Tiberius.[36] The Roman Senate turned down the argument of the Ephesians on the grounds that the city already concentrated its civic worship upon the cult of Artemis. In the end, Smyrna received permission to build the temple. This episode indicates how intensely the cities of the province often competed over such issues as the size of asylum areas of temples, the construction of imperial temples, and honorific titles granted to the cities by the Roman government during the first through third centuries AD. These struggles were not simply sterile contests over empty titles and privileges. The existence of an imperial temple in a city, for example, could bring many pilgrims to a city during imperial festivals, and these pilgrims would have to purchase materials for sacrifice, including animals and incense. Sometimes costly dedicatory statues or statuettes were bought as well. The competition over titles and offices and buildings among the cities of Asia not only brought increased status within the greater Roman world, but promised immediate economic rewards for the winners.

We can see this intersection of economic self-interest, religious belief, and practical politics very clearly again during the reign of Claudius. Around AD 44, the proconsul of Asia, Paullus Fabius Persicus, issued an edict intended to stop the sale of priesthoods by public officials at Ephesos.[37] City officials apparently had auctioned off these priesthoods to the highest bidders, who not only received the perquisites of the office in return, but were allowed to borrow from the temple revenues in addition. The proconsul probably discharged these priests from office, and the city was instructed to pay back the priests' bids on their offices at 1 per cent of the price paid. He further prohibited priests or members of the town council from giving or receiving money in connection with the sales. Perhaps most importantly, Persicus established that loans negotiated by a public official had to be repaid out of the current year's revenues, and funds earmarked for endowments had to be invested properly, with no diversions for other purposes.

Most of Persicus' measures were directed toward Ephesian attempts to raise money through sales or loans which, should the fortunes of the people who borrowed money from temple revenues falter, might ultimately lead to the bankruptcy of the temple of Artemis. If the temple of Artemis went bankrupt, the consequences for the city and the province would be financially disastrous, since the temple also functioned as a kind of bank for the province. The Roman government could not let this occur, even if it meant direct interference in the internal affairs of Ephesos. Persicus' intervention into the financial affairs of the city was based upon his stated obligation to make provision for the welfare, both of the province and the cities in it for all time, but the tacit priority was Roman self-interest. This aggressive Roman policy of scrutinizing the finances of Ephesos, which were intimately connected with the cults of the city, was a clear harbinger of further Roman action, two generations before Pliny embarked upon his special office in Pontos and Bithynia.

It was also during the reign of the emperor Claudius that the Apostle Paul spent two full years in the city of Ephesos, and caused the famous riot of the silversmiths led by Demetrios. This incident, which, following the account of the author of the *Acts of the Apostles* 19.23–41, has generally been interpreted in light of the economic threat to the livelihood of the silversmiths that Paul posed, perhaps would be understood more clearly against the background of the aforementioned debate over Jewish civic status within the Greek cities of the province. Paul's message that gods made by human hands were not gods at all, presented an immediate threat to the peace and security of the Jewish community at Ephesos, which had lived for centuries on the razor's edge of pagan tolerance. We should also not forget that during the riot, the Jews of the city put forward a certain Alexandros, to make an apology to the Greeks of Ephesos. No doubt Alexandros attempted to disassociate the Jewish community of Ephesos from both the words and deeds of Paul, a Jew from Tarsos.[38]

Paul's success in spreading the news of the resurrection throughout the province – a success which cannot be quantified – must be set against the less well publicized expansion and growth of the imperial cult, to which the establishment of the worship of Claudius in Kos and Prusa at least gave further impetus.[39] At the same time, from the numerous instances of the name Klaudioi found in the inscriptions of the province, we can assume that many natives of Asia gained citizenship during the rule of Claudius. Further, the creation of a new tribe named Sebaste at Ephesos, as well as subdivisions of the tribes called chiliastyes, with names such as Kaisarion, Tiberion, and Klaudion, provides clear evidence, not only of how much goodwill there was directed toward the various Julio-Claudian emperors, but, more importantly, of the extent to which Roman terms and categories had penetrated the defining nomenclature of citizen status at Ephesos. Alongside the more familiar expansion of Roman citizenship, and the increased opportunities for promotion in the imperial administration for natives of Asia, whether through the equestrian or senatorial orders, which scholars have detailed,[40] discovering ever more senators at even earlier dates, came what can only be called a Romanization of local citizenship and offices. At Ephesos, a tribal affiliation named after a Roman emperor, and service in imperial priesthoods, became part of the local cursus, and appeared as such on honorary inscriptions, dedications, and tombstones.

Roman worries about the financial affairs of the province come into sharp focus again during the reign of Nero. The proconsul Barea Soranus dredged the harbor of Ephesos, no doubt in an effort to help relieve the silting from the Kaystros River. For his troubles, his enemies later accused him of popularity hunting in the province, with a view toward winning Asia for the cause of revolution.[41]

During the same period (c. 54 to 59 AD), the Ephesians erected a fishery toll-house at the harbor, apparently built through the efforts of private subscribers.[42] Finally, from 8 July AD 62, we have a long (unpublished) text, which shows that a reorganization of the customs of Asia took place, the record of which was posted at the Artemision. Thus the city of Ephesos and the province in general survived, and even prospered during the reigns of the Julio-Claudians, safely removed from most of the court intrigues and treason trials at Rome.

Further centralization and prosperity marked the impact of the Flavian dynasty upon the province of Asia. The transference of the collection of indirect taxes from agents of the publicani to government officials with the title of promagister has often been attributed to the reign of Vespasian.[43] At the same time, the office of the procurator increased in importance, which suggests greater control of the province by the emperor himself. The appointment of Eprius Marcellus, the prosecutor of Thrasea Paetus during the reign of Nero, to the proconsulship of Asia per triennium also indicates imperial encroachment upon the public province.

Vespasian also pursued a policy of developing urban centers and improving communications between them, through the improvement or construction of roads. Ephesos profited directly from this policy by being located on the route of a new road constructed in AD 75, which ran from Pergamon southward along the coast to Smyrna through Ephesos to Thyateira and Sardeis. As a result of these and other benefactions, it is probable that a temple of the Augusti was erected at Ephesos by the province of Asia during the reign of Vespasian. This temple was later dedicated to Domitian among others, and then rededicated after Domitian suffered damnatio memoriae.

The unfavorable portrait of Domitian which we find in contemporary sources, in fact, should not bias our evaluation of his provincial administration in Asia. On the whole, Domitian kept a tight grip on governors in Asia, and this ensured both honesty and a degree of justice in the province. The execution of Civica Cerialis, proconsul of Asia around AD 84, on a charge of conspiracy, perhaps served as a more general warning to those who might consider oppressing the provincials.

Domitian also hastened the process whereby talented natives of Asia, such as Julius Quadratus and Celsus Polemaeanus from Sardeis, the dedicatee of the library at Ephesos, advanced through the imperial administration: Celsus was adlected into the Senate under Vespasian, became suffect consul in AD 92 under Domitian, and finally was proconsul of Asia in 105/106 during the reign of Trajan.[44]

The gigantic statue of Domitian placed within the temple of the Augusti at Ephesos gives some evidence that the province was not totally ungrateful for the benefits the emperor bestowed at least upon the upper classes. Indeed, Domitian's reign, and that of the Flavian dynasty in general, saw a period of great urban growth and architectural development in the cities of Asia, matched only by what had occurred during the reign of Augustus.

When Domitian died on 18 September AD 96, Ephesos acted quickly to erase his name from all public monuments following the official decree of the Roman Senate. Such a show of solidarity with the Senate could not as easily erase the tangible debts of the city and the province to the emperor whose reign brought Ephesos to the point where it 'had increased in size beyond all the cities of Ionia and Lydia and, having outgrown the land on which it was built, had advanced into the sea'.[45] At the beginning of the second century, during the years when Salutaris perhaps first conceived the idea of his great foundation, the city of Ephesos had become the most prosperous and important Greek city in the eastern Roman empire.

Thus Ephesos, and the province of Asia, eventually found peace and prosperity under Roman rule – but only after both had shared fully in the prolonged political crisis which we call the fall of the Roman Republic. In the beginning, the Roman Senate, on behalf of the Populus Romanus, but really for its own interests, had put into place all of the ingredients which were essential to their own peaceful exploitation of the province: an administrative system of free and subject cities with direct and indirect taxes and courts assigned accordingly, a governor and a small staff with defined powers and limited duration of office, the conventus centers, and at least the threat of Roman arms to back up these arrangements. From the provincial point of view, however, these ingredients alone could not guarantee either peace or prosperity, for too much still depended upon the ability and character of individual Roman governors, tax-collectors, and soldiers, all of whom could not, and did not wish to, escape from the demands of politics at home. Thus Asia during the late Republic became a place where ambitious governors might make a fortune to buy an election – or perhaps pay for one in the past. Many governors turned a blind eye to the excesses of the publicani, or colluded. If the provincials brought their grievances to Roman tribunals, the politicized courts at Rome usually voted in favor of their colleagues, friends, and kinsmen rather than their subjects.

Roman exploitation thus encouraged the cities of the province to seek alternative masters, including Mithridates. In his disastrous wake, the fierce competition of the great Roman dynasts brought alternatively fortune or disaster to individual cities, which placed their political bets according to affection or compulsion, but stability to none.

The defeat of Antony and Kleopatra at Actium gave the province of Asia a second life. The framework of administering the province was not radically altered; in theory, Asia was given back to the Roman people, and the governor still went around the conventus centers with his small staff, supplemented at times by a few imperial appointees, who were usually financial officials of some kind. Roman soldiers became a relatively rare sight. But the application of government, especially the collection of taxes, was regularized, and, most importantly, all accounts suddenly were rendered to one man.

Centralization of power, therefore, may have helped to destroy the old senatorial aristocracy, but it also gave birth to an era of unprecedented economic prosperity for the cities of Asia. The pace and scale of monumental building within the old cities of Ionia during the early empire is perhaps only the most enduring evidence of a prosperity which may well help to explain the rapid growth of the imperial cult in Asia as well. Along with this prosperity came vastly increased opportunities for participation in the imperial system of government at every level for the provincials – as Roman citizens, as equestrians, as senators. Clearly, large numbers of Asians aspired to, and took advantage of, these opportunities. The success of the talented, the well-connected, or the lucky within the imperial administration, in turn, was advertised on thousands of honorary inscriptions put up in the cities of Asia, which not only satisfied the vanity of honorands, but also set out an ideal of service to be imitated or admired by social and economic inferiors.

The study of such historical trends, which ancient historians have rightly seen as resulting in the emergence of a fully Mediterranean ruling class in place of a strictly Roman or Italian elite, may, at the same time, disguise, in some sense, how precisely such opportunities to participate in the Roman system of citizenship and government must have raised crucial questions of religious, social, and historical identity, especially among those very provincials, such as Salutaris, who took greatest advantage of the system.

THE FOUNDER

The man behind this foundation largely remains a shadow; at the end of the day, we know him better through his foundation than his cursus. Nevertheless, evidence provided in his foundation and a series of honorary inscriptions on statue bases dedicated at Ephesos between AD 104 and 107/108 or 109/110 allows us to reconstruct an outline of his family background, his career, and some of his activities and friends at Ephesos before the foundation of AD 104.[46] Problems of chronology and interpretation persist even within this outline, but do not seriously affect either our overall conclusions about his life or our interpretation of his foundation.

C. Vibius Salutaris was born a Roman citizen and a member of the equestrian order.[47] His family, which perhaps was connected with the organization of Roman businessmen at Ephesos, conferred distinction upon him;[48] the character of his father apparently was well known within the city in AD 104.[49] Salutaris and perhaps his family owned estates near Ephesos, which were generating interest in AD 104.[50] He had living heirs at the time of the foundation, but probably no son, and he survived until at least A.D 107/108.[51]

Although all of the honorary inscriptions which describe

Salutaris' cursus give the same offices in the same order, the rarity and configuration of the offices he held within the imperial administration must make conclusions about his career tentative. The offices detailed in the inscriptions recording his career begin with the unusual post of promagister which should mean, not a public office, but a post as local manager in a company of tax-collectors. He probably served his promagistracies in Sicily during the early eighties AD, first as *promagister portuum provinciae Siciliae*, where he collected the port taxes of Sicily. His second promagistracy, in the same province, as *promagister frumenti mancipalis*, or perhaps supervisor 'of the collection of the rent in kind from the ager publicus',[52] reveals personal interest and (no doubt) competence in the general area of tax collection. It was surely no accident that Salutaris began his career as a financial expert in a Greek-speaking province.

Next, an overlooked passage in the foundation itself suggests that Salutaris' military service and subprocuratorships occurred either wholly during the reign of the emperor Domitian, or perhaps during the reigns of Domitian and Trajan.[53] Salutaris probably became *praefectus* of *cohors Asturum et Callaecorum* (prefect of the cohort of the Astures and Gallacei) in Mauretania Tingitana around AD 85, at a time when the province was highly militarized.[54] This military duty implies some capacity for leadership and knowledge of Latin. His military tribunate, in *legio XXII Primigenia Pia Fidelis Domitiana*, stationed at Moguntiacum (Mainz), took place after the revolt of Saturninus in AD 89 and before AD 96, when the epithet of the legio, Domitiana, was removed.[55] There is no evidence that he went on to become the *praefectus* of an *ala* of cavalry. Therefore, Salutaris never completed his equestrian military career and his service record looks, at best, ordinary.

He then became subprocurator of Mauretania Tingitana around AD 93. Subprocurators were extraordinary appointees for particular tasks.[56] Thus Salutaris returned to the same region where he held his military tribunate. The honorary inscriptions do not reveal his duties as a subprocurator, although these probably were financial. Not much more can be asserted confidently about Salutaris' subprocuratorship of Belgica. The office must have been held near the end of the reign of Domitian. There is no evidence of family connections in the area, and no information about where he may have lived, or what he did in the province.

Before AD 104, Salutaris conferred benefactions upon the city of Ephesos, where he was both a citizen and a member of the boule.[57] In AD 104, he sought out the confirmation and sanction of the proconsul and his legate for his foundation, and also chose where the decree of the demos should be incised.[58] His choices – which I will discuss later – reveal a strong desire for self-advertisement.

His friends included C. Aquillius Proculus, the proconsul of Asia in AD 103/104, and the legate from the same year, P. Afranius Flavianus.[59] A recognition of common interests, if not genuine affection, is likely at least in the case of Flavianus. The Ephesians also made Flavianus, destined for a career which would lead ultimately to the proconsulship of Asia, possibly in AD 130/131, a citizen.[60] Thus Salutaris could rely personally upon the two highest ranking Roman officials in the province to support, ratify, and sanction his foundation. But Salutaris made other friends with brilliant careers – and important connections.

L. Nonius Calpurnius Torquatus Asprenas, the son of the legate of Galatia and Pamphylia under Galba, possibly became proconsul of Asia in AD 107/108;[61] a dedication from Salutaris to his 'best friend' Torquatus dates from that year.[62] The inscription proves that Salutaris survived until at least AD 107/108, and the existence of a friend from a famous family, the Nonii Asprenates, twice a consul ordinarius, perhaps close to the imperial ear, enhances our estimation of Salutaris' access to the center of power.

Finally, Salutaris declared M. Arruntius Claudianus a 'friend and personal benefactor'.[63] What Arruntius, the man from Xanthos with the double career, first equestrian, then senatorial, did for Salutaris and when, we cannot know. His name, M. Arruntius M. F. Teretina Claudianus, implies that his father received citizenship, name and tribe under the imperial procurator M. Arruntius Aquila, procurator of Pamphylia in AD 50.[64] He belonged first to the equestrian order, and his career took place under Domitian; the absence of a mention of Domitian under his military honors strengthens the case. Salutaris put up the inscription for his friend after AD 96. The earlier, equestrian career of Arruntius perhaps provides our closest chronological parallel to the career of Salutaris.

Therefore, it is difficult to assess the career of Salutaris. He served twice in Sicily, twice in North Africa, and twice in Belgica – but nowhere else. His subprocuratorships either are otherwise unattested or *were* unique. He did not complete the *tres militiae equestres*, the three junior rungs of the equestrian military career. Salutaris evidently was no soldier. While his career appears to have been relatively limited in scope (as far as we are able to assess it), the geographical range of his offices, from Sicily to North Africa to Belgica, does at least give some indication of the considerable integration of the administration of the empire. The talents of the man were probably financial; a tax expert, comfortable in Greek, with important friends emerges. His dual citizenship, both Ephesian and Roman, was in no way extra-ordinary in this world, where men could be citizens of a Greek city and Rome, or many Greek cities simultaneously. Parallel examples, such as the Apostle Paul, who was a citizen of Tarsos and Rome, and happened also to be Jewish, abound. Nor was Roman citizenship incompatible with very active local patriotism: as we shall discover, it was precisely the men who had served the Roman government throughout the Mediterranean world who were responsible for the architectural transformation of Ephesos at the end of the first century AD. The local patriotism of Roman citizens throughout the eastern Roman empire was, in fact, one of the most important reasons why the cities of the East, from Athens to Alexandria, flourished under Roman imperial rule. To the honor roll of these local Roman patriots, we should add the name of Salutaris – who chose not to adorn his city with a new bath or gymnasium, but expressed his love of Ephesos and Rome through the creation of a grand lottery and procession.

TEXT AND CONTEXT

If prosopographers have struggled to reconstruct the career of Salutaris, editors have labored no less hard to restore the text of his foundation. Thus, since J. T. Wood discovered the series of documents inscribed on the 'eastern wall' of the southern entrance to the Great Theatre at Ephesos in February of 1866, E. L. Hicks, R. Heberdey, and H. Wankel, aided by the many linguistic repetitions in the foundation, have contributed decisively to the restoration of the fragmentary text.[65] The *lacunae* which remain do not obscure the reading of the main provisions of the foundation, largely because of the heroic efforts of R. Heberdey in 1912.[66] A Greek text of the main body of the Salutaris foundation, with a facing English translation, is printed as Appendix I, on p. 152.[67]

But while epigraphists have expended much time and effort upon the restoration of this long and difficult text, they have seldom paused to ask any of the functional questions about the role of the inscription in the life of the city, which may be just as important for our interpretation of the foundation, as a series of brilliant emendations.[68] We can at least measure the value of asking such functional questions about inscriptions from comparison to studies of ancient Egypt and early medieval Scotland where scholars, who have seen monumental displays of writing essentially as mediating statements between monuments in an archaeological field and actors in a social context, have been able to establish connections between the production and use of such displays, and the emergence of powerful, self-conscious aristocracies.[69]

In the case of the Salutaris foundation, it is obviously important not to transfer *our* preconceived ideas about the uses of monumental writing in our culture, or other ancient societies, on to first-century AD Ephesian society; every society has a unique relationship to its own public displays of writing. Nevertheless, unless we believe that the main value of such texts derives from their ability to provide ancient historians with corroborating evidence for literary texts, we can and should ask at least some of the basic functional questions about the various *contexts* in which the inscription might mediate between other objects and other actors, which may help us to interpret the inscription itself.

To treat the inscription as a mediating object within various fields of discourse is not to elevate stones to the level of conscious social actors, but merely to recognize that the Ephesians expressed themselves often by non-verbal means. Thus, I hope to show that the Salutaris inscription should be interpreted essentially as a symbolic statement, which can only be fully understood within a physical, and social context.

The physical characteristics of the inscription, as it was intended to appear at Ephesos, justify this interpretive approach. First of all, the inscription, which was inscribed on the marble wall of the south parados of the theatre (and the most suitable place in the Artemision), would originally have appeared at a height such that almost all of the inscription would have been inscribed well above the eye level of a man or woman who stood 1.6 m (5 feet 6 inches) tall.[70] Further, the small size of the variable letters (1–4 cm), the variable height (left 208 cm, right 430 cm) and breadth of the engraved stones (494 cm), together with the length and complexity of the long text of the seven documents (568 lines) in six columns, constitute decisive indications about the relationship between the text of the inscription, and any possible audience.[71]

Without imposing any of *our* notions about reading habits upon the Ephesians, or even raising the issue of literacy, we may safely conclude that the majority of Ephesians did not read *this* text consistently. They simply could not do so physically, nor did Salutaris intend them to. If neither Salutaris nor the demos intended the text to be consulted for the details of the foundation, at least on any regular basis, what role then did this enormous display of writing play within the life of the city?

The answer, I believe, lies in the physical and social setting of the inscription. Our concentration upon the *linguistic* text of the foundation has led us to forget that the text itself is also an archaeological artefact; 'like a pot or a bowl', an inscription must be interpreted in relation to the other artefacts in its physical vicinity.[72] In other words, unless we are prepared to accept the unlikely idea that the Ephesians placed their monumental displays of writing throughout the city randomly, we must assume that these displays were matched to specific architectural and topographical contexts, which may help us to interpret these texts. Choices were made, both with respect to the display of the inscription, and the civic rituals it represented, which we must attempt to explicate.

The text of the foundation strongly supports this idea: we are told that Salutaris himself chose exactly the places where the decree of the demos and boule which ratified his foundation should be engraved, in order that his generosity toward the city and his reverence toward the goddess Artemis might be apparent.[73]

What then was it about these settings which would make his generosity and reverence apparent? Apart from the obvious reply, that these were major monuments in the city, if not the province, and could be expected to expose thousands of people to the inscription, and thus satisfy the vanity of Salutaris, a more subtle answer might lie within the architectural character of these two buildings.

Salutaris' selection of a wall of the theatre and somewhere on the Artemision framed the record of his generosity to the city upon monuments designed architecturally, and used socially, for public performances such as plays, mimes, and public meetings, and rituals such as sacrifices, prayers, and dedications in the city. As we shall discover, not only were these precisely the kinds of public ceremonies which Salutaris' foundation created, but the ceremonies literally *took place* throughout the year directly underneath the inscriptions themselves. Thus we may tentatively posit at least an intended visual congruence between the public, ceremonial setting of the Artemision and the theatre, the massive display of writing, and the performance of Salutaris' rituals. The demos of the Ephesians evidently considered this display of writing, perhaps by virtue of its unprecedented size and content, an appropriate iconographic element for the ceremonial contexts where it was incised. On those many days during the Ephesian year when Salutaris' civic rituals were performed, like a series of well-timed eclipses, the ceremonial contexts, the displays of writing, and the rituals came into alignment, and cast, I will argue, social, historical, and theological meanings over the whole performance which were absent in the discrete parts.

The inscription, though, was not only an artefact placed in a physical setting; it also represented a fixed moment within a social discourse between the founder and the city over the question of whether, and by what terms, Salutaris would legally be able to transfer some of his wealth to the beneficiaries. We should not pass over this assertion about the function of the text without some explanation of why such a symbolic validation of a legal process may have been necessary. The transfer of property at Ephesos, while not creating quite the social uncertainty that death would produce, by permanently removing an actor from the web of social relations, nevertheless would call into question the relationship between the owner of the property and his relatives, and would require, if not rituals to resolve the possible sense of chaos following death, certainly defined legal processes designed to re-establish social relationships on the basis of the new distribution of property.[74]

In a case where heirs were being passed over in preference to various civic groups, the need for a symbolic statement which would allow there to be peace between the donor and his heirs, and his heirs and the city, might be particularly acute. Thus the symbolic validation of the process might help the society of Ephesos to reproduce itself under new economic conditions.

Much more will be said about the legal and comparative aspects of this social discourse on pages 24–30. Here it is important to state that *publication* of the record of this discourse only mediated between all of the personal, legal, and legislative steps which were necessary before the record of this transaction could be carved on to the wall of the Artemision and the theatre, and all of the civic ceremonies which resulted from its legislative adoption. The whole social discourse about Salutaris' bequest expanded outward from the donor himself to his heirs, to his friends, to the Roman governors, to the secretaries of the boule and assembly, to the boule and the assembly, to the thousands affected by the bequest, and ended, or rather was repeated, when those affected performed Salutaris' civic rituals throughout the Ephesian year. One inscription, therefore, linked together thousands of people interacting with each other in the city, the province, and, indeed, the greater Roman world. The bulk of this book will be taken up in explicating how those various links may be shown to compose a coherent view of the world of Ephesos in AD 104.

At the same time that the inscription functioned within the city as a public and permanent validation of the power of the boule and demos to transfer the property of Salutaris to the various beneficiaries by means of a legal process, it also symbolized and legitimated the various power relationships in the city and the province which made such a transfer of property and such endowed rituals possible. The text fixed a statement about the ability of Salutaris and his supporters to effect the transfer in a form which was intended to make that statement and the people who stood behind it somewhat less open to change – since the statement was written in stone.

Thus we may link this monumental display of writing to the appearance of a visible and self-conscious elite at Ephesos during the early second century AD, which was able to muster all of the legal, political, cultural, and material resources necessary to make such a statement about its own power to control such property transactions.[75] At the same time, we should not forget that the founder and his friends needed to convince the boule and the assembly of the basic validity of that statement, if not their own positions of authority. Long before the display of writing was incised on the wall of the theatre and somewhere in the Artemision, Salutaris had to enter into a process of negotiation with the demos over the terms of that statement. Therefore, the technology of monumental writing at Ephesos was not purely an instrument of repression, as Lévi-Strauss would have it;[76] rather Salutaris' display of writing made a symbolic statement about the power, grandeur, and identity of the demos.

THE FOUNDATION

Scholars have also located the foundation of Salutaris within the generic context of other bequests from Ephesos and the Roman empire.[77] Salutaris' *diataxis*, probably a Greek translation of *constitutio*, fell within the category of annual allocations 'of public funds or a permanent arrangement (by testament or deed of gift) for the use or ownership of what has hitherto been private property',[78] and thus C. P. Jones has grouped it within a set of essentially public foundations, characteristic of the civic revival of the principate, where the city or some subdivision of it directly or indirectly benefited, and the city administered the terms of the foundation.[79]

Within this set of public foundations, Laum placed Salutaris' bequest among a set of other 'sacred' foundations from the Hellenistic and Roman periods, such as the foundation of Ptolemaios of Phaselis (who left perpetual gifts to his fatherland for votives, spectacles, and distributions), whose character and purpose was directly connected to the dedication and care of images of deities, sacred ornaments, or votive offerings.[80] As we shall see, most of the procedural processes and legal stipulations which governed the execution of Salutaris' foundation can be paralleled at Ephesos, or elsewhere in Asia Minor, during the Hellenistic or imperial periods. The form of Salutaris' foundation was shaped from familiar legal idioms. What cannot be surpassed among analogous foundations is the scale and complexity of Salutaris' foundation. But the relative size of Salutaris' bequest is not the aspect of the foundation which sets it apart from other foundations, and makes it such a valuable source for the history of Ephesos. The intimate involvement of the demos of Ephesos at every step in the process of creating the foundation, which the text reveals, and then the decision of the demos to represent the whole legal process of the foundation monumentally, at the most visible points in the city, using language drawn from the vocabulary of the sacred, was unprecedented in the city, if not the province, and shows the full extent to which the demos itself stood behind the terms of the foundation. The foundation, in other words, was a self-representation of the demos of Ephesos.

Salutaris proposed his foundation as a private citizen by December of AD 103, and asked that the proposal be ratified by a decree of the demos and boule.[81] Although more than one-third of the founders Laum identified in Asia Minor during the Hellenistic and imperial periods were individuals who had held, or were holding, various priesthoods, magistracies, or public liturgies, such as the agoranomoi Artemidoros and Diogenes, from Tralleis in Lydia, who endowed a covered walk, an office, a colonnade, an archive, and shops, before they ended their magistracies,[82] nevertheless, private citizens, such as Tiberius Claudius Ktesias, who provided 11,000 denarii for distributions to the boule, the tribes, and prokleroi of Aphrodisias, also were not uncommon.[83] No doubt the formal proposal of a private citizen, who wished to make a public foundation, and had made no promises to gain a local magistracy, or fulfil its duties, was preceded by much serious negotiation – in this case, between Salutaris and the boule at least, as well as the Roman governors, all of whom would have carefully reviewed the terms of the foundation. In fact, it is impossible to believe that the various boards and institutions touched upon by the foundation of Salutaris did not have prior knowledge of the stipulations which would have affected them; it is quite possible that a lengthy, and, perhaps, not always completely amicable process of suggestions and counter-suggestions took place before Salutaris brought the results of the discussions before the boule and demos as a motion.[84] There is, indeed, just the slightest hint, in the letter of the legate, Afranius Flavianus, that Salutaris may have proposed a previous gift to the city, which was overlooked, and possibly even rejected.[85]

After these initial negotiations were completed, Salutaris came into the assembly, proposed his foundation as a private citizen, and asked that it be ratified by a decree (psephisma) of the boule and demos.[86] Once the demos and boule officially ratified the proposal, the main foundation in January, and the addendum in February of AD 104, it became a *diataxis*, a technical legal term used commonly to describe a bequest made while the founder was still alive, which was intended to be perpetual.[87] It was then normal practice at Ephesos and elsewhere for the details of such an accepted proposal to be embodied in a public decree of the demos and boule,[88] which was displayed on stone somewhere in the city. Thus, Salutaris' foundation was proposed and ratified according to legal and legislative procedures applicable to other foundation proposals in the city and the province during the imperial period.

What distinguishes Salutaris' foundation from other analogous foundations during the time, is not the legal steps by which his proposal became an official decree of the assembly, but the willingness of the demos to devote an unprecedented amount of highly prized visual space within the city to the record of this normal legal procedure, and this type of foundation. Although there are antecedents and parallels to the publication of the legal process behind foundations which involved additions to pre-existing processions, or newly created ones, and cash distributions to civic bodies, timed to coincide with celebrations of the birthdays of deities, emperors, founders, or their relations, from the Hellenistic period onwards in Asia Minor, none of the surviving inscriptional portfolios equal the Salutaris foundation in terms of the combination of line length, civic space used, or centrality of physical position of the record in the city.[89] The decision of the demos of Ephesos to permit a private founder to choose two of the most conspicuous surfaces in the city on which to inscribe the longest inscription in the history of the city demands an explanation which goes beyond the desire of the demos to advertise the continuing vitality of its legislative procedures. An aspect of the language of the foundation, which has not been so much overlooked, as not set against the background of other similar foundations, may help to supply part of the explanation of why the demos chose to give Salutaris' foundation such a prominent place in the city.

Unlike other foundations involving processions or distributions on birthdays during the imperial period, such as the foundation of C. Iulius Demosthenes from Oinoanda during the reign of Hadrian,[90] while the legal term used to describe the proposal throughout the seven documents of the Salutaris foundation was *diataxis*,[91] the text of the foundation and the letter of the legatus, Afranius Flavianus, refer to Salutaris as a dedicator.[92] What Salutaris actually *did* under the terms of his proposal was to dedicate[93] certain type-statues and images,[94] and money,[95] both referred to as dedications throughout the documents, *to* Artemis and *to* various civic bodies and individuals in the city.[96] As if to leave no doubt about the nature of the statuary in particular, the type-statues and images are also explicitly referred to as sacred in the text.[97]

While forms of the same verb used to describe Salutaris' act of dedicating images and money can be paralleled at Almoura and elsewhere in Asia Minor in analogous foundations, the other foundations do not refer to the act of making the foundation as a dedication, designate the objects paid for as dedications throughout, and call the material objects sacred as well.[98]

Next, Salutaris consecrated landed property in order to guarantee the revenues which made his dedications possible.[99] This practice can be paralleled in the case of similar foundations at Oinoanda, Nysa, and Philadelphia during the second and third centuries, and indeed seems to have been a preferred method of financing foundations generally.[100] The explicit purpose of Salutaris' dedications was to adorn and exalt the sacred and public possessions of Ephesos, and to honor and reverence 'the most mighty goddess Artemis and the imperial family'.[101] In fact, the capital sum donated by Salutaris was officially designated as an endowment of the goddess.[102]

The sanctions meant to ensure the execution of the terms of the foundation brought the foundation under the jurisdiction of temple law. If Salutaris died, his heirs were charged to fulfil the terms of the foundation, and were liable to the terms of contracts for loans applicable in the sacred affairs of the goddess and in business with the gerousia.[103] Furthermore, the consecration of the property of the foundation meant that anyone who attempted to make changes in the administration of the dedicated statues in particular was subject to prosecution for temple robbery and sacrilege.[104] The Ephesians therefore would look upon a breach of the conditions laid down by Salutaris as an act of impiety toward Artemis and the emperor.[105]

The sanctions and penalties laid upon those who *did* violate the terms of the foundation further connected the foundation to the temple of Artemis and the imperial treasury. A double fine fell upon transgressors: 25,000 denarii for the adornment of Artemis and another 25,000 denarii to the fiscus of Caesar.[106] Other foundations from the Greek provinces during the imperial period stipulated such fines, to be paid not only to the chief temple of the city, but also the fiscus, including the Peplos foundation from the territory of Ephesos itself, where the fine was 20,000 denarii.[107] As C. P. Jones has pointed out, it is difficult to assess the gravity of such fines; however, comparative material from Greater Termessos in Pisidia would suggest that although larger fines for the violation of a tomb existed (up to 100,000 denarii), the 50,000 denarii fine stipulated in the case of the Salutaris foundation would place it among the most expensive group of fines known.[108] If we also remember that such a fine (50,000 denarii or 200,000 sesterces) equaled one-half the minimum wealth for an *eques*, or twice the minimum for a town councillor at Comum,[109] we may argue that the gravity of the fine also indicates the relative size and importance of the Salutaris foundation.

Indeed, within the group of public foundations referred to at the beginning of this section, apart from benefactions specifically earmarked for the purchase of land, or the construction of major public buildings, which necessarily involved large sums of money, and detailed inventories, such as the well known example of the Opramoas benefaction from Rhodiapolis in eastern Lykia from the middle of the second century AD,[110] in terms of investment, Salutaris' endowment, which consisted of 21,500 silver denarii for lotteries and distributions, and at least 124 pounds, ½ ounce, and 8 grammes of gold and silver for type-statues and images,[111] would appear to fall into the middle range of expenditure among foundations from Asia Minor during the imperial period. Salutaris expended far less than the 300,000 denarii Megakles spent (through his mother) for the training of the *paides* at Sillyon in Pamphylia,[112] but far more than the 3,333 denarii Marcus Aurelius Euarestos dedicated to be distributed to the Claudian Boule of Tralleis in AD 206.[113]

The proconsul of Asia, Aquillius Proculus, and his *legatus*, Afranius Flavianus, confirmed the foundation in separate letters.[114] Since permission from the governor and his legate either to make or accept such a proposal was neither necessary nor often requested, the acceptance of the Roman governors placed the foundation of Salutaris within a special category of sanctioned endowments.[115] The precedent for imperial confirmation of foundations at Ephesos, however, dated from the very beginning of the principate. Augustus himself confirmed the foundation of his friend Vedius Pollio at Ephesos, certainly after 27 BC.[116] The confirmation of the proconsul placed Salutaris' foundation under the jurisdiction of Roman law and the Roman courts of the province.

Thus, the Salutaris foundation was proposed, ratified, sanctioned, and propagated according to legislative procedures which can be paralleled in similar foundations at Ephesos and elsewhere in Asia Minor during the imperial period. While the size and complexity of the Salutaris foundation stand out in comparison to other foundations concerned with processions and distributions on birthdays,[117] size alone is not the only, or most important argument, for a thorough study of the provisions of the foundation. Less noticed, but perhaps more important, is the *relentlessly* sacred language used to describe every step of that legislative process. From proposal to promulgation, the language of the process of founding belonged to the semantic context of dedications, sacrilege, and sacred law: in other words, to the sphere of the divine. The foundation becomes a sacred, public act, embodied in law, and displayed on stone.

Once we recognize the essentially public, and sacred nature of the act of foundation, we may understand the genesis of the foundation outside the utilitarian, gift, or institutional models of 'euergetism' which are usually employed to explain this social phenomenon,[118] and within the more specific and dynamic context of the pervasive, and persistent expectations, needs, and goals of the demos of Ephesos in AD 104.

We have already seen that Salutaris did not exchange his wealth for public honor outside of a social context. Although Salutaris no doubt gained some public honor from his bequest, the boule, the demos, and the Roman governors all were intimately involved in the creation, approval, ratification, and confirmation of the foundation. Thus, a purely utilitarian model of exchange between an elite and the masses in the city cannot account for Salutaris' benefaction.

Nor, indeed, as we shall see in Chapters 2 and 3, did Salutaris alone dispense collective benefits to beneficiaries without discrimination, the notion at the core of the gift model. The demos ultimately saw to it that Salutaris' *euergesiai*, to borrow a term from Veyne, were dispensed differentially in the city, based upon one version of the sacred and secular history of the city. The demos itself then objectified those differences by setting them in stone, and dramatized and reinforced the differences by having them acted out in public through the civic rituals of the foundation. The social, historical, and theological discrimination at the very heart of the foundation ultimately represented the attitudes of the demos of Ephesos.

Finally, we have already seen that, while the separate legal and semantic components of Salutaris' foundation did arise from well-known institutional idioms, those components were combined in an unprecedented way, a way which broke the institutional mould at Ephesos. Much more importantly, we shall see later that the origins of Salutaris' foundation cannot be understood within an institutional model which separates out institutions and benefactors from broader historical, social, and theological trends at Ephesos during the empire.

Now that we have suggested at least some of the reasons why the Salutaris inscription should be interpreted primarily as a symbolic statement of the demos, understandable only in a specific physical, social, and semantic context, let us try to set the civic rituals which acted out the world view of that symbolic statement within the dynamic context of Ephesos in AD 104.

NOTES

1. Transliterations of Greek nouns such as Ephesos in this book are based upon the spellings to be found in the *Geography* of Strabo, except in cases where other forms have become so common in English usage that to adopt the transliterated form might confuse the reader.

2. See Jones (1983) 116. Throughout this book I have taken a bold, but necessary decision with regard to my citations of both ancient evidence and modern scholarship. Because Ephesos has become, in the words of one Turkish scholar, 'a factory of scholarship', I have decided to base my arguments as much as possible upon the ancient evidence itself – the inscriptions, the coins, the texts, the excavation reports – both for my own sake and the sake of readers. In the notes, I have made a conscious effort, nevertheless, to at least indicate where the initial, definitive, or most recent discussion of the evidence or problem can be found. For those who wish to explore the huge bibliography of research on the site (which ran to 1,535 titles by 1987), they can do no better than to start with R. Oster, *A Bibliography of Ancient Ephesus* (Metuchen 1987).

3. Particularly important are the topographical, architectural, and archaeological studies contained in the *Forschungen in Ephesos* volumes, published by the Österreichisches Archäologisches Institut in Vienna: various articles in I (Vienna 1906); 'Das Theater in Ephesos', II (Vienna 1912); 'Die Agora', III (Vienna 1923); 'Die Marienkirche in Ephesos', IV,1 (Vienna 1932); 'Das Cömeterium der Sieben Schläfer', IV,2 (Vienna 1937); 'Die Johanneskirche', IV,3 (Vienna 1951); 'Die Bibliothek', V,1 (Vienna 1953); 'Das Monument des C. Memmius', VII (Vienna 1971); 'Die Wandmalerei der Hanghäuser in Ephesos', VIII/1 (Vienna 1977); 'Römische Mosaiken aus Ephesos I: Die Hanghäuser des Embolos', VIII/2 (Vienna 1977); 'Das Mausoleum von Belevi', VI (Vienna 1979); 'Der Staatsmarkt',

IX/1/1 (Vienna 1981); 'Das Hadrianstor in Ephesos', XI/1 (Vienna 1989); the inscriptions are published in the series, *Inschriften Griechischer Städte aus Kleinasien*, under the title, *Die Inschriften von Ephesos*, Ia (Bonn 1979); II (Bonn 1979), III–VI (Bonn 1980); VII, 1–2 (Bonn 1981); VIII, 1–2 (Bonn 1984).

4. In the most recent text of H. Wankel, *IE*, 27, the inscription is 568 lines long.

5. Florus, *Epitome*, 1.35.2f.; Strabo, *Geography*, 13.4.2; Justin, *Epitome*, 36.4.5; on the creation of the Roman province and the role of Ephesos in the province down to the time of the Sullan settlement, see (most recently in English) Sherwin-White (1984) 80–8; 235–49.

6. Strabo, *Geography*, 14.1.38.

7. Thus, *not* included in the new province were: much of Great Phrygia, granted to the King of Pontos, all Lykaonia, ceded to the King of Kappadokia, possibly Phrygia Epictetos, which may have been given to King Nikomedes of Bithynia, the cities and peoples of Karia and Lykia south of the Maeander, which never were part of the Kingdom of Pergamon (and remained free to the time of the first Mithridatic war), and the territories of free Kyzikos and the small cities of the Troad in the north, although the interior of Mysia had been part of the original grant to Attalos in 189 BC. The eastern boundaries of the province have not been determined. For a detailed discussion of the land included in the province see Sherwin-White (1984) 88–92.

8. Strabo, *Geography*, 13.4.12.

9. Cities such as Priene and Ephesos, which had been free under Attalos III, retained their freedom, despite the fact that they lay within the geographical boundaries of the new province. The reason for this was that the Roman Senate generally preferred to maintain relations with cities on the basis of the legal and political circumstances which obtained when those relations began, even if this meant, as it did when the province of Asia was formed, that various autonomous cities were located within the borders of the new province. On this point, see J. Reynolds, 'Cities', in D. Braund (ed.), *The Administration of the Roman Empire 241 BC – AD 193*, (Exeter 1988) 17–18.

10. For this point see G. P. Burton, 'Proconsuls, Assizes and the Administration of Justice under the Empire', *JRS*, 65 (1975) 92.

11. Strabo, *Geography*, 14.1.26.

12. For the edict of Scaevola see Cicero, *Letters to Atticus*, 6.1.15; for the date of Scaevola's governorship, see R. Kallet-Marx, 'Asconius 14–15 Clark and the Date of Q. Mucius Scaevola's Command in Asia', *Classical Philology*, 84 (1989) 305–12, who argues that Scaevola went out in 98/97 or slightly earlier.

13. Cicero, *Letters to Atticus*, 6.1.15, 'ut Graeci inter se disceptent suis legibus'.

14. *IE*, 7.

15. *OGIS*, 438.

16. Magie, I (1950) 174.

17. Appian, *The Mithridatic Wars*, 21.
18. *ibid.*, 22–3.
19. Strabo, *Geography*, 14.1.23.
20. *IE*, 8.11–12.
21. Appian, *The Mithridatic Wars*, 12.61–2; see also Sherwin-White (1984) 143–8 on the settlement after the decisive battle at Orchomenos.
22. Caesar, *Civil Wars*, 3.105; Appian, *Civil Wars*, 2.89.
23. *IE*, 251.
24. Plutarch, *Life of Antony*, 24; for the reception of Antony at Ephesos see C. Pelling, *Plutarch: Life of Antony* (Cambridge 1988) 176–81.
25. Appian, *Civil Wars*, 5.4–5.
26. Strabo, *Geography*, 14.1.23.
27. Plutarch, *Life of Antony*, 56; for commentary see C. Pelling, *Plutarch: Life of Antony* (Cambridge 1988) 255.
28. Cassius Dio, *Roman History*, 51.2.1.
29. On the issue of Augustus' transfer of certain provinces back to the Populus Romanus, not the Senate, in 27 BC, see, most recently, F. Millar, '"Senatorial" Provinces: An Institutionalized Ghost', *Ancient World*, 20 (1989) 93–7.
30. Cassius Dio, *Roman History*, 51.20.6.
31. *IE*, 1522.
32. Strabo, *Geography*, 14.1.23.
33. See *IE*, 19B b4; 3501; 3502.
34. Josephus, *Jewish Antiquities*, 16.6.4.
35. *ILS*, 156.
36. Tacitus, *Annals*, 4.55.
37. *IE*, 17–19.
38. See G.M. Rogers, 'Demetrios of Ephesos: Silversmith and Neopoios?' *Belleten* (1987) 877–82.
39. See Price (1985) 249; 266.
40. H. Halfmann, 'Die Senatoren aus den kleinasiatischen Provinzen des römischen Reiches von 1. bis 3. Jahrhundert', in *Epigrafia e ordine senatorio*, II (Roma 1982) 603–49.
41. Tacitus, *Annals*, 16.23.
42. *IE*, 20.
43. Magie, I (1950) 566–7.
44. H. Halfmann, *Epigrafia e ordine senatorio*, II (Roma 1982) 631.
45. Philostratus, *Life of Apollonius*, 8.7.28.
46. *IE*, 27.14–16; H. Devijver, *The Equestrian Officers of the Roman Imperial Army* (Amsterdam 1989) no. 77, 292, 298; the honorary inscriptions include *IE*, 28–36A–D; 37.
47. *IE*, 27.14–15.
48. *IE*, 27.15.
49. *IE*, 27.17–18.
50. *IE*, 27.305–8.
51. *IE*, 3027.
52. P. Brunt, *Roman Imperial Themes* (Oxford 1990) 391.
53. *IE*, 27.15–16: στρατείαις τε καὶ | ἐπιτροπαῖς ἀ[πὸ] τοῦ

κυρίου ἡμῶν αὐτοκράτορος κεκοσμημένος. At first glance, the imprecision of the phrase, 'adorned by our lord the emperor with military posts and procuratorships', would appear to be resolved 9 lines later in the inscription by the use of a similar formula, τοῦ κ[υ]ρίου ἡμῶν αὐ[τοκράτορος] | Νέρουα Τραϊα[νοῦ (25–6), clearly referring to the emperor Nerva Trajan.

But, if we suppose that the emperor referred to in lines 15–16 is Trajan, Salutaris would have to have held his military posts and subprocuratorships, four posts in all, between AD 98 and 104, the date of the foundation. Since this is highly unlikely, due to the average lengths of the military offices held, two other possibilities arise. First, the imprecise phrasing at lines 15–16 reflects a deliberate blurring of the chronology of his career designed to hide the fact that Salutaris advanced first under Domitian, and then subsequently under Trajan. It is also possible that, in fact, Salutaris held all four appointments under Domitian, a reconstruction of his cursus which would allow sufficient time for Salutaris to confer other benefactions upon the city before AD 104, and to be rewarded with membership in the boule of Ephesos.

Therefore, while the possibility cannot be excluded that the phrase refers to the reigns both of Domitian and Trajan, if the phrase means that Salutaris was appointed to these positions by Domitian, the following tentative conclusions ensue. Salutaris was *praefectus coh. Asturum et Callaecorum, trib. mil. leg. XXII Primigenia P. F., subproc. provinc. Mauretaniae Tingitanae* and *item provinc. Belgicae* between 81 and 96 AD. When he was *promag. provinc. portuum Siciliae* and *promag. frumenti mancipalis eiusdem provinc.* remains open to question.

54. Tacitus, *Histories*, 2.58.
55. The legion abandoned the epithet after Domitian suffered *damnatio memoriae*. Hence Salutaris was military tribune after AD 89 and before AD 96.
56. T. Mommsen's original estimation of this obscure office still persuades; not all procurators had subprocurators on their staffs and subprocurators were special appointees. See *Römisches Staatsrecht*, II (Leipzig 1877) 977 n.2.
57. *IE*, 27.17–21.
58. *IE*, 27.412–13,123–6.
59. *IE*, 27.341–2, 372–7.
60. *IE*, 430.28–9.
61. *IE*, 3027; W. Eck, *Senatoren von Vespasian bis Hadrian* (Munich 1970) 168.
62. *IE*, 3027.5–6.
63. *IE*, 620.25–6: this inscription is now set up on the Embolos, near the 'temple of Hadrian', on the northern side of the street.
64. See C. Habicht, 'Zwei Römische Senatoren aus Kleinasien', *ZPE*, 13 (1974) 3; H. Halfmann, *Die Senatoren aus dem östlichen Teil des Imperium Romanum bis zum Ende des 2. Jahrhunderts n. Chr.*

(Göttingen 1979) no. 28.
65. The major editors include C. Curtius, 'Inschriften aus Ephesos', *Hermes*, 4 (1870) 201–3; Wood (1877) appendix VI, no. 1; Hicks (1890) 481; Heberdey (1912) *FiE*, II 27; Laum, II (1914) 82–8; F.H. Marshall, *Ancient Greek Inscriptions in the British Museum*, IV (Oxford 1916) 481; F. F. Abbott and A. C. Johnson, *Municipal Administration in the Roman Empire* (Princeton 1926) 387–89; Oliver (1941) 55–69; H. Wankel, *IE*, 27.
66. The edition of H. Wankel, *IE*, 27, incorporates readings from Wood, Hicks, and Heberdey.
67. I base my text upon examination of the main fifteen stone fragments which compose the foundation, conducted at Ephesos from 1 through 7 August 1988, and at the British Museum in London from 29 to 31 March 1989. I would like to thank B.F. Cook and S. Walker at the British Museum for permission to work upon the Salutaris inscription, and W. Cole for his help in the inscription room.

The Greek text of the Salutaris foundation which appears as Appendix I is based upon the text printed as *IE*, 27, and incorporates the later corrections of R. Merkelbach and J. Nollé published in *Addenda et Corrigenda zu den Inschriften von Ephesos I–VII, 1 (IK 11, 1–17, 1)* (Bonn 1981) 2. I have presented the Greek text of the foundation without the fragments, the apparatus criticus, and appendix to the apparatus (which can be found in *IE*, 27: 205–7 and 217–22), because the fragments as understood thus far do not significantly change our understanding of the foundation, and because the text I offer is mainly intended to serve as an accurate, up to date, working text for readers, to be read and consulted in relation to my interpretation of the foundation. I have nothing to add to the very complete apparatus criticus of the *IE* editors. My facing English translation is based upon the translation of Oliver (1941) 69–80.
68. On all issues related to the use and interpretation of inscriptions in the Classical World see F. Millar, 'Epigraphy', in M. Crawford (ed.), *Sources for Ancient History* (Cambridge 1983) 80–136; for pioneering studies on the social function of written documents, compare M. Clanchy, *From Memory to Written Record: England 1066–1307* (Cambridge 1979); J. Barrett, 'Fields of Discourse, Reconstituting a Social Archaeology', *Critique of Anthropology*, 7 (1987/1988) 5–16.
69. See J. Baines, 'Literacy, Social Organization, and the Archaeological Record: the Case of Early Egypt', in J. Gledhill, B. Bender, and M. Larsen (eds.), *State and Society* (London 1988) 192–214; and in the same volume, S. Driscoll, 'Power and Authority in Early Historic Scotland: Pictish Symbol Stones and other Documents', 215–33.
70. Based upon my measurements conducted at Ephesos on 1 August 1988, and at the British Museum on 29 March 1989. See also the British Museum photograph of the inscription and the accompanying diagram.

71. No evidence exists that the Ephesians ever read such monumental texts in public places straight through. Even an audience with very different reading habits from those common in our culture would have had a very difficult time reading the text as it appeared on the wall of the theatre, mostly for physical reasons; the bulk of the inscription would have appeared well above the heads of pedestrians, the crowds shuffling in and out of the theatre during the day would have interfered with the sight lines, and the sun of the late afternoon would not have provided the best shadows for reading the text.

72. For inscriptions as archaeological objects see M. Gibson, 'The Archaeological Uses of Inscribed Documents', *Iraq*, 34 (1972) 113–23.

73. *IE*, 27.117–26.

74. On the possible reasons for creating monumental symbols representing property arrangements see S. Driscoll, 'Power and Authority in Early Historic Scotland: Pictish Symbol Stones and other Documents', in J. Gledhill, B. Bender, and M. Larsen (eds.), *State and Society* (London 1988) 215–33.

75. With one possible exception, *IE*, 4, an inscription which scholars have dated anywhere from 297 BC until the first century BC, all published and dated Ephesian inscriptions over 70 lines long belong to the imperial period: *IE*, 17–19, the edict of Paullus Fabius Persicus, 77 lines from AD 44; *IE*, no. 20, the Fishery-Tollhouse inscription, 71 lines from AD 54 to 59; no. 22, an honorary inscription for T. Aelius Alkibiades, 70 lines from the time of Antoninus Pius; 27, the Salutaris inscription, 568 lines from AD 104; 47, expenditures of the prytaneis for the gerousia and Kuretes, 117 lines from the time of Commodus. Even allowing for statistical distortions owing to random survival, the question remains: why do all Ephesian inscriptions which might be deemed monumental come from the period between AD 44 and, at the outside, AD 192? Is it possible to connect the production of such displays of writing with the appearance of a bilingual aristocracy in the city, anxious to exhibit both its local patriotism and love of Rome through the media of these inscriptions? Further excavation may produce large displays of writing from other periods, but the phenomenon of monumental displays of writing during the imperial period at Ephesos and throughout the Greek east would repay further study.

76. C. Lévi-Strauss, *Tristes tropiques* (Paris 1955) 266.

77. See Laum, II (1914) 82–8; Oliver (1941) 55–85; J. and L. Robert, *Hellenica*, IX (Paris 1950) 14–18; Oliver (1953) 963–5; Atkinson (1962) 261–89; Jones (1983) 116–25.

78. See Oliver (1953) 964; for *diataxis* as a translation of *constitutio* see Atkinson (1962) 271.

79. See Jones (1983) 116.

80. See Laum, I (1914) 65 for the sacred nature of Salutaris' bequest; other examples from this sub-set of sacred foundations include Laum, II (1914) 128, an honorary inscription from Miletos from 306–293 BC for Antiochos, whose revenues were to be used for

building furnishings at the sanctuary of Didyma; no. 108, an imperial honorary decree from Aphrodisias for Marcus Ulpius Carminius Claudianus, who provided monies for perpetual votive offerings; and no. 140, an imperial honorary decree from Phaselis (cited in text, p. 24) for Ptolemaios.

81. Although the bequest was formally dated to January of AD 104, as is made clear by the consular dating in lines 134–6, it is equally clear that Salutaris had made his proposal by December of 103, since the letter of the proconsul, dated to Poseideon as well, refers to the proposal in lines 327–30. At lines 447f. we are told that the addendum to the foundation, which was ratified by the boule and demos at line 568, was dated to February of AD 104. Thus the minimum time period between initial proposal and acceptance of the foundation in its final form was something over two months, and the boule and demos was involved in each step of the process.

82. *Tralleis*, 146; for the endowments of agoranomoi while in office, see L. Robert in *Laodicée du Lycos* (Paris 1969) 259; Laum, I (1914) 18–20, for a survey of priests, magistrates, and public officials in Asia Minor, who had made foundations; and P. Veyne, *Bread and Circuses* (London 1990) 10f., who calls this kind of euergetism *ob honorem*, since the notables made their expenditures on the occasion of their election to a public honor, magistracy, or function in the city.

83. For founders who made their endowments as private citizens, see Laum, II (1914) no. 110, for Poseidonios of Halikarnassos, at the end of the third century BC; Laum II, no. 110, for Ktesias of Aphrodisias, as cited in the text, during the post-Claudian period; *Tralleis*, 220, for Soterichos of Tralleis, probably during the second century AD; Pleket (1970) 61–74, for P. Aelius Menekrates, from Almoura in the post-Hadrianic period; on voluntary euergetism in general see Veyne, op. cit., 10–11.

84. On negotiations between donors and civic officials, see L. Robert, *Hellenica*, I (Paris 1940) 50–1.

85. At line 378, the legate stated that, '[Salutaris] has appeared to be a most intimate and kindred friend to us, it has been recognized on many occasions, if the majority have overlooked it, how he maintains goodwill and purpose toward you'. It is uncertain whether this is an echo of a previous rejection of one of Salutaris' proposals, or perhaps a reference to an honor not voted to Salutaris by the city.

86. At line 22 we are told that Salutaris actually came into the assembly, which must have taken place in the theatre. The private nature of Salutaris' proposal is emphasized at line 74.

87. *IE*, 27.1–133 is the decree of the demos; for the legal definition of *diataxis* see Laum, I (1914) 125.

88. *IE*, 27.134–332; *Iasos*, 248; for the practice see Atkinson (1962) 285.

89. See Appendix II.

90. In line 49 of the Demosthenes bequest the founder is simply referred to as the one who δι[αταξά]μενος τὴν πανήγυριν, or founded the festival.

91. *IE*, 27.68, 73, 120, 321, 329–30, 332, 555–6.
92. *IE*, 27.153–4, κ[αθι]ερωκότι, 400, καθιερούντος.
93. *IE*, 27.332, καθιέρωσα.
94. *IE*, 27.163, καθιερωμένα; see also lines 317, 421, 473, 554–6.
95. *IE*, 27.126–7, τῶν καθιε[ρωμένων] ὑπ' αὐ-| [τοῦ χρ]ημάτων; see also lines 220–1, 317–18, 464, 485.
96. *IE*, 27.141–8, 453–9.
97. At lines 90–1, the dedicated statuary is called ἱε-|ρῶν [εἰδ]ων.
98. In the foundation of P. Aelius Menekrates from Almoura, discussed by Pleket (1970) 61–74, the verb used in lines 11–12 to describe Menekrates' selection of certain ergasteria to provide revenues for incense was καθι-| έρωσεν. Forms of καθιερόω were used frequently in other types of foundations at Ephesos, notably the foundation of Stertinius Orpex, *IE*, 2113.9; but also in the testamentary bequest of Pompeius Euprosdectus, *IE*, 3216.4; and at Teos during the first century, *CIG*, II 3080.9–10; and see generally the comments of Pleket, 62–3 on the uses of the verb.
99. *IE*, 27.305–11; examples from the Hellenistic period onward parallel the consecration of property in foundations: see Laum, I (1914) 169–78.
100. See Wörrle (1988) 4, lines 15 and 28, for land set aside to finance the festival of Demosthenes; Laum, II (1914) 130.18–20 for horse-pastures earmarked to finance the distributions of Aelius Alkibiades of Nysa at the time of Hadrian; Laum, II, no. 83.2–3 for land made over to the boule for the sake of distributions by Cornelia from Philadelphia at the end of the second or beginning of the third century AD; on the different types of property founders designated to generate revenues for foundations, see Laum, I (1914) 134–5; also L. Robert, *Opera Minora Selecta*, II (Amsterdam 1969) 1055 n.2.
101. *IE*, 27.382–4.
102. *IE*, 27.248–9.
103. *IE*, 27.304–11.
104. *IE*, 27.217.
105. A foundation from Eleusis during the second century AD parallels this feature of the Salutaris foundation; see Laum, II (1914) no. 19b.
106. *IE*, 27.108–16, 321–5.
107. See Laum, I (1914) 202; *Iasos*, 248; *IE*, 3214.
108. See Jones (1983) 121.
109. Pliny, *Letters*, 1.17.
110. *IGR*, iii 739; J. J. Coulton, 'Opramoas and the Anonymous Benefactor', *JHS*, 107 (1987) 171–8.
111. At line 219, we are told that the weight of the dedicated statuary was 111 pounds; add to this Athena Pammousos at lines 465–7, weight of 7 pounds, ½ ounce, 8 grammes, and Sebaste Homonoia Chrysophoros at lines 470–3, weight of 6 pounds at least and we arrive at a total of not less than 124 pounds, ½ ounce, 8 grammes. Of this total, 3 pounds was gold, lines 158–60, 2 pounds, 10 ounces, and 5 grammes was silver overlaid with gold, lines 159–60, and the rest was silver.

112. See Laum, II (1914) no.150; expenditures over 100,000 denarii on public foundations are not particularly rare during the second century: e.g. Aurelius Hermippos from Philadelphia in Lydia who gave 500,000 denarii to his fatherland, 50,000 to the boule, and 10,000 to the gerousia alone, at the time of Marcus or later, see Laum, II (1914) no. 86.

113. *Tralleis*, 66; for other public foundations of 10,000 denarii (value) or less see, *Magnesia*, 20; Laum, II (1914) nos. 81, 84, 85, 93, 95=*Tralleis*, 145; Laum, nos. 106, 109, 112, 113, 124=*Iasos*, 248; Laum, nos. 132, 184, 185, 191, 193, 202.

114. *IE*, 27.333–69, 370–413.

115. See J.H. Oliver, 'The Roman Governor's Permission For a Decree of the Polis', *Hesperia*, 23 (1954) 165–6; see also Wörrle (1988) 31–3 for analogous practices in Lykia-Pamphylia.

116. See Atkinson (1962) 283; and generally, P. Herrmann, 'Kaiserliche Garantie für Private Stiftungen', *Studien zur Antike Sozialgeschichte* (1980) 339–56.

117. See Appendix III.

118. The utilitarian, gift, and institutional models of euergetism are exemplified by the works of D. Johnson, 'Munificence and Municipia: Bequests to Towns in Classical Roman Law', *JRS*, 75 (1985) 105–6; Veyne, op. cit., 10–13; P. Gauthier, *Les cités grecques et leurs bienfaiteurs (IVe–Ier siècle avant J.-C.): contribution à l'histoire des institutions* (Paris 1985) 1–6.

2

THE LOTTERIES
AND DISTRIBUTIONS

INTRODUCTION

Although historians of the Middle Ages,[1] the Renaissance,[2] and Early Modern Europe,[3] have extensively explored the terms of various charities, public distributions and lotteries, have identified complex patterns of altruism, exchange, and social control between benefactors and beneficiaries, and have set their results within dynamic social contexts, with the notable exception of the recent study of the festival foundation of C. Iulius Demosthenes from Oinoanda,[4] no ancient historian has attempted a similar analysis of one scheme of distributions which involved cash distributions to civic bodies, timed to coincide with celebrations of the birthdays of deities, emperors, founders, or their relations, from the Graeco–Roman world. The failure to study such ancient schemes within wider social contexts is all the more strange, in light of the considerable amount of evidence for such distributions at Nysa, Thyateira, Philadelphia, Tralleis, and other cities in Asia Minor during the imperial period.[5]

Studies of these distributions conducted thus far show that donors included prominent men in the city, such as T. Aelius Alkibiades from Nysa during the Antonine period, who organized distributions to be made every year on the birthday of the god Hadrian, but also women, such as Cornelia, from Philadelphia, who set aside land so that the boule would take a distribution on the birthday of her brother.[6] Many distributions were made by individuals who either had held, or were holding public offices, perhaps as one of the official duties of the office,[7] but private citizens also organized distributions.[8] Roman citizens also appear frequently in the list of those who made distributions during the imperial period.[9]

Members of the larger civic bodies, such as the boule and the gerousia, often benefited from these distributions at Thyateira or Philadelphia, although the entire citizen body seems to have received money for sacrifices to celebrate the birthday of the emperor Antoninus Pius at Ephesos in AD 138.[10] The money for the sacrifices in AD 138 probably came from public revenues, but individual donors also spent thousands of denarii as well.[11] Thus far, however, none of the privately financed distributions which have been discovered rival Salutaris' in terms of expenditure, or the number of different civic bodies involved.

In the case of Salutaris' foundation, which we certainly cannot consider a charity, previous scholars usually have addressed only the thorniest financial questions raised by Salutaris' scheme of lotteries and distributions.[12] J.R. Melville Jones, in particular, has shown that various references to payments of 9 or 13½ assaria within the list of lotteries and distributions organized by Salutaris, which have been adduced as evidence that the denarius at Ephesos at the beginning of the second century AD contained 18, not 16 assaria,[13] have produced a misunderstanding: in fact, other references[14] presuppose a denarius of only 16 assaria, and the apparent discrepancy is explained by the term 'silver assaria' which must refer to an accounting unit, since the assarion was never a silver coin.[15]

But while scholars have explicated some of the financial issues related to the scheme of lotteries and distributions, no other historian has carefully investigated the timing of the lotteries and distributions, the location, and the identities of the various beneficiaries. Nor has the scheme been located within a social context. The importance of this can be measured from comparison to other historical contexts where private benefactors designed schemes of benefactions to help guide youths into various social, political, and religious structures.

In quattrocento Florence, for instance, lay benefactors often exercised the firmest control over confraternities of youths through their financial support. 'By corporate segregation from public life, biologically mature adolescents could be indoctrinated and taught to act out the ideal and even seamy daily needs, thoughts and gestures of their elders, male or female, without losing their innocence'.[16] Later those adolescents in Florence emerged as the male 'saviors' of society.

Thus, only the synthesis of all the different provisions which governed the execution of the lotteries and distributions of Salutaris, set within the context of the history of Ephesos, can reveal the inner logic, the purpose, and the significance of this part of the foundation. As we shall discover, unlike the example from quattrocento Florence, Salutaris' scheme specifically did *not* separate the youth associations of the city from public life: rather, the lotteries and distributions forced the paides and the ephebes of the city to act out a civic hierarchy along *with* their elders. Acting out the hierarchy of the scheme taught the young men of Ephesos, as well as their fathers, to look (metaphorically) to the institutional structure of their city, to its Ionian foundation, and to the birth of the goddess Artemis, for their sense of social and historical identity in the complex and changing Roman world. If they played their roles according to the script of the scheme, they would become, not the male 'saviors' of society, but good and true Ephesians, the sons of Androklos and Artemis.

THE LOTTERIES AND DISTRIBUTIONS

Before readers consider my discussion of Salutaris' scheme of lotteries and distributions, they may wish to turn to my translation of the foundation text (printed as Appendix I) and read through those sections of the foundation, particularly lines 220–352 and 485–553, which set out the terms of the lotteries and distributions. As readers work their way through these sections, I hope they will come to recognize just how involved the arrangements governing the lotteries and distributions were; in my discussion, I hope to show that these detailed arrangements, often involving very small sums of money, did not contradict the essentially religious focus of the whole scheme. At Ephesos piety and careful accounting went hand in hand. In order to simplify the terms of the scheme for readers here, I produce below a table of the lotteries and distributions endowed by Salutaris, first in the decree of the boule and the demos and then in the addendum to the decree, followed by a key.[17]

As we can see from Table 1, in the decree of the demos and boule, the total capital endowment was 20,000 denarii. This 20,000 denarii yielded 1,800 denarii yearly for lotteries and distributions at the standard 9 per cent interest.[18] In the addendum, 1,500 denarii was the total capital endowment; 9 per cent of this 1,500 denarii yielded 135 denarii yearly for additional lotteries and distributions.

Table 1 Main Endowment

Ben	Ls	M	P	D	Cap	YI	R	F	Por
Boule	222–31	d	t	5th	5000	450	450+	?	1
Gerousia	231–8	1	?	6th	4250	382½	309+	?	1
Neokoroi	238–40	d	?	?	?	7½	?	?	?
Asiarchs	240–6	1	?	?				5	11
Phylarchs	246–52	1	?	?	8333⅓	750	1500+	?	½
Ephebes	253–8	1	?	6th	1400	125	250	?	½
Ephebarch	257–8	d	?	6th	?	1	1	?	1
Theologoi	258–65	1	t	6th	275	24¾	9	?	2¾
Priestess	265–8	d	?	6th	200	18	?	?	?
Neopoioi	268–73	d	?	as	33⅓	3	2	c	¼
Beadle	268–73	d	?	as	33	3	1	c	¼
Paides	273–9	1	t	6th	175	12¼	49	c	¼
Paidonomoi	273–9	d	t	6th	175	3¼	7	?	½
Cleaner	279–84	d	?	proc	333⅓	30	1	c	30

Addendum to the Main Endowment

Ben	Ls	M	P	D	Cap	YI	R	F	Por
Boule	488–97	1	t	6th	?	55	5	s	11
Gerousia	497f.	1	?	?	?	27½	5	?	5½
Chrys.	500b–d	1	?	?	?	6¾	9	?	¾
Paides	519–31	1	t	6th	?	15¾	63	s,p	¼
Thesmodoi	532–5	d	t	6th	?	7	14	?	½
Acrobatai	536–9	d	?	6th	?	15	20	?	¾
Custodian	546–9	d	?	yr	?	8	1	c	8

Key to Table
Ben: Beneficiary; Ls: Lines in text; M: Method of distribution; P: Place of distribution; D: Date of distribution; Cap: Capital endowment for beneficiaries in denarii; YI: Yearly interest on capital endowment in denarii; R: Number of recipients; F: Function stated for distributions or lotteries; Por: Individual portions; d: distribution; l: lottery; t: Temple of Artemis; th: Thargelion; as: assemblies; proc: processions: s: sacrifices; p: prayers; c: care of statues; Chrys: Chrysophoroi and Sacred Victors; ?: unknown; yr: yearly

Therefore Salutaris' total capital endowment was 21,500 denarii, the interest from which each year was distributed to the various beneficiaries.

Timing

We can see from Column D of Table 1 that most of Salutaris' lotteries and distributions took place on 5 or 6 Thargelion.[19] Thargelion was the ninth month of the Ephesian year, which probably began on 23 September, the birthday of the emperor Augustus.[20] At the beginning of the second century AD, the Ephesians celebrated the birthday of their patron goddess Artemis on 6 Thargelion.[21] Thus, Salutaris specifically associated his scheme of lotteries and distributions with the celebration of the mysteries of Artemis, one of the most important festivals of the city, which took place in the late spring of each year. Salutaris possibly timed the lotteries and the distributions which took place on 5 Thargelion to avoid crowding in the temple on the birthday of the goddess.[22] Until quite recently, we have mainly known about the celebration of this festival from a brief description by the first-century geographer Strabo.

> For here is the mythical scene of the birth, and of the nurse Ortygia, and of the holy place where the birth took place. . . . Above the ground lies Mt Solmissos, where, it is said, the Kuretes stationed themselves, and with the din of their arms frightened Hera out of her wits when she was jealously spying on Leto, and when they helped Leto to conceal from Hera the birth of her children. A general festival is held there annually; and by a certain custom the youths (neoi) vie for honor, particularly in the splendor of their banquets there. At that time, also, a special college of the Kuretes holds symposiums and performs certain mystic sacrifices.[23]

Now, as a result of recent studies of the site,[24] and the re-editing of an important inscription,[25] we can at least glimpse the annual celebration of Artemis' mysteries at Ephesos from the time of the Hellenistic king Lysimachos until the reign of the emperor Commodus. Elsewhere, I hope to clarify how celebration of Artemis' birth helped to articulate the relationship between the ruling power and the city. For our immediate purposes here, it is important to emphasize the obvious importance of the Kuretes in the city – a group which would find no place at all in Salutaris' scheme of lotteries and distributions.

The Location

All the lotteries and distributions endowed by Salutaris took place in the temple of Artemis in the instances where the location was specified:[26] in the case of the distribution to 450 or more members of the Ephesian boule, Salutaris further designated the pronaos of the temple as the exact location of distribution within the temple.[27] The pronaos of the temple of Artemis, which measured 20.45 m × 21.5 m with eight columns *in antis*,[28] certainly did not provide much space for the 450 or more members of the boule, who received a donation amidst the statuary dedicated by Salutaris, which was stored in the pronaos as well, particularly on the same day that other lotteries and distributions probably were taking place in the same location. Thus Salutaris chose that his lotteries and distributions should take place at the very center of the old celebration of the mysteries of Artemis. He consciously associated his benefaction with the Temple of Artemis – rather than the prytaneion perhaps, which had asserted increasing control over the celebration of the mysteries of Artemis through the direction of the prytanis since the time of Strabo.[29]

The Civic Hierarchy of the Lotteries and Distributions

In AD 104 Salutaris endowed lotteries and distributions which totalled at least 2,702 allotments; he distributed most of his allotments to the beneficiaries during the celebration of the mysteries of Artemis in the Artemision. A careful review of Column F (for function) on our Table 1 reveals that we can divide all of the beneficiaries of the endowment into three functionally differentiated groups: those beneficiaries enjoined to take care of the dedicated statuary, those directed to spend their allotments on specific ritual tasks during the celebration of the mysteries, and those who were not ordered to take care of any statues or to perform any ritual tasks. Based upon an analysis of what Salutaris ordered the beneficiaries to do – and, much more importantly, what he did not order some of them to do – I hope to show that the purpose of these benefactions was essentially symbolic and educational. Since part of demonstrating that the purpose of the scheme was educational and symbolic depends upon knowing who the beneficiaries in the city were historically and socially, for each set of beneficiaries, as the evidence permits, I have tried to furnish some historical background, and to indicate how the individual or group actually functioned in the city. Inevitably, there are gaps in the backgrounds I provide; the Ephesians were not necessarily interested in informing us at what age a young man entered the ephebeia at Ephesos in AD 104, or how the boule of the city set its legislative agenda. Nevertheless, I hope these historical and social sketches of the sets of beneficiaries do provide at least a framework for understanding Salutaris' complex scheme of lotteries and distributions.[30]

Group I

The first group comprised those beneficiaries Salutaris enjoined to take care of his dedicated statuary. To assess the relative importance of individuals within this group of beneficiaries and the group as a whole in relation to the other lot-winners, we can relate the amount of interest designated for these beneficiaries both to the total amount of denarii earmarked for the care of the statues and to the total interest on the endowment (1,935 denarii).

Table 2 Group I

Beneficiary	Interest	% for Care Statues	% of Total Interest
1 Cleaner	30 dn.	0.6185	0.0155
1 Custodian	8 dn.	0.1649	0.0041
(?) Neokoroi	7.5 dn.	0.1546	0.0038
2 Neopoioi and Beadle	3 dn.	0.0618	0.0015
at least 7	48.5 dn.		0.0249 of total

From the main endowment, Salutaris gave 30 denarii to the individual who cleaned the statues of the goddess each time they were carried back to the temple of Artemis before they were put back into the pronaos of the temple.[31] C. Picard has identified this individual with the custodian of the deposits, a beneficiary of 8 denarii each year for the care of the statues and the purchase of argyromatic earth in the addendum, a hieros or sacred slave of Artemis.[32]

The neokoroi were either private individuals charged with taking 'religious care of the images in the house of the donor Salutaris' (line 239), or were actual temple wardens from the first neokorate temple of Domitian (later changed to Vespasian). Some of the leading Roman citizens of Ephesos since the time of Claudius are found in their ranks, including the wealthy benefactor Tiberius Claudius Aristio, in whose trial before the emperor at Centum Cellae Pliny took part.[33] The total restoration of the line perhaps makes the problem moot, but arguments exist for either identification. Certainly the language of an earlier passage which outlined the conditions on which Salutaris dedicated statues of Trajan and Plotina suggests that individuals who were not actually officials of a temple could perform the *functions* of a neokoros.[34] In this case, Salutaris would simply have religious care of the statues of Trajan and Plotina – and there is no evidence whatsoever to suggest that Salutaris was a neokoros or official temple officer.

However, the fact that the statues represented the emperor and his wife may hint that the neokoroi mentioned in line 239 were actual wardens. There are, in fact, no other examples from Ephesos of the use of the title neokoros designating an individual other than as a temple warden of Artemis or an emperor. Thus the use of the verbal form *neokorontai* in line 153 (in the case of Salutaris) simply refers to a religious task performed by a private citizen and not an official office, whereas the (restored) neokoroi were actual temple officials.

From the absence of any other official charged to carry out the distribution to these temple wardens, we can assume that the secretary of the gerousia performed this function on the birthday of the goddess in the pronaos of the temple of Artemis.[35] It is not certain how the neokoroi were to spend their distributions. However, the lottery of the registered asiarchs (officials of the provincial koinon, not the city) which followed, specifically designed so that they could buy materials for sacrifice (lines 240–3), suggests a distribution with a function in mind. Since statues of Trajan and Plotina were involved, it is likely that the neokoroi were being paid for their services, or that Salutaris intended a sacrifice on behalf of the imperial images.[36] Elsewhere, for the imperial festival of Gytheion in Lakonia, painted images of Augustus, Livia, and Tiberius were set up in the theatre with a table and incense burner in front where sacrifices were offered.[37]

The money distributed to the neokoroi perhaps subsidized purchases of wine or incense for sacrifices before the images of Trajan and Plotina on the birthday of the goddess Artemis. If this was the case, Salutaris' distribution is evidence for part of the process whereby the celebration of the birth of Artemis was also used to honor the emperor. By the time of Commodus, at any rate, there were sacrifices made to the emperor at the celebration of Artemis' mysteries.

The 4½ asses given to the neopoioi and to the beadle at each regular assembly was a payment for carrying the type-statues of the goddess and the other images from the pronaos of the temple into the theatre and back on the same day.[38] Beginning in the Hellenistic period, the neopoioi were charged with inscribing the names of new citizens on the wall of the Artemision.[39] Around 300 BC the neopoioi recommended the goodwill and enthusiasm of Melanthios, an officer who received citizenship,[40] and also recommended citizenship for Euphronios, an officer in the army of Prepelaos, who captured Ephesos for Lysimachos in 302 BC.[41] During the imperial period, the neopoioi at Ephesos composed a board of elected officials called a sunhedrion or a sunagoge.[42] The board, which included prominent Roman officials since at least the time of Domitian,[43] probably comprised twelve members – two men elected annually from each tribe in the ekklesia.[44]

In Salutaris' endowment, the neopoioi appear as guardians of the statues dedicated by him: two of the neopoioi 'attend' the statues which were carried from the pronaos of the temple of Artemis into the theatre and back at every assembly, during gymnastic contests, and on other days determined by the boule and demos.[45]

The epigraphical evidence surveyed therefore associates the neopoioi with two general functions in the city. First, and historically prior, the institutional process whereby citizenship was recommended and formally conferred in the city, and, second, the guardianship and preservation of the dedicated furniture of the temple of Artemis.[46] It may well be an accident of evidence survival that we only hear about the neopoioi inscribing names of citizens on the Artemision during the Hellenistic period; they may well have carried on in this job during the imperial period and, equally, may have taken care of the furniture of the temple during the Hellenistic era.

The appearance of the neopoioi in the endowment reinforces

the link between Salutaris and the temple of Artemis. The involvement of the beadle and the guards strengthens this link further. Both in the Salutaris endowment, and related inscriptions, the beadle is consistently associated with temple officials and servants.[47] The beadle evidently maintained order in the temple and its precincts, and performed the same job during processions.[48]

Outside the Salutaris endowment, the beadle is mentioned only once in the epigraphical corpus,[49] but an archiskeptouchos appears frequently, especially in association with the neopoioi,[50] and the title clearly designated the annually elected chief beadle, who supervised the guards in the temple.[51] The guards appear only in one inscription outside of the Salutaris endowment,[52] and were subalterns of the beadle; they guarded the temple and its treasures continually.[53]

The provisions which governed the activities of this first group of beneficiaries show how Salutaris and the demos used the temple administration to implement the terms of the foundation. Salutaris provided a payment for a service which advertised Artemis, the temple administration and, of course, the donor. Beyond this, my breakdown of the allotted endowments in Group I shows that Salutaris earmarked less than 3 per cent of his capital endowment for the care of his dedicated statues. Salutaris obviously did not organize his lotteries and distributions merely to take care of his statues. Not surprisingly, given the purpose of this group of donations, the cleaner of the statues received the greatest percentage of funds by far.

Group II

The second group comprised those beneficiaries whom Salutaris directed to spend their allotments on specific ritual tasks during the celebration of the mysteries. Once again, we can relate the

Table 3 Group II

Beneficiary	Interest	% for Ritual Tasks	% of Total Int.
6 Asiarchs	66 dn.	0.4826	0.0341
5 Boule members	55 dn.	0.4021	0.0284
63 Paides	15.75 dn.	0.1151	0.0081
74 allotments	136.75 dn.		0.0706

amount of interest designated for these beneficiaries both to the amount of denarii earmarked for ritual tasks and to the total interest on the endowment.

Through the lottery of the registered asiarchs, Salutaris provided money for sacrifice by provincial officials of the imperial cult during the celebration of the mysteries. These priests of the imperial cult came from the elite of the province and were among the most important individuals in Asia, let alone the city.[54] In fact, the generosity of the priests largely made the various activities of the cult possible.[55]

The registered asiarchs received 11 denarii apiece, the largest individual allotments given, except the sum given to the individual who cleaned the statues in the main endowment (lines 279–84). This alone should stand for Salutaris' estimation of their rank. The asiarchs perhaps bought materials for sacrifice with their allotments, but the lacuna at line 242 makes this uncertain. Salutaris' grouping of the asiarchs with the neokoroi in charge of the statues of Trajan and Plotina strengthens this argument.[56] Whether Salutaris was simply honoring the asiarchs or he provided money for sacrifices to Artemis (or on behalf of the emperor), his inclusion of the asiarchs shows that Salutaris projected important officials of the Roman imperial cult into the middle of Artemis' festival.

In the addendum, Salutaris provided 55 denarii for a lottery of five members of the boule to take place on the birthday of the goddess.[57] He allotted 27½ denarii for the purchase of materials for sacrifice, and another 27½ denarii for some unspecified purpose. Although I shall discuss the role of the boule in the endowment at length later in this chapter, it is worth emphasizing here that the provision in the addendum which ordered members of the boule to buy materials for sacrifice supplies the clearest indication that Salutaris wished to associate his endowment ritually with the celebration of the mysteries of Artemis.

The lottery of the 63 paides, who formed part of one of the official youth organizations in the city (which I shall review later), included a provision that they should sacrifice and pray in the temple of Artemis, probably on 6 Thargelion.[58] Their inclusion in the addendum and the clear direction of their activities on the day of the festival shows that Salutaris led them directly into the geographical center of one of the most important festivals during the year in the city.[59]

In conclusion, from our analysis of the second group of beneficiaries, we can see that Salutaris set off approximately 7 per cent of his capital endowment for ritual tasks performed during the celebration of the mysteries; there is no evidence whether these ritual tasks formed part of the official celebration or not. The money Salutaris set aside for this group was easily more than double the amount he endowed for the care of his statues; nevertheless it still added up to less than 10 per cent of the endowment. This relatively low percentage of investment demonstrates that Salutaris did not design his foundation primarily to subsidize the performance of rituals during the celebration of the mysteries. Within this group, the asiarchs and the five members of the boule received equal individual allotments. These comparatively high individual portions no doubt were related to the expenses involved in sacrifices.

Group III

The third group consists of those beneficiaries who were not ordered to take care of any statues or to perform any ritual tasks to our knowledge.

Table 4 Group III

Beneficiary	Interest	% of Unenjoined	% of Total Interest
1500 citizens	750 dn.	0.4286	0.3875
450 members of Boule	450 dn.	0.2571	0.2325
309 + 5 members of Gerousia	336.5 dn.	0.1923	0.1739
250 Ephebes	125 dn.	0.0714	0.0645
9 Theologoi	24.75 dn.	0.0141	0.0127
1 Priestess for Hymnodoi	18 dn.	0.0102	0.0093
20 Acrobatai	15 dn.	0.0085	0.0077
49 Paides	12.25 dn.	0.0070	0.0063
14 Thesmodoi	7 dn.	0.0040	0.0036
9 Chrysophoroi and Sacred Victors	6.75 dn.	0.0038	0.0034
7 Paidonomoi	3.5 dn.	0.0020	0.0018
1 Ephebarchos	1 dn.	0.0005	0.0005
at least 2624	1749.75		0.9037

Before we consider how various sub-groups of beneficiaries can be separated out from this large third group, we should stop and highlight a few conclusions which emerge from a preliminary inspection of this list of beneficiaries and their allotments. Most importantly, from the figure at the bottom of the column which represents the percentage of total interest, it is irrefutably clear that Salutaris earmarked over 90 per cent of his endowment without any specific tasks imposed upon the recipients. Within this third group, the citizens of the tribes received by far the greatest percentage of interest – almost 43 per cent – and nearly 39 per cent of the interest on the whole endowment. Salutaris clearly saw to it that his generosity to the city in AD 104 could not be overlooked. After the citizens of the tribes, only the members of the boule (23 per cent), the members of the gerousia (17 per cent), and the ephebes (6 per cent) received more than 5 per cent of the foundation.

Therefore, if we consider the endowment of the lotteries and distributions as a whole, we may conclude that Salutaris devoted the least amount of interest to the care of his statues, about 2.5 per cent, only 7 per cent to ritual tasks performed during the celebration of the mysteries of Artemis, and a striking 90 per cent of the endowment for purposes unrelated to either, but during the celebration of the mysteries. This comparison alone should demonstrate, once and for all, that the purpose of this part of the foundation was *not* a 'general distribution of money'; on the contrary, in terms of investment, the lotteries and distributions were *overwhelmingly* weighted toward the third group of the beneficiaries, all of which, in turn, can be divided into four quite distinct sub-groups in the city: functionaries of the imperial cult, functionaries of the Artemision, members of the youth associations in the city, and adult members of civic institutions. As we shall see, this unenjoined group of beneficiaries is the most important for our understanding of how the Ephesians wished to represent the civic hierarchy of their city both to themselves and to others.

A simple mathematical breakdown of the allotted endowments, expressed in terms of the percentage of the endowment devoted to the beneficiaries, both within and between various sub-groups yields a series of comparative tables. We can then establish various relative hierarchies of importance within each sub-group and an overall hierarchy for the unenjoined group of beneficiaries from these tables.

No one should suppose that the amounts of money involved were too small either for the Ephesians or for us to recognize such hierarchies, or that the mental blueprint which lay behind the overall hierarchy of the city especially was only an insubstantial ideal. Rather, the very modesty of the sums involved makes the minute differences allotted to the beneficiaries chosen by Salutaris all the more socially significant. Further, the civic hierarchy of the lotteries and distributions itself was as real and tangible as the preliminary registration of the beneficiaries, the actual lotteries and distributions which took place in the Artemision on 6 Thargelion, and the denarii the beneficiaries received. The Ephesians themselves *acted out* the blueprint of Salutaris' contemporary civic hierarchy. A denarius received from Salutaris during the celebration of the mysteries validated the civic hierarchy of the city just as much as a vote cast in the assembly to honor a member of the boule or an emperor with an inscription or a statue – and perhaps more so, since the recipient of the denarius probably participated in Salutaris' hierarchy with less overt political reflection, and certainly more immediate profit.

Therefore, precisely because the beneficiaries performed no tasks and received very small amounts of money, we should see their participation in the scheme of lotteries and distributions primarily as a hierarchical validation of the importance of the beneficiaries during the festival. The omission of certain important civic institutions from the overall hierarchy of the city perhaps discloses more about Ephesian self-representations than the list of who was included: I shall return to this point at the conclusion to this chapter, where I hope to show that there was a discernible pattern to the omissions as well, a pattern which is as consistent as it is revealing about Ephesian attitudes to the relationship between different kinds of wealth and status in the city. In any case, we should remember at all times that Salutaris' civic hierarchy was an ideal representation of the city, promoted and carried to fruition by Salutaris and the elite of the city to be sure, but also implicitly ratified by the boule and demos and approved by the Roman governors. As such an ideal, which found widespread assent, if not enthusiastic support in the city, it is of exceptional value for our understanding of how the demos wished to see itself and be seen by others in AD 104.

Salutaris further associated his foundation with the imperial cult through the lottery of the nine theologoi, organized by the

Table 5 Sub-group I

Functionaries of Imperial Cult	Interest	% within Group	% of Total Int.
9 Theologoi	24.75 dn.	0.7795	0.0127
14 Thesmodoi	7 dn.	0.2204	0.0036
23 allotments	31.75 dn.	0.0181	0.0163

archiereus in the temple of Artemis on her birthday.[60] The theologoi at Ephesos composed a sunhedrion,[61] and could include Roman citizens.[62] Inscriptions from outside Ephesos indicate that the theologoi should be associated with hierophants and declaimers of the sacred litanies at celebrations of mysteries.[63] Although the theologoi originally were servants of gods or goddesses particular to Asia Minor, they later were attached to the imperial cult at Smyrna, Pergamon, and Ephesos.[64]

It may be guessed that the nine theologoi who benefited from the lottery of the high priest actually prayed at the festival, although there is no evidence. While the capital endowment of the theologoi was only the fifth largest, at 275 denarii, their individual shares, 2¾ denarii, were the third largest. Clearly the theologoi were important in Salutaris' scheme. Whether they performed or not, their lottery, directed by the archiereus,[65] on the birthday of the goddess in the temple of Artemis, clearly signifies an attempt to include the priestly hierarchy of the imperial cult, and other important occasional servants of the cult in the celebration of the festival.

The fourteen thesmodoi received 7 denarii in the temple of Artemis on the birthday of the goddess.[66] At Ephesos, the thesmodoi comprised a sunhedrion of special singers for the emperor, attached to the provincial temple of the emperors by AD 104.[67] There is no evidence, however, to indicate that a particular activity was endowed by Salutaris. Their appearance in the addendum is only a clear sign of Salutaris' design to associate his endowment with the imperial cult – even if the impetus came from the thesmodoi themselves.

Functionaries of the imperial cult therefore received less than 2 per cent of the endowment, the smallest percentage of Group III. The theologoi received almost 78 per cent of the interest expended on officials of the imperial cult and large individual portions as well: 2¾ denarii apiece. Clearly the theologoi were far more significant than the thesmodoi in Salutaris' Group III hierarchy. This may perhaps reflect the fact that the theologoi were associated particularly with hierophants and declaimers of sacred litanies at celebrations of mysteries – such as the mysteries of Artemis. The thesmodoi, on the other hand, were more specifically attached to the temple of the emperors in AD 104. Left out of consideration are the asiarchs because of their functionally related endowments. The size of their individual allotments (11 denarii apiece) may adjust our picture of where Salutaris ranked functionaries of the imperial cult in his hierarchy. Nevertheless, it is striking that Salutaris set aside the least amount of his capital for the use of officials or servants of the imperial cult, who were clearly among the most prominent men in the city, if not the province or the empire.

Table 6 Sub-group II

Functionaries of Artemision	Interest	% within Group	% of Total Int.
Priestess for Hymnodoi	18 dn.	0.4528	0.0093
20 Acrobatai	15 dn.	0.3773	0.0077
9 Chrysophoroi and Sacred Victors	6.75 dn.	0.1698	0.0034
at least 30	39.75 dn.	0.0227	0.0204

The provision of 18 denarii for the priestess of Artemis on behalf of the goddess on the birthday of the goddess brought the endowment back into the center of the temple hierarchy.[68] There is no sign of the ancient eunuch priest of Artemis, the megabyzos, at this time.[69] Rather, the priestess of Artemis appears as the chief official of the cult of AD 104. She was in charge of the liturgy of the cult, and several different priestesses claimed to have celebrated the mysteries during the first and second centuries AD.[70] Priestesses also appear frequently at the beginning of Kuretes' lists,[71] and one unidentified priestess from the third century claimed to have renewed all the mysteries of the goddess and re-established them on the old customary basis.[72] These priestesses came from prominent local families of wealth, and represented in inscriptions spread throughout the city as the daughters and wives of asiarchs, neopoioi, and Roman citizens, often for generations.[73] Often, but not exclusively, family wealth was used to fulfill the functions of the priesthood, which included the erection of buildings, and other civic projects, entailing great expense.[74]

The hymnodoi were associated with the priestess of Artemis in the same provision of the foundation.[75] According to C. Picard, the hymnodoi of Ephesos were attached primarily and directly to the Artemision,[76] and included Roman citizens such as C. Aquileius Severus since at least the time of Tiberius.[77] As support for this conclusion, Picard adduced three instances in the Salutaris endowment where the hymnodoi appeared among the servants of the temple: lines 146-7, 266-7, and 295-6. This conclusion may be correct, but it should be noted that two of the instances require complete restoration.

If we step outside the endowment, we can clearly distinguish the hymnodoi of Ephesos from the sunodos of hymnodoi at Pergamon, founded specifically to sing the praises of Augustus on his birthday,[78] and the hymnodoi of the gerousia at Smyrna.[79] At Ephesos, the hymnodoi are attested as associated with the temple of Artemis from the early first century AD until the time of Philip of Arab,[80] when they composed a sunhedrion.[81] In this capacity, a hymnodos such as M. Aurelius Artemidoros sang songs in praise of Artemis on cult occasions.[82]

However, there is also evidence of attachment to the temple on the Embolos dedicated to Artemis, Hadrian, and the demos,[83] and further evidence of a direct connection between all the hymnodoi of Asia and the imperial cult as early as the reign of Tiberius, when all the hymnodoi came together to Pergamon for sacrifices to the deified emperor.[84]

Perhaps the best hypothesis for explaining this confusion is that although an original group of hymnodoi remained directly attached to the Artemision from the early empire until the third century AD, and primarily served Artemis, by the time of Hadrian, at the latest, a second group of hymnodoi developed (probably out of the first at a time when the services of the original hymnodoi were increasingly utilized for imperial celebrations), and became directly attached to the imperial cult of the temple.

Salutaris' endowment therefore involved the direct participation of the priestess of Artemis, who probably retained control of the ritual aspects of the celebration. It is unlikely in any case that Salutaris could have arranged any of the lotteries and distributions to take place in the temple without the full co-operation of the priestess. The distribution to the hymnodoi involved another group of temple functionaries during the celebration of the festival, although which hymnodoi and how many cannot be known. It is also impossible to tell whether the hymnodoi sang for their distribution or merely received a distribution.

The provision of 15 denarii for a distribution to 20 acrobatai of the goddess on her birthday indicates a distribution during the festival.[85] The acrobatai belonged to the administration of the Artemision,[86] and were associated with other temple servants including the neopoioi, until at least AD 160.[87] Their appearance in several Kuretes' lists supports the conclusion that they participated in the festival,[88] and the recurrent formulation of their title 'akrobates epi thumiatrou' in the inscriptions strengthens Hesychios' claim that the acrobatai fulfilled the duties of their office through sacrifices.[89] Based on Hesychios' statement, E. L. Hicks connected them with the Lares, representations of small boys who moved on their tiptoes, and held up rhytons to pour wine on altars,[90] and C. Picard concluded that the acrobatai were sacrificial dancers, perhaps related to dancers in the cult of Cybele, who danced in front of altars and sacred processions,[91] although it is more generally agreed now that they derived their name from walking on mountain tops. The foundation, however, does not order a specific activity of the acrobatai. The significance of their inclusion in the addendum therefore rests upon their connection with the Artemision.

The fragmentary nature of the text beginning at line 479 prevents us from concluding whether Salutaris endowed the lottery of the chrysophoroi for participation in the celebration of the mysteries or as a payment for services. In Document E (lines 419–25) Salutaris granted the chrysophoroi of the goddess the right to bear his statues into assemblies and competitions.[92]

The relationship between the chrysophoroi and the hieroneikai is problematic. At Ephesos, the chrysophoroi formed a sunhedrion during the empire, but also appear as a sunodos near the end of the first century BC.[93] Judging from the names which appear among the lists of chrysophoroi, Roman citizens served among their numbers.[94] According to Picard, the chrysophoroi were subalterns of the Artemision charged with guarding the objects of the goddess.[95] Other inscriptions from Ephesos where the chrysophoroi are associated with the neopoioi support this conclusion.[96] The existence of an agonothete of the chrysophoroi proves that the chrysophoroi took part in competitions,[97] and in

AD 170 there may have been a hymnodos attached to the sunhedrion.[98] Roman citizens are found in the sunhedrion,[99] and the chrysophoroi may have 'borne gold' to the emperor Hadrian when he visited the city.[100]

Elsewhere the term designated a privilege given to members of a royal family or distinguished individuals.[101] In mainland Greece, the privilege was granted to eminent benefactors,[102] but also earmarked a privilege certain priests and magistrates enjoyed ex officio.[103] From these parallels, E. L. Hicks concluded that at Ephesos the chrysophoroi were victors in contests which brought the same privilege held by certain priests.[104]

Unfortunately, it is not easy to untangle the relationship between the chrysophoroi at Ephesos and the Hieroneikai. The 'sacred victors' formed a sunodos by 20/19 BC,[105] which included foreigners such as the Alexandrian Ischyrion,[106] and, later, Roman citizens.[107] Not surprisingly, most of the references to the sacred victors in the inscriptions from Ephesos come from the context of athletic competitions, such as the honorary inscription for the athlete Kallikrates, a sacred victor at the time of Hadrian.[108]

In the Salutaris endowment, the sacred victors are associated with the chrysophoroi in every case except one, which led E. L. Hicks to conclude that they were the same association, C. Picard that a brotherhood had developed, and L. Robert that the 'sacred victors' and the priests formed a sunhedrion with a place reserved in the theatre.[109]

Given the fact that a sunodos of the hieroneikai existed, independent of the priests and chrysophoroi at the end of the first century AD, it is reasonable to suppose that the later athletes who triumphed for the city at sacred games were rewarded with the same title of chrysophoroi which had previously been reserved for certain priests. Thereafter, these two groups formed a powerful sunhedrion – powerful enough to provoke two decrees of the boule which created a role for them in Salutaris' procession of statues.[110]

Functionaries of the Artemision therefore received only 2 per cent of the total endowment – statistically equivalent to the amount spent on functionaries of the imperial cult. The hymnodoi received about 45 per cent of the interest set off for the temple functionaries, the acrobatai 38 per cent, and the chrysophoroi and sacred victors around 17 per cent. The high percentage of interest expended upon the hymnodoi reflects their clear importance: singers of songs of praise of Artemis attached directly to the

Artemision. The percentage expended upon the shadowy acrobatai is more intriguing and less explicable. It should be recalled, however, that the acrobatai may have danced in front of altars and sacred processions.

As previously asserted, it is impossible to believe that Salutaris could have used the temple to effect his distributions without the agreement of the temple authorities, making his rather small contribution to temple officials all the more surprising. Nor can this be explained by large individual endowments. The acrobatai and chrysophoroi and sacred victors received only ¾ of a denarius, only 4½ asses more than the ephebes. Salutaris was not concerned with subsidizing temple officials, and the priestess herself received nothing.

Table 7 Sub-group III

Youth Associations	Interest	% within Group	% of Total Int.
250 Ephebes	125 dn.	0.9107	0.0645
49 Paides	12.25 dn.	0.0892	0.0063
299	137.25 dn.	0.0784	0.0708

The ephebes received the fourth largest capital endowment, although the individual lot-winners received only 9 asses, exactly the same sum won by the citizens of the tribes. Strabo had not mentioned the ephebes participating in the celebrations of the mysteries, and, in fact, the ephebes were carefully distinguished from the neoi (who did participate) in inscriptions at Ephesos. The two youth associations sometimes acted together – such as the time when they honored the gymnasiarch Diodoros in the second century BC.[111] Numerous honorary inscriptions set up for the gymnasiarchs at Ephesos were the natural result of the central place the gymnasium held in the education of young men in the city, although the relative dearth of ephebic lists from the site may seem to indicate otherwise.[112] As far as we are able to judge, the Ephebic gymnasium at Ephesos served as the center for young men engaged for a year or more in compulsory training, which was originally military and athletic, but later became literary and cultural.[113]

An ephebarchos, perhaps an annual official, whose duties often involved heavy expenditure, probably worked under the supervision of the gymnasiarch.[114] Some were Roman citizens.[115] Under the direction of the ephebarchos, the ephebes had a prominent role in the religious ceremonies of the city. In *c.* AD 44, the proconsul Paullus Fabius Persicus ordered the ephebes to sing suitable hymns for the house of the emperor without pay, a liturgy taken over from the hymnodoi.[116] Persicus did not specify the exact occasion of these hymns, but the birthday of the emperor must remain a strong possibility. It is surely no coincidence that later we find the ephebes singing for the emperor Hadrian in the Great Theatre of Ephesos.[117]

It is possible that the 9 asses for each of the 250 ephebes constituted a payment to the ephebes for singing hymns to Artemis and the emperor at the celebration of the mysteries. This does not exclude other possibilities: that the ephebes used their portion for a common meal or that they simply held on to their bronze coins. However the young men expended their money, this endowment broadened youth participation during the celebration of the festival.

The term paides clearly designated an age category at Ephesian festivals which had existed from the time of King Eumenes II of Pergamon,[118] including athletic and musical competitions, as numerous examples demonstrate, such as the child pankratiast, victorious in the children's division at the Ephesian Barbilleia,[119] or the victor in the children's cithara competition at the Great Artemisia.[120]

Although Salutaris provided small individual allotments (¼ of a denarius) to the 49 paides, through this provision he brought another important youth organization in the city into the temple of Artemis during the celebration of the mysteries. Certainly Salutaris' order that the paides were to pray in the temple of Artemis on her birthday reveals a determination to encourage reverence for Artemis among the children of the city.

Salutaris expended about 7 per cent of his endowment on youth associations in the city. This constitutes the second highest total spent on a sub-group of beneficiaries. Within this sub-group the ephebes received more than 90 per cent of the funds and also individual allotments twice as large as those given to the paides. This may be due to the age difference of the beneficiaries, but the strong validation of the importance of the ephebes appears again in Salutaris' 'Procession of Statues' (Chapter 3), where the ephebes escorted the statues within the city walls on the 'Map of

Foundations'. The paides did not march in Salutaris' procession. There is also no sign of the neoi in Salutaris' hierarchy, another youth association so prominent in Strabo's description of the celebration of the mysteries during the first century.[121] Rather Salutaris was vitally concerned with the position of the ephebes in his hierarchy.

Table 8 Sub-group IV

Adult Members of Civic Institutions	Interest	% within Group	% of Total Int.
1500 Citizens	750 dn.	0.4866	0.3875
450 Members of Boule	450 dn.	0.2920	0.2325
309 + 5 Members of Gerousia	336.5 dn.	0.2183	0.1739
7 Paidonomoi	3.5 dn.	0.0022	0.0018
1 Ephebarchos	1 dn.	0.0006	0.0005
2272	1541 dn.	0.8806	0.7962

Salutaris' lottery of the six tribes of Ephesos in AD 104 clearly expanded the numerical scope of his foundation;[122] it must also have evoked the Hellenistic past, and indeed the Ionian foundation of the city, since five of the tribes, those of the Ephesians, Karenaeans, Teians, Euonumoi, and Bembinaeans, originated during the period of the foundation of the city by Androklos, according to Ephoros.[123] The Ephesians added the sixth tribe, Sebaste, sometime during or after the reign of the emperor Augustus.

Salutaris did not specify the exact date of this yearly lottery; we can only infer from parallel cases that the lottery was to take place on 6 Thargelion.[124] Nor does the inscriptional record indicate the location or the purpose of this lottery. We can only balance the small sum involved, 9 asses for the lot-winners, against the fact that the capital endowment of the tribes was by far the largest, 8,333⅓ denarii. The citizens of Ephesos received the smallest individual allotments in the main foundation except for the paides, but there were far more allotments to be distributed than for any other group.

The most significant revelation of this provision is the clause which stated that the capital sum donated by Salutaris was officially designated as an 'endowment of the goddess'.[125] This should mean that the endowment was the possession of Artemis, or the Artemision in her place. Salutaris clearly deserved his epithet of 'philartemis', his statues in the temple of Artemis and the most conspicuous places in the city, and his golden crown.[126] Finally, this lottery would certainly increase the recognition of Salutaris' generosity toward the city: a measure which Salutaris perhaps took to ensure that this benefaction would not be overlooked 'as others had been in the past'.[127] At least 1,500 citizens pocketed Salutaris' coins, however small. The name of Salutaris must have been on Ephesian lips for at least one day every year.

The capital endowment of the boule in the main foundation for distribution to the members of the boule was the second largest total, and generated enough interest each year for at least 450 beneficiaries at one denarius apiece. The relative size of this endowment compared to the other capital endowments must speak for Salutaris' estimation of the importance of the boule. Salutaris himself was a member of the body, and therefore not a completely disinterested donor.

The first appearance of the Ephesian boule in the epigraphical corpus of the city dates from the early Hellenistic period, although the Ephesian boule clearly was in place at least as early as the classical era.[128] During the early empire there were at least 450 members, who received distributions during the imperial period on several other occasions.[129]

The imperial boule of Ephesos decreed statues for numerous distinguished Ephesians and Romans, including most of the emperors, as well as honorary inscriptions for various athletes, flute players, poets, and philosophers.[130] It also honored other civic institutions, such as the Ephesian demos.[131]

We know little about how the boule financed such statues or honorary inscriptions; a fund of unspecified origin existed which was used to honor the archiereus Aurelius Athenaios.[132] One rather limited source of income may have been the fines paid to the boule by individuals who tampered with the sarcophagi specifically put under the sanction of the boule.[133] A more considerable source of income may have been the entry fees paid by new members of the boule, such as the ship captain L. Erastos in AD 128/129.[134] In the case of Erastos, the emperor undertook to pay the entry fee, but the amount is not stated. At Bithynia, Pliny states that it had been the usual practice for supernumerary members of the boule to pay one or two thousand denarii.[135] The existence of a dokimasia attests to the relative degree of autonomy maintained by the Ephesian boule at the beginning of the second century. Subject to some pressure from the emperor, the Ephesian boule had control over its membership.[136]

Individuals often belonged to several boulai at once. The pantomime Tiberius Julius Apolaustos claimed membership in seventeen different boulai.[137] In none of the cases of multiple boule membership which involved Ephesos do we hear that the individuals served among the officers of the body. At Ephesos, these officers included a boularchos, best understood as chairman of the boule during the late second and third centuries AD,[138] and more commonly during the empire a secretary.[139]

Salutaris did not specify how the lot-winners of the boule in the main foundation were to spend their allotments. The distribution took place in the pronaos of the temple on 5 Thargelion. Therefore Salutaris' endowment of the boule created activity focused upon the temple. It is difficult to believe that this was possible unless the administration of the temple agreed to Salutaris' plans.

The capital endowment of the gerousia amounted to 4,250 denarii, the third highest total among the capital endowments. The gerousia also received the second highest total in the addendum, an endowment which generated 27½ denarii per year, although this money may have been set aside for ritual activities. The 9 per cent interest on the capital endowment made 382½ denarii available for the lottery of the gerousia. Since the lottery extended to 309 named individuals, at least this many members during the imperial period can be assumed.[140] In fact, the clause which provided for additional lots if the rate of interest on the endowment should be greater, proves that the gerousia had more than 309 members.[141] Salutaris did not specify either in the main foundation or the addendum exactly how the members were to spend their one-denarius allotments.

The Ephesian gerousia was one of the oldest and most important civic bodies in the city. During the early Hellenistic period, in fact, the gerousia and the epikletoi ruled Ephesos for Lysimachos according to Strabo.[142] Almost no information about the gerousia of at least 309 hereditary members during the empire exists until the time of Salutaris' endowment,[143] although Roman citizens such as T. Pedoukaios Kanax, who served as priest of

Rome, and of Publius Servilius Isauricus, the heroified victor over the Kilikian pirates, achieved membership by the end of the first century.[144] In the foundation, one major concern of the imperial gerousia emerges in the clause which outlined the obligation of Salutaris' heirs in the event of his death before the complete settlement of Salutaris' estate. The heirs were 'subject to the methods of collection according to the terms of contracts for loan applicable in the sacred affairs of the goddess and in the business of the elders'.[145] Evidently, the gerousia was involved in lending money, although the source of the capital is unknown.

From a later period, the same activity is attested in a letter of Hadrian to the Ephesian gerousia, where the emperor attempts to smooth out financial difficulties incurred when the heirs of borrowers from the gerousia refused payments on the grounds that they were creditors of the deceased rather than liable legal heirs![146] Hadrian's reply of 27 September AD 120 makes clear that the money was lent considerably earlier – perhaps as early as Salutaris' endowment of AD 104, and also highlights a corollary of lending conducted by the gerousia: trouble in the collection of debts.[147] We can perceive similar problems in AD 162/163 from a rescript of Marcus Aurelius and Lucius Verus to the financial commissioner of the gerousia, M. Ulpius Apuleius Eurykles.[148] Apparently, financial difficulties of the gerousia had led to the appointment of a logistes or financial commissioner by the proconsul who wrote to Marcus Aurelius and Lucius Verus concerning these matters: the possibility of changing images of old emperors to likenesses of present ones (lines 11–14) and simply melting down silver statues (lines 8–9, 23) (these measures presumably to save money on the creation of new imperial images and to create additional capital); second, the actions of a public slave Saturninus, who, without proper authority, had collected money owed to the gerousia (lines 28–30); and third, the problem of postponement of debts owed to the gerousia for three generations by the family of Sabinus (line 43). If this debt arose three generations previous to the rescript it surely proves that the gerousia was lending money at the time of Salutaris, if not before. The eventual appointment of a financial commissioner by the proconsul shows the importance of the gerousia's financial stability in Roman eyes.[149]

The sources of money of the gerousia remain problematic. Individual members of the gerousia certainly benefited from distributions and lotteries such as the Salutaris foundation.[150] Those who tampered with sepulchral inscriptions under the sanction of the gerousia may have also contributed something to the finances of the gerousia.[151] An inscription from the time of Commodus, which refers back to the era of Lysimachos, shows that 'common funds' of the Ephesian gerousia existed from the early Hellenistic period, from which funds members received unspecified amounts for feasts and sacrifices to the goddess Artemis.[152] We do not hear of any such common funds under the empire, and a certain Tiberius Claudius Nikomedes now provides funds for a banquet and sacrifices of the gerousia during the celebration of the mysteries.[153]

The background to the preceding inscription delineates another of the most important traditional activities of the gerousia. At the time of Lysimachos, the gerousia was intimately involved in the celebration of the mysteries of Ortygia and Mt Solmissos, the annual re-enactment of Artemis' birth.[154] At some point, the ceremonies were interrupted due to a lack of funds – presumably a lack of funds of the gerousia.[155] The ceremonies were renewed through the generosity of Nikomedes, the general advocate of the gerousia, who provided funds for worship and sacrifice to Artemis and to Commodus.[156]

The renewal of these practices through private funding at the end of the second century AD shows that the gerousia, while not directly in charge of funding of the ceremonies, nevertheless supported the ceremonies financially. The lack of funds for such practices beginning at some unspecified time indicates financial problems and a possible interruption of the celebration of the mysteries. The generosity of Nikomedes in one sense merely continued the private sponsorship of the celebration of the mysteries: such private sponsorship may have begun with Salutaris. In the case of Nikomedes, however, the renewal of the traditional sacrifices to Artemis also included a new development, sacrifice directly to the emperor Commodus at the same time (line 9), an innovation (as far as we know) which must earmark a significant change of theological perspective.

The gerousia apparently had connections with the imperial cult throughout the second century, as proved by its possession of a whole series of imperial images in the sunhedrion of the gerousia, and by their association with the asiarchs.[157]

The paidonomoi received 9 asses each.[158] In general, paidonomoi in Asia Minor were city officials elected for a year to be in charge of the education of the paides.[159] They organized athletic contests for the boys of the Greek cities, chose, and often led boys and girls who participated in processions and other civic ceremonies at Miletos, Magnesia-on-the-Maiandros, Notion, Pergamon, Priene, Teos, and Kyzikos.[160] At Ephesos, the paidonomoi were connected with the athletic contests of the paides from the second century BC,[161] and exercised control over the sons of citizens when they appeared on public occasions at the beginning of the second century AD.[162]

The ephebarchos, an annual official whose duties have been reviewed already in the section on the ephebes, received 1 denarius from Salutaris. The ephebarchos received his allotment on 6 Thargelion, but Salutaris did not impose any particular task upon this official.

If we now look back upon sub-group IV as a whole, we discover that Salutaris earmarked 80 per cent of his endowment for adult members of civic institutions with no specific tasks imposed. The members of the tribes stood at the very top of this sub-group and received almost 39 per cent of the total endowment. The tribal structure and history of Ephesos also figured prominently in the 'Procession of Statues'. Just below the tribes, the members of the boule and the gerousia received relatively equal shares of the endowment, 23 per cent to 17 per cent, especially when considered on the basis of individual portions. Both percentages are far higher than any other except the citizens'. Clearly Salutaris ranked the tribes and then the boule and the gerousia at the top of his hierarchy at Ephesos. The seven paidonomoi received by far the smallest individual allotments in this sub-group – in some sense parallel to the small portions given to the paides among the youth associations. Conspicuously missing from this sub-group are the Kuretes or any other officials connected with the prytaneion. It should be recalled that the Kuretes were intimately involved in the celebration of the mysteries at the time of Strabo and the prytaneion had asserted some control over the celebration of the festival since the early first century AD. Neither the Kuretes nor the prytanis found a place in Salutaris' hierarchy.

CONCLUSION

The members of the tribes stood at the top of the civic hierarchy of Ephesos in AD 104 according to the scheme of lotteries and distributions. This tribal organization ultimately derived from the Ionian foundation story of the city: the tribes of the Epheseis, Karenaeans, Teians, Euonumoi, and Bembinaeans were said to have come into being at the time of the Attic colonization or shortly thereafter, when settlers from Athens, following the oracle of Apollo from Delphi, founded the new Greek city on the spot a fish showed them and to which a wild boar led the way.[163] Behind this lottery of 1,500 citizens, which also ensured that Salutaris' *philotimia* could no longer go unrecognized, lay an implicit affirmation of the Greek character of the city in AD 104: the organization of tribes in Roman Ephesos, even after the addition of the sixth tribe, Sebaste, inevitably reflected a social reality which had persisted since the very beginning of the group's identity as Ephesians. In fact, the tribal structure of the city was grounded not only in a historical event, but indeed in a divine oracle, which preceded the existence of a city called Ephesos. Thus, a citizen of Ephesos during the early Roman empire could claim affiliation with a tribe whose origins preceded the era of the Diadochoi, before the golden age of Perikles, before Xerxes set foot on Hellenic soil – indeed before the invention of Greek history itself. In a world where new tribes could be invented overnight, without the aid of ancient oracles, such an affiliation might give a citizen a pre-eminent sense of belonging to a city and its past.

The boule and the gerousia ranked just below the tribes in the contemporary hierarchy of Ephesos. No doubt wealthy and prominent men in the city, if not the province or even the empire, filled these most ancient institutions in AD 104. Members of the gerousia, along with the epikletoi once ruled Ephesos for a Hellenistic king; during the early empire the gerousia was heavily involved in lending money to individuals in the city and trouble collecting payments invited the interest of Roman proconsuls who were forced to appoint special financial commissioners to oversee their affairs from time to time. Their sources of money included distributions and lotteries, collected fines and 'common money'. The gerousia apparently had connections with the imperial cult throughout the second century. The boule Salutaris endowed was a co-opting body of 450 members or more filled with at least some members who could afford a substantial entry fee. Control over membership lay with the boule itself. Most of the time of the Ephesian boule apparently was spent considering proposals and voting for honorary decrees and statues. Its sources of income were the entry fees of new members, fines related to sanctioned burials and other sources of unknown origin. It may be inferred that its general character was at once plutocratic and timocratic.

Salutaris placed the paidonomoi and the ephebarchos at the bottom of the first level of his hierarchy. The position of the ephebarchos, however, may be somewhat deceptive. His individual portion matched those of the members of the boule and gerousia, and most importantly, the ephebarchos trained the ephebes.

The omission of the prytaneion from this level of civic institutions is at first surprising. Certainly the prytaneion occupied a central position in the Upper Agora, and was the home of Hestia Boulaia with the sacred fire of the city. But the Kuretes were also attached to the prytaneion. Perhaps their traditional role in the celebration of the mysteries described by Strabo in the passage reviewed accounts for Salutaris' omission.

Nevertheless, the absence of officials of the prytaneion and the Kuretes from the hierarchy is significant given the context of the distributions. Salutaris' endowment did not validate the importance of the Kuretes during the celebration of the mysteries.

Youth associations formed the next and most important level of the civic hierarchy. This is somewhat surprising, since this puts the youth associations above functionaries of the imperial cult and the Artemision. In fact, the unexpectedly prominent position occupied by the youth associations in the civic hierarchy leads to the inevitable conclusion that this part of the foundation functioned primarily as a tool of social, political, historical, and even religious acculturation. Salutaris and the demos designed this instrument mostly for the sake of the ephebes and paides of the city, but the foundation also reminded the adults of Ephesos of the answers to some of the most persistent questions of identity in the city, largely because the process of acculturation within a society is, by definition, never complete.[164] Acculturation into the ethos of Ephesos, which Salutaris designed to take place through mass participation in his civic rituals, may have been particularly important in the case of a city without any formal system of education. There were no civics lessons at Ephesos, there was no clerical training;[165] citizens learned about their city and its history by performing its civic ceremonies together. When the citizens of Ephesos performed the civic rituals of the city together at the birthday party of Artemis, a time of mirth as well as great piety, they also acted out the social structure of the city. The performance at the festival *was* the civic hierarchy of Ephesos.

If we leave aside our analysis of the civic hierarchy, and briefly recreate what was performed on 6 Thargelion as a result of Salutaris' foundation, perhaps we can understand exactly what kind of acculturation Salutaris intended the paides and ephebes to acquire. When the 250 ephebes and 49 paides assembled, probably at the Artemision, to receive their bronze coins on 6 Thargelion, the whole city of Ephesos would have been decked out to celebrate the birthday party of Artemis. No doubt the Kuretes were polishing their armour, preparing for their symposia, ready to frighten Hera out of her wits again, as she tried to spy upon Leto in labour on Ortygia. The neoi and their families perhaps grilled the choicest bits of animals from the sacrifices of the day. Clouds of incense billowed into the sky from altars in every section of the city. Visitors from around the whole Greek-speaking world, who had come to see the annual re-enactment of Artemis' birth and, perhaps, if they were lucky, to become initiates into her mysteries, could hear hymns and prayers wafting out from temples.

What then could the youth associations of the city learn through their participation in the scheme of lotteries and distribution while they were enjoying themselves at the 'drama of the nativity'?[166] First, the scheme helped to lead the ephebes and paides into a civic structure which implicitly validated the importance of the tribes, the boule, and the gerousia above all other institutions. The political acculturation of the ephebes in particular would take place as the ephebes moved upward in this validated civic hierarchy: entry into the tribes marked the beginning of citizenship, the boule was the civic body they would enter during their mature years, and the gerousia, the traditional repository of wisdom and experience in the city, was the institution some would serve during old age. Historical instruction, also a product of the ephebes' participation in the 'Procession of Statues' (Chapter 3), was linked to the histories of those ancient institutions which helped to establish a sense of order, direction, and point for the lives of the young Ephesians. The tribes at least went back to the city founder Androklos, to King Kekrops at Athens, and to the oracle of Apollo. The legitimation of the civic hierarchy of AD 104 rested securely upon a divine oracle delivered more than a thousand years before Salutaris' foundation.

Before the foundation of the Ionian city at Ephesos, which tied the Ephesians to latter-day Ionians from around the Greek world, there was only the birth of the goddess Artemis in the grove at Ortygia, an event which, by definition, lay well beyond human calculation or the contingencies of human activity and meaning. Thus her birth at Ephesos was the ultimate legitimation of the civic hierarchy of Roman Ephesos, because her birth related a human and therefore precarious social construction of the present to an unchangeable reality.[167]

The scheme of lotteries and distributions then taught the young Ephesians assembled at the Artemision on 6 Thargelion to look to the institutional structure of their city for a social sense of rightness about the roles they would play in Ephesian public life, to the Ionian foundation of the city for a historical sense of where those roles came from, and the order in which the roles should be played, and finally, to the birth of the goddess Artemis at Ephesos, for a theological sense of how Ephesian social and historical identity was grounded in a 'sacred' reality, which was impervious to all humanly wrought challenges. The answer to such challenges, other contenders in 'the struggle for the real',[168] lay in the sacred past of Ephesos. Well might the silversmiths of Ephesos shout, 'Great is Artemis of the Ephesians'.[169]

If we now return to the civic hierarchy, we find that, omitted from this level of youth associations in the city were the neoi. Once again, this may be connected somehow with their traditional role in the celebration of the mysteries. There is also some evidence that the neoi received other endowments for their banquets at the festival. The neoi probably did not need Salutaris' distribution. But neither was their importance validated, and the gerousia, for instance, also received endowments other than Salutaris' for celebrating banquets during the mysteries. Among youth associations, the ephebes were the most important and the neoi found no place whatsoever.

The rather low position of temple functionaries in the hierarchy surprises, due to the location of the majority of the distributions. Salutaris was not concerned with subsidizing or validating the importance of temple officials. The priestess merely distributed allotments of the hymnodoi. Her role can stand for the unvalidated role of women in general in the hierarchy. There are no specifically female sets of beneficiaries in the endowment. In fact, women hardly appear in the hierarchy. Perhaps this is not surprising, since the endowment was structured to help bring *young men* into a male-dominated civic structure.

Equally striking is the rather low position of functionaries of the imperial cult. While images of Rome figured prominently at the front of Salutaris' procession, which wound its way through the streets of Ephesos, the imperial cult did not figure as prominently in the scheme of lotteries and distributions. When the ephebes of the city looked to the institutional structure of their city, to the Ionian and sacred past of Ephesos for their sense of identity, as the scheme of lotteries and distributions taught them, the image of the emperor was noticeably absent. Ephesos and 6 Thargelion still belonged to Artemis in AD 104.

Thus we may be able to explain the low position of functionaries of the Artemision in the civic hierarchy, and the total absence of the Kuretes and neoi by their involvement in the official celebration of the festival. As for the rest of the possible list of beneficiaries in the city, we cannot know precisely why Salutaris passed over certain groups, partially because so many civic bodies performed so many different tasks in the city; the essenai, for instance, enrolled new citizens into the tribes and chiliastyes from the Hellenistic period,[170] managed the money paid by new citizens,[171] and also carried out sacrifices to Artemis.[172] In other words, because Ephesian institutions were structurally so undifferentiated, it is difficult, if not impossible, to isolate any functional reasons why Salutaris may have *not* included a particular board in his scheme. The omission of *sets* of boards or institutions with at least some shared characteristics, however, may be explicable in terms of the educational purpose which we have identified as the primary motivation for the structure of the scheme of lotteries and distributions.

From this point of view, the absence of some of the most important financial officials in the city is conspicuous. Surely the oikonomoi, who were treasurers in charge of the sacred monies of the gods from the time of Demetrios Poliorketes to Augustus,[173] might have been held up to the ephebes and paides as deserving of respect and imitation in the city. Why, further, was there no mention in the endowment of the agoranomos, who supervised the sale and purchase of all commodities in the city,[174] who set the all-important price of the different kinds of bread in the city,[175] and among whose numbers we find none other than the great Tiberius Julius Celsus Polemaeanus, the dedicatee of the library in the city?[176] The case of Celsus may indicate that it was not the men who filled these positions that constituted the issue for Salutaris and the city fathers, but the offices themselves. Is it possible that Salutaris avoided including these offices in the civic hierarchy precisely because these offices focused upon financial matters, especially in the case of the agoranomos, financial matters relating to commerce and trade? A more glaring group of omissions from the civic hierarchy may support this idea, and perhaps explain why Salutaris and the city should wish to exclude from their ideal civic hierarchy a set of offices and institutions which clearly were critical to the economic prosperity of the city.

Unlike the cases of so many other cities in Asia, the epigraphical corpus at Ephesos does at least give some indication of the wide range and number of guilds in the city during the imperial period. In addition to the silversmiths, so familiar to us through the famous passage in the *Acts of the Apostles* (19.23–41), there seem to have been a considerable number of people working in the textile industries in the city: we hear of wool-workers,[177] wool-dealers,[178] and cloak-dealers.[179] Flax-workers may have labored in the so-called Stoa of Servilius,[180] and cobblers no doubt fashioned and repaired the sandals of Ephesians in the agora.[181] Luxury items, such as perfumes, were produced by a guild of famous perfume-makers.[182] These guilds – and there were no doubt many such guilds in the city – brought the guild-members wealth, of course, and certain low-level social privileges, such as reserved places in the latrines of the gymnasia of the city,[183] but their occupations rarely were deemed honorable enough to be included in cursus inscriptions.

The guilds, however, did not just engage in light industries. Indeed, their labor was central to the economy of the city. An incident from the very end of the second century neatly illustrates this point. A strike of the bakers from around AD 200 eventually elicited a strongly worded edict from the proconsul (probably), which prohibited the bakers from holding unauthorized meetings, or causing further disturbance, and also commanded them to obey the regulations made for the general welfare, and to supply the city unfailingly with the labor necessary for bread-making.[184] While the proconsul implicitly recognized the vital contribution of the bakers to the welfare of the city in this edict, the clear message of the proconsul to the bakers was to keep to their place – the bakeries, not the political assembly. This episode sums up precisely the essential reason why the guilds of Ephesos were not part of Salutaris' civic hierarchy at the beginning of the second century. The wealth of the members of the guilds came from the wrong sources, and their commercial occupations, however critical to the city even feeding itself, were not appropriate ones to hold up to the paides and ephebes as worthy of their social and political aspirations. Thus, although the guilds fulfilled a fundamental role in an economy which we may glimpse, but probably never completely describe or understand, they became invisible when Salutaris and the Ephesian aristocracy explicated their civic ideal.

Such a civic ideal, which completely ignored the labors of a substantial percentage of the population, a percentage which contributed much to the economy of the city, may seem artificial or even deceptive to us, especially since institutions such as the Artemision and the gerousia, which did hold prominent positions in the civic hierarchy, apparently were constantly in financial trouble from AD 44, when Paullus Fabius Persicus published his edict prohibiting the sale of priesthoods, until the time when Hadrian felt compelled to appoint two logistoi (financial commissioners) to audit the finances of the gerousia.[185] To the Ephesian aristocracy, however, which was more interested in reproducing itself in the next generation at Ephesos than in the social mobility of cobblers, wool-workers, and silversmiths, Salutaris' civic hierarchy no doubt seemed to represent the world they imagined themselves to live in – and rule – very well indeed. The guilds could not belong to the ideal civic hierarchy; if they were admitted, the club of the aristocracy would no longer be worth joining for the ephebes and paides.

NOTES

1. For example, M. Mollat, *The Poor in the Middle Ages* (New Haven 1986) 87–145, trans. A. Goldhammer.
2. Trexler (1974) 200–64.

3. K. Norberg, *Rich and Poor in Grenoble, 1600–1814* (Berkeley 1985) 81–168.
4. Wörrle (1988) 151f.
5. See Appendix II.
6. See Laum, II (1914) nos. 83 and 130.
7. See Laum, II (1914) 85 for Diogenes, who had been strategos; also *Tralleis*, 66 for M. Aurelius Euarestos, who held seven offices.
8. See Laum, II (1914) 81 for P. Aelius Aelianus; also 83 for Cornelia.
9. See Laum, II (1914) nos. 81; 83; 130; also *Tralleis*, 66.
10. For the boule as partial or conditional beneficiary at Thyateira see Laum, II (1914) 81; 83; 85; also *Tralleis*, 66; for the gerousia, Laum no. 85; for the citizen body at Ephesos, *IE*, 21 I 29.
11. See Laum, II (1914) no. 81 for 6,500 denarii given to the boule and municipal officials of Thyateira.
12. See, especially, Hicks (1890) no. 481; Heberdey, *FiE*, II (1912) no. 27; Oliver (1941) 80–5; Melville Jones (1971) 99–105.
13. *IE*, 27.231–79, 495, 520, 535, 539.
14. *IE*, 27.301–2.
15. Melville Jones (1971) 100.
16. Trexler (1974) 232.
17. The decree of the boule and demos is *IE*, 27.134–332; the addendum comprises lines 447–568. My table is based on Oliver (1941) 83–5; *FiE*, II (1912) 127–47, 188–98.
18. The same interest rate is assumed in Pliny, *Letters*, 10.54; also in *IE*, 4123.9
19. The lines in the text that correspond to the allotments received on 5 or 6 Thargelion are *IE*, 27.224–5, 234–5, 255, 261, 267, 275, 277, 313, 493–4, 524, 535, 538–9.
20. On the calendar at Ephesos during the early Roman empire see Merkelbach, 'Die ephesichen Monate in der Kaiserzeit', *ZPE*, 36 (1979) 157.
21. See Picard (1922) 294; *FiE*, IX/1/1 (1981) 73 for the identification.
22. These lotteries and distributions were for the members of the boule and the asiarchs, *IE*, 27.225–6, 242–3.
23. Strabo, *Geography*, 14.1.20.
24. Especially D. Knibbe, 'Ursprung, Begriff und Wesen der ephesischen Kureten', *FiE*, IX/1/1 (1981) 70–92.
25. *IE*, 26.
26. *IE*, 27.223–5, 261–2, 275–8, 532–5.
27. *IE*, 27.223–5.
28. See A. Bammer, *Die Architektur des jüngeren Artemision von Ephesos* (Wiesbaden 1972) abb. 5.
29. See *FiE*, IX/1/1 (1981) 75–6.
30. Such historical sketches, however brief, are all the more necessary due to the lack of basic studies of Ephesian civic institutions, without which it is extremely difficult to interpret any single inscription, let alone the massive Salutaris foundation.
31. *IE*, 27.279–84.
32. *IE*, 27.546–9; Picard (1922) 246–7.

33. See *IE*, 3801.6–9 for Alexandros, neokoros during the reign of Claudius; 424.1; 424A.1; Pliny, *Letters*, 6.31.1 for Aristio; and *IE*, 710.1–5; 2069.5–8 for Cn. Pompeius Hermippus and his son Cn. Pompeius Quartinus, each neokoros.

34. *IE*, 27.150–4.

35. This should follow from the restored present subjunctive verb, διδόσθ[ω, which follows the restored future, [δώ-]‖[σει (lines 231–2), and the restored present subjunctive, [ὅπως ἐπιτελῆ] (line 234). Salutaris instructed the secretary of the Gerousia to perform the last two.

36. For sacrifices and imperial images see Price (1985) 188–9.

37. *SEG*,11.923, cited by Price (1985) 188.

38. *IE*, 27.268–73.

39. *IE*, 1405.12; 1408.5 and 15; 1409.4; 1411.8; 1412.6; 1413.5; 1440.7; 1441.8; 1442.7; 1443.7–8; 1447.17–21; 1449.1; 1450.9; 1452.4–5; 1453.15–16; 1454.6–7; 1455.8–9; 1458.6–7; 1461.2; 1466.6–7; 1470.2–3; 1471.3; 2004.14; 2005.12; 2008.5.

40. *IE*, 1408.7–9.

41. *IE*, 1449. 1–2; for Prepelaos see Diodorus, *World History*, 20.107.

42. Sunhedrion of neopoioi at Ephesos: *IE*, 28.2 from AD 104; 943.5; 951.10 from the late second century AD; 966.1–2, undated; 2083.c2, post Augustan; 3263.1, undated; 4330.3, third century AD; sunagoge of neopoioi: *IE*, 419a. 8–9, AD 92/93; cf. *BE* (1949) 150; (1969) 508; (1977) 418, 421.

43. See *IE*, 1812 for Tiberius Claudius Clemens, a freedman and epitropos of Domitian who served as a neopoios; also *IE*, 3066 for C. Licinius Maximus Iulianus, neopoios and prytanis of AD 105.

44. *IE*, 1578a.1–26 apparently gives a complete list of 12 neopoioi for a year during the first century AD. See also 1590b.

45. *IE*, 27.543–4.

46. See E. Haenchen, *The Acts of the Apostles* (Philadelphia 1971) 571–2 for the neopoioi and the temple of Artemis.

47. *IE*, 27.48, 94, 147, 209, 270, 299–300, 543–4, 561–2; 34.23.

48. See Hicks (1890) 87.

49. *IE*, 187.I 13, a subscription list probably from the first century BC.

50. *IE*, 622.21; 940.2; 943.2; 1256.3; 1581; 4327.8–9.

51. For this point see Picard (1922) 105.

52. *IE*, 3214.5.

53. See Hicks (1890) 86.

54. See Rossner (1974) 101–11; Price (1985) 62.

55. See Price (1985) 122.

56. Salutaris' endowment of the gerousia, the neokoroi, and the asiarchs is presented as a group in lines 231–6.

57. *IE*, 27.488–97.

58. *IE*, 27.519–31.

59. I will discuss the paides further in my section on their allotments in the main foundation.

60. *IE*, 27.258–65.

61. *IE*, 645.6.

62. *IE*, 3015.2.
63. *CIG*, II 3199; 3200; see also Picard (1922) 250.
64. For Smyrna see *CIG*, II 3148; at Pergamon, *BCH*, 9 (1885) 125.4; and at Ephesos, *IE*, 22.4.
65. The title archiereus designated the functional aspect of the office of the asiarch. See Rossner (1974) 106, 'Die Beste Erklärung est wohl, das "asiarch" mehr als titel und "archiereus Asias" mehr als Benennung der Funktion verwendet wurde'. But see also the recent arguments of R. Kearsley, 'The Archiereiai of Asia and the Relationship of the Asiarch and the Archiereus of Asia', *GRBS*, 27 (1986) 183–92.
66. *IE*, 27.532–5.
67. For the sunhedrion of the thesmodoi see *IE*, 645.4–7 (third century AD); for attachment to the provincial temple of the emperors by AD 104, see *IE*, 27.457–8.
68. *IE*, 27.265–8.
69. See Picard (1922) 182.
70. *IE*, 213 from *c*. AD 88/89; 987.9–13, Vipsania Olympias who celebrated the mysteries of Artemis before the first neokorate; 3072, Vedia fulfilled the mysteries, mid second century AD.
71. *IE*, 1012 from AD 92/93; 1017 from AD 97 to 100; 1044 from the time of Pius.
72. *IE*, 3059.
73. *IE*, 411, the daughter of the rich freedman Stertinius Orpex; 617, Julia Atticilla, wife of the asiarch Daphnos, at the time of Macrinus; 637, Aufidia Quintilia, wife of the asiarch Aelius Crispus, who fulfilled many liturgies after AD 130; 661, the father of the priestess Julia was a neopoios between c. AD 140 to 150; 690, the father and husband of the priestess Hordeonia Paulina were Roman citizens at the time of Hadrian or Pius; 892, Claudia Caninia Severa was priestess of Artemis, prytanis, and theoros to the Olympic games; her father Tib. Claudius Severus was a consul, and descended from consuls; 894 Pia [?] Paula Aratiane, was a priestess, and theoros to the Olympics, and her husband was a procurator ducenarius; 897, a priestess, daughter of M. Aurelius Agathokles from Thyateira [?], asiarch under Macrinus; 980, Claudia Crateia Veriane, priestess, and prytanis, of the senatorial order from a consular family of the second century AD; 983, Julia Pantima Potentilla, priestess and daughter of an asiarch at the time of Marcus and Commodus; 984, Hordeonia Pulchra, the daughter of a sophist *c*. AD 140; 1068, two daughters of prytanis and gymnasiarch Plutarch are priestesses; 3072, the priestess Vedia, daughter of an equestrian, mid third century AD, family includes priestesses and asiarchs since AD 130.
74. For the wealth of the family being used to meet the expenses of the priesthood see *IE*, 989; 1139; 3072; but also note 492, the dedication of a building by the priestess Helvidia Paula in AD 89/90, from her own funds.
75. *IE*, 27.267.
76. Picard (1922) 254.

77. See *IE*, 1002.5; *FiE*, IX/1/1 (1981) 119.
78. *IE*, 3801.
79. *CIG*, II 3170; 3201.
80. *IE*, 18 d.4–7, the hymnodoi at Ephesos lose a paid liturgy to the ephebes in AD 44; 645, the hymnodoi of Artemis at the time of Philip the Arab; 1004, the hymnodoi in a Kuretes' list at the time of Tiberius, therefore suggesting an association with the celebration of the mysteries; 1061, hymnodoi in a Kuretes' list at the time of Commodus; 1600, a hymnodos in a list of priests from the time of Commodus; 3247, a hymnodos of Artemis.
81. *IE*, 645.4–5.
82. *IE*, 3247.7–9.
83. *IE*, 742; 921.
84. *IE*, 3801 I 10; II 13.
85. *IE*, 27.536–9.
86. *IE*, 27.459, 537.
87. *IE*, 941; 943; 1569; 4327.
88. *IE*, 1022.9; 1023.8; 1024.21–2; 1025.7–8.
89. See *IE*, 1022–5; and Hesychios, s. v. ἀκριτοβάται.
90. Hicks (1890) 85.
91. Picard (1922) 255–6.
92. *IE*, 27.414–30.
93. For the sunhedrion see *IE*, 28.3 in AD 104; 943 from the time of M. Aurelius; 951 from the second century; 991.1 from the time of Caracalla; 3263; 4330 from AD 231 to 234; as a sunodos see *IE*, 940, but this requires full restoration.
94. e.g. *IE*, 907.4, Gellius Priscus; also 1081A, a citizen of the tribe Quirina.
95. Picard (1922) 242–3.
96. *IE*, 943; 958; 959.
97. *IE*, 1618.15.
98. *IE*, 1604.4–6.
99. e.g., in *IE*, 1081a.
100. *IE*, 1145.7–8; cf. *BE* (1953) 178.
101. I Maccabees 10.89; 11.58; 14.43, 44.
102. See *Tralleis*, 90.
103. Artemidorus, *Oneirokritika*, 2.9.
104. Hicks (1890) 85.
105. *IE*, 902.9–10.
106. *IE*, 3005.8.
107. *IE*, 650.14.
108. *IE*, 11a.9; cf. 14.25–7 (60 denarii for the sacred victors crowned at the Great Ephesian Augusta at the end of the first century AD); 17.46–8 (sacred victors called hieroi of Artemis receive honoraria until AD 44); 276.11 (sacred victors honor Hadrian); 650.14 (Tiberius Claudius Tuendianus, agonothete of priests and sacred victors).
109. *IE*, 27.455–7, 474–5, 500 c, 561; Hicks (1890) 85; Picard (1922) 340; 690; J. and L. Robert, *BE* (1977) 420; the Roberts called the formulation at lines 474–5, 'le titre complet et solennel'.

110. *IE*, 27.413–30, 431–46.
111. *IE*, 6.25.
112. *IE*, 903; 904a; 905a.
113. See Picard (1922) 328–9, 691; J. and L. Robert, *BE* (1954) 158.
114. *IE*, 734.10; 936b; 965; 1020.7; 1145.11; 1150.6; 1579.7; 2288b; 3014.2; 3016.2.
115. e.g. the son of the asiarch Tiberius Claudius Aristio during the reign of Hadrian, *IE*, 1145.11.
116. *IE*, 17.54–63.
117. *IE*, 1145.4; J. and L. Robert, *BE* (1953) 178.
118. *IE*, 1101.
119. *IE*, 2072.1; for other athletic competitions of children see also *IE*, 1082; 1092; 1101; 1115; 1130 from AD 174; 1132; 1416; 1608; 1615; cf. J. and L. Robert, *BE* (1967) 249; on the age qualifications for paides in agonistic festivals, see L. Robert, *Opera Minora Selecta*, II (Amsterdam 1969) 623–7.
120. *IE*, 3813; for other musical competitions of children see 1606.8–9, an honorary inscription for Titus Flavius Sarpedon from Akmonia in Phrygia, from the second half of the second century AD, which shows that children from other cities could take part in these competitions at Ephesos; 3814, for M. Aurelius Nicephoros, victor in the children's tragedy competition; cf. J. and L. Robert, *BE* (1971) 307.
121. Strabo, *Geography*, 14.1.20.
122. *IE*, 27.246–52.
123. Ephoros quoted in Stephen of Byzantium s.v. Βέννα.
124. The phrase Salutaris used to describe when the lottery of the tribes should take place in line 247 is the same repeated elsewhere (232–4, 252–4, 260, 261) in connection with lotteries which clearly took place on the birthday of the goddess.
125. *IE*, 27.248–9.
126. *IE*, 28.87–90.
127. *IE*, 27.376–9.
128. *IE*, 1435.2; 1437.3, both citizenship decrees from 322 BC. See also Hicks (1890) 71–4.
129. *IE*, 1151; 2111; 4123.
130. *IE*, 789; 1123; 1126; 1470; 3067.
131. *IE*, 2052.
132. *IE*, 3057.8–10.
133. For example, *IE*, 2299b.
134. *IE*, 1487.
135. Pliny, *Letters*, 10.112.
136. For an exact parallel to the example of L. Erastos see *IE*, 1488, a letter of Hadrian for the captain Philokyrios, also from AD 128/129.
137. *IE*, 2070. 1–70.
138. *IE*, 645; 740; 743; 892; 928; 1061; 1071; 1080a; 1136; 1586; 1600; 2086b; 2119; 3059; 3071; 3074; 3083e; 3247; 4336; references to the office: *IE*, 816.4; 928.5; 1037.4; 3040.9; 3057.II; the boularchos may have been an annual officer on the analogy of *CIG*, 2882; 2930b;

3419; at Thyateira a boularchos for life is an exception to the rule of *CIG*, 3494; the office was also used to date the year elsewhere, *CIG*, 1725; 3424.

139. *IE*, 8.17, 21, 46 (86/85 BC); 712b; 839; 1074; 1380.
140. *IE*, 27.234–8.
141. *IE*, 27.235–8.
142. Strabo, *Geography*, 14.1.20; see also Oliver (1941) 9–20.
143. The gerousia appears in a citizenship decree for Euphronios at the end of the fourth century BC, *IE*, 1449.2; in an honorary inscription during the Hellenistic period, 1470.3–4; and again at the time of Eumenes II (197–160 BC) 1101.9; for the hereditary nature of this body see Picard (1922) 91–8; Oliver (1941) 9–27; D. Berchem, 'La Gérousie d'ephèse', *Museum Helveticum*, 37 (1980) 25–40.
144. *IE*, 702.
145. Trans. Oliver (1941) 75.
146. *IE*, 1486.
147. In Hadrian's letter it is clear that the trouble collecting payments occurred under the proconsul of AD 119/120, Mettius Modestus, but the reply of the emperor came while Sextius Subrius Dexter Cornelius Priscus was proconsul in AD 120/121.
148. *IE*, 25.
149. For the appointment of another logistes under the emperor Hadrian see *IE*, 618.
150. Distributions to the gerousia under the empire include *IE*, 47.3–4; 987.20–1; 988.23–4; esp. 2113 where Stertinius Orpex set up a distribution and lottery; see also 411; 720; 4123; and possibly 3214.3.
151. See *IE*, 1636; 1648; 2299b; 2514; 4117; the gerousia also undertook the care of certain graves, *IE*, 2109; 2266; 2437; 4117.
152. *IE*, 26.5–6.
153. *IE*, 26.7.
154. *IE*, 26.2–4; Strabo, *Geography*, 14.1.20.
155. *IE*, 26.6.
156. *IE*, 26.8–12.
157. For the images see *IE*, 25.11–12; for the association of the gerousia with the asiarchs see 27.238–46.
158. *IE*, 27.273–9.
159. See Magie, II (1950) 853.
160. Magie, II (1950) 853.
161. *IE*, 1101, a victory list for the contests of the boys from the time of Eumenes II (197–160 BC), in which the paidonomoi made a dedication to Hermes (probably), Herakles, and Eumenes II; cf. J. and L. Robert, *BE* (1953) 178.
162. See Hicks (1890) 82 for this role of the paidonomoi.
163. Athenaeus, *Deipnosophistae*, 8.361.
164. Berger (1969) 16.
165. For the social implications of this lack of a formal system of education for children in the Greek polis see M. Weber, *Economy and Society* (Berkeley 1978) 1143–5.
166. Picard (1922) 278.

167. For this idea see Berger (1969) 33–4.
168. Geertz (1973) 316.
169. *Acts of the Apostles*, 19.23–4.
170. *IE*, 1408; 1409; etc.
171. *IE*, 2001.10.
172. *IE*, 1448.
173. *IE*, 3513.7.
174. *IE*, 1455.
175. *IE*, 923; 924; 929; 934; 938; 3010.
176. *IE*, 5102.5.
177. *IE*, 727.
178. *IE*, 454; 3803d1.
179. *IE*, 3063.11.
180. *IE*, 445.
181. *IE*, 2080; 2081.
182. Athenaeus, *Deipnosophistae*, 15.38f.; Pliny, *Natural History*, 13.10; 20.177.
183. *IE*, 454.
184. *IE*, 215.
185. *IE*, 618; 1486.

3

THE PROCESSION OF STATUES

INTRODUCTION

Processions meandered through the narrow streets of the Roman world almost daily.[1] In these processions, celebrants often carried statues or ritual objects of the honored deity along a prescribed route in the city 'stopping at certain points for specific acts of ritual, heading toward the god's temple or sacred precinct'.[2] Such processions usually began and ended at the primary temple of the honored deity, and temple or civic authorities carefully regulated participation in the processions.

An important example from the early Hellenistic period illustrates this last point. Because the Ptolemaic kings in Egypt adopted and publicized a view of Alexander the Great in their 'Grand Procession' which 'enhanced their position as the legitimate heirs of Alexander in Egypt and endowed them with a convenient legitimization of the divine status of their dynasty',[3] the Ptolemies paid very careful attention not only to the order of participants, but to the route and timing of the procession as well. The Ptolemies devoted such care to the regulation of the procession because the procession served their dynastic intentions: the presentation of Alexander in the procession as a conqueror of the East and a god with a special relationship to the Ptolemies placed the Ptolemies on an equal footing with the Seleucids within the eastern parts of Alexander's empire.

Salutaris' 'procession of statues' at Ephesos in AD 104 also proceeded along a circular route which began and ended at the temple of Artemis. However, we should carefully distinguish Salutaris' civic procession from festival processions initiated and directed by a central authority such as the 'Grand Procession' of

Ptolemy Philadelphus, or, especially, the lectisternial processions at Ephesos, whereby sacrificial meats were brought to the goddess at the celebration of the mysteries.[4] First, no ritual acts took place during the performance of Salutaris' procession. The procession did not form one of the constituent parts of one of the major religious festivals in the city. Second, although Salutaris proposed his procession to the demos and boule of Ephesos as a private citizen, the demos and boule of Ephesos ratified Salutaris' procession. No one can argue that Salutaris imposed his procession upon the city from above. Salutaris may have conceived the procession, but the demos *as a whole* approved the conception.

We can measure the significance of such civic approval from comparison with more recent examples.[5] In Renaissance Venice, sixteenth-century Lyon, and quattrocento Florence, scholars have seen the careful civic regulations which governed the order of participants, the routes, and timing of processions as important expressions of civic ideology.[6] In the absence of a written constitution, the ducal processions of Renaissance Venice represented the constitution of the city.

> More than merely reinforcing the ideology of Venice, the ducal processions helped create that ideology by serving as a conscious, visible synthesis of the parts of society: each symbol or person in the procession corresponded to a specific principle or institution; placed together and set in motion, they were the narrative outline for the myth of Venetian Republicanism.[7]

In Lyon, Catholic festival processions privileged certain groups in the city, certain areas and routes within the city, and certain times of the year.[8] The very separation of certain participants from the amorphous crowd in the city along a route marked off as significant at times outside of normal time in the city created a privileged mental map of the city – a map which could be remembered by onlookers anywhere in the city at any time. The Catholic festival processions of Lyon dramatized the identity of the city and gave protection to the body of the town during the festival and afterward.[9] In quattrocento Florence, the public procession was the typical outdoor ritual, a linearly designed spectacle of intermeshing parts meant to 'display the assembled political or social order'.[10] Essentially, these processions helped to create and confirm a civic identity for each city.

We must, of course, understand Salutaris' civic procession of statues within its ancient context: in fact, only when we locate the statues, the timing, the logistics, and the route of this procession within the specifically pagan context of Ephesos in AD 104 can we begin to grasp the purpose of Salutaris' procession. To begin to appreciate the historical significance of the procession, we need, however, to do more than establish who the images in the procession represented, where the procession went, when it took place, and how. We should follow my approach to the interpretation of the foundation inscription, and analyse the procession itself as yet another non-verbal means of communication, by which the Ephesians negotiated their personal and social identities over space and time.

In other words, we need to place the procession within a wider social framework, in which the donor, the city authorities, the participants in the procession, and the audience all played roles for their own reasons: for it was the actions of these social actors which endowed the procession with whatever social significance it held for Ephesians. This is simply to say that, just as in the case of the epigraphical display of Salutaris' foundation, part of the intended meaning of the procession depended upon the various identities and social statuses of those who saw to it that the images were carried around the city throughout the year.

Finally, as we establish where, when, and how the procession took place within that wider social context, we must remember that all of Salutaris' and the demos' positive choices in these matters implied many more negative decisions as well. The route of the procession implied one way for young Ephesians especially to see the city, and also many ways not to see Ephesos, the timing of the procession implied one way to experience the passage of time during the year in the city, but still more ways not to, and performing the procession implied one way for the participants to act in public, and innumerable ways not to.[11] My hypothesis about the *combination* of choices taken, which led to the actual performance of the procession as we know it, will eventually lead to some important conclusions about the historical significance of the procession. To the various choices involved in the organization of the procession I turn now.

THE STATUARY

Salutaris promised to dedicate nine type-statues in the decree of the demos which was dated to 6 Poseideon in the Ephesian civic year, during the prytany of Tiberius Claudius Antipater Julianus.[12] The date 6 Poseideon would fall near the end of December on our calendar.[13] One of these type-statues was silver overlaid with gold, the rest were silver alone.[14] Salutaris also dedicated twenty silver images.[15] This group of twenty silver images contained one likeness of Trajan, one of Plotina, one of the Roman Senate, one of the equestrian order, one of the people of Rome, and fifteen others which represented the city of the Ephesians: one of the demos, one of each tribe, one of the boule, one of the gerousia, and one of the ephebeia. Five of the twenty-nine type-statues and images promised by Salutaris are missing from this enumeration and certainly lines 31–47 in Document A, now lost, would have completed the list of images.

We may restore the five missing silver images from the foundation itself and related inscriptions: Augustus; probably an image of the city founder Androklos; Lysimachos, the Hellenistic dynast; Euonumos, the son of Kephisos or Uranos and Ge; and Pion, the mountain god.[16] Therefore we can propose a complete list of type-statues and images including known weights from the main foundation and the addendum (Table 9, below).

Salutaris' procession of statues threaded its way through the streets of Ephesos on the day when the high priest of the common temple of Asia in Ephesos took office,[17] during the twelve sacred and regular assembly meetings fixed by law and custom,[18] at the time of the Sebasteia, the Soteria,[19] and the penteteriç Great Ephesia,[20] during all gymnastic games, and on other occasions determined by the demos and boule.[21] At Ephesos these gymnastic contests could be either penteteric[22] or annual, such as the matches which took place at the Great Artemisia during the month of Artemision.[23] Based upon these terms, the procession probably would have taken place at least once every two weeks in the city throughout the year. If such repetition lessened the immediate impact upon participants and spectators, this suggests that the purpose of the procession was connected with its regularity: the less immediate emotional impact the procession perhaps made upon the city, the more thorough the internalization of the message would have been. That the procession was

Table 9 Main Endowment

T		Rep	Ls	Ded	L	O	G	M
1	E	Trajan	150–2		?	3	–	S
2	E	Plotina	152–3		3	–	–	S
3	A	Artemis	158–60	Artemis & Boule	3	–	–	g
		2 Deer	159–60		2	10	5	o
4	E	Senate	160–1		4	2	–	S
5	E	Boule	161–3		4	–	9	S
6	A	Artemis	164–5	Artemis & Gerousia	6	–	–	S
7	E	Roman People	165		?	–	–	S
8	E	Gerousia	166		?	–	–	S
9	A	Artemis	168–9	Artemis & Ephebes	6	5	?	S
10	E	Equestrian Order	170–1		3	½	3	S
11	E	Ephebeia	172		?	–	–	S
12	A	Artemis	173–4	Artemis & Tribe Sebaste	?	?	?	S
13	E	Augustus	174–5		?	?	?	S
14	E	Tribe Sebaste	175–6		?	–	–	S
15	A	Artemis	177–8	Artemis & Tribe of Ephesians	?	?	?	S
16	E	Demos	179		?	–	–	S
17	E	Tribe of Ephesians	180		?	–	–	S
18	A	Artemis	182–3	Artemis & Tribe of Karenaeans	?	9	–	S
19	E	Androklos	183		?	–	–	S
20	E	Tribe of Karenaeans	183–4		?	?	3	S
21	A	Artemis	186–7	Artemis & Tribe of Teians	?	–	–	S
22	E	Lysimachos	187		?	–	3	S
23	E	Tribe of Teians	187–8		?	–	–	S
24	A	Artemis	189–91	Artemis & Tribe of Euonumoi	?	3	½	S
25	E	Euonumos	191		?	–	–	S
26	E	Tribe of Euonumoi	191–2		3	½	?	S
27	A	Artemis	194–5	Artemis & Tribe of Bembinaeans	?	?	–	S
28	E	Pion	195		?	–	–	S
29	E	Tribe of Bembinaeans	195–6		?	–	–	S

Addendum to the Main Endowment

T		Rep	Ls	Ded	L	O	G	M
30	E	Athena Pammousos	465–7	Artemis & Ephesian Boys	7	½	8	S
31	E	Sebaste Homonoia Chrysophoros	470–3	Artemis & Chrysophoroi	6	–	–	S

Key
T: Type of statue; Rep: represents; Ded: dedicated to; Ls: Line in text; L: Pounds; O: Ounces; G: Grammes; M: Metal; E: Eikon; A: Apeikon; S: Silver; g: Gold; o: Overlaid with gold.

intended to be taken seriously by the masses at Ephesos when it was performed, is explicitly stated in the decree of the demos itself, first of all at line 91, when we are told that the conveyance of the statues was to take place in front of the koinon, and second, at line 212 when we learn that the ephebes were to receive and escort the procession with all due dignity.

On these days temporally associated with the calendar and celebration of the imperial cult, meetings of the assembly and important national and civic festivals, the guards of the Artemision,[24] two neopoioi, the beadle,[25] the chrysophoroi,[26] and Musaios, a sacred slave of Artemis and assistant to the weight-master Hermios,[27] picked up the thirty-one gold and silver type-statues and images dedicated by Salutaris from the pronaos of the temple of Artemis.[28] The procession began then from a specifically sacred setting, located outside the walls of the city in AD 104.[29] From the pronaos of the giant 'younger' temple of Artemis (130 m long by 68 m wide, with 127 columns according to Pliny the Elder),[30] the procession proceeded southward along the sacred road to the limits of the temenos which had been fixed by Augustus, and probably set most recently by Domitian.[31] Where the procession crossed the specifically sacred boundary of the temenos on its way to the Magnesian Gate remains uncertain; however, somewhere between the temple and the gate the procession must have passed over the bridges which forded the Selinous and the Marnas. The brook known as the Marnas was often represented on the coinage of the city and provided a major source of water for the city,[32] including the fountain house of the theatre. Today fields of fat yellow melons, heavy peaches, and ripe green figs still bear witness to the fertility of this land.

After the procession left the sacred temenos of Artemis behind, it marched along the sacred road through a space that monumental remains defined as neither sacred nor secular, before reaching the Magnesian Gate.[33] The Magnesian Gate, built in the third century BC at the same time as the city walls, and remodeled during the reign of Vespasian, formed the main south entrance to the city, and derived its name from the nearest town, Magnesia-on-the-Maiandros. The imposing towers of this gate flanked three passages, and two marble lions symbolically guarded this entrance to the city.[34] The Ephesian authorities apparently reserved two of the passages for chariots and wagons; Salutaris' procession probably passed through the passage reserved for pedestrians alone. When the procession entered this gate, it also crossed through the city wall built by Lysimachos, whose silver image was borne along in the middle of the procession as well.[35] The procession of statues thus entered the ancient Greek city at its most south-easterly terminus point, as had been determined during the early Hellenistic period.

Within the protective shell which the city wall provided, the ephebes of the city received the procession, and escorted the statues from the Magnesian Gate into the theatre, and from the theatre in the same manner right up to the Koressian Gate.[36] Since there were at least 250 ephebes in the city in AD 104, the procession now numbered at least 260 individuals. Such a throng of participants, bearing conspicuous silver and gold statues through the narrow streets of Ephesos, must have impeded, if not altogether halted traffic within the city at procession time.

THE ROMAN ROAD

Once the procession reassembled inside the Magnesian Gate, to the north, construction work on the East Gymnasium would have been visible by the early second century AD, but probably after the date of the foundation.[37] Proceeding on the road from the Magnesian Gate almost due east, the procession probably passed a heroon on the left, a rotunda from the first century, now called the grave of St. Luke.[38] A fountain built by Tiberius Claudius Aristio, along with Iulia Lydia Laterane, between AD 102 and 117, stood slightly further down the same road before the procession entered the area of the city centered around the large Upper Agora.[39] The Upper Agora lay in the valley between Bülbül-Dağ and Panayir-Dağ.

The Upper Agora formed a rectangle within the valley 160m by 56m, and, while its plan may have gone back to the fourth century BC,[40] it had been paved around 66 BC by the agoranomos Timon.[41] Salutaris' procession probably passed along its northern side, where an Augustan basilika occupied the entire length of the agora.[42] A chalcidicum was apparently added at the time of Nero.[43] C. Sextilius Pollio, along with his wife Ofillia Bassa, and their children, dedicated this basilika to Artemis, Augustus, Tiberius, and the demos of Ephesos between AD 4 and 14 in a bilingual inscription.[44] The façade of the basilika was originally composed of closely placed Ionic columns with bulls' heads decorating the capitals.[45] Between the columns stood statues of prominent individuals in the city: under the floor tiles of the eastern part of the building, statues of Livia and Augustus were found (which are now displayed in the Ephesos Museum).[46] The excavators also discovered the plinths of statues of Sextilius Pollio and his wife Ofillia Bassa. At this point then, the procession was moving almost directly westward under the shadow of a building which belonged specifically to the Augustan era.

First, to the north of the agora, the procession passed the bouleuterion, the center of political power in the city at the beginning of the second century AD.[47] A bouleuterion existed in the city from at least the first century BC, although the present structure on the southern slope of Panayir-Dağ was dedicated to Artemis, and probably to the emperor and the polis of Ephesos by P. Vedius Antoninus, the Roman senator, and his wife Flavia Papiane, in the middle of the second century AD.[48] Its tiered marble seats on the two levels, separated by a diazoma, could accommodate around 1,400 individuals, although the boule in Salutaris' time had around 450 members. Salutaris not only provided for a distribution to the members of the boule, he also dedicated a silver image of the boule. This image now passed directly in front of the bouleuterion for the members of the council to reflect upon.

After the bouleuterion on the north came the temples of Dea Roma and Divus Iulius, the sanctuaries for the cults of the goddess Roma and C. Iulius Caesar which Octavian Caesar specifically allowed at Ephesos and Nikaia.[49] These two temples, built around 29 BC, rose from a podium situated between the bouleuterion and the prytaneion, and had four columns on their eastern façade.[50] The prytaneion was the home of Hestia Boulaia with the sacred fire of the city, and comprised the religious and political center of the upper city.[51] The building on the site in AD 104 was constructed during the time of Augustus, and had been renovated several times during the first century AD.[52] On the eight plain, thick Doric columns of the façade, which supported the architrave, were engraved the names of the Kuretes who watched over the sacred fire[53] which burned on the basalt altar, and who celebrated the mysteries of Artemis in the grove of Ortygia.

Next, on the north side of the 'Domitian' square, proceeding westward, the procession moved past the Memmius Monument, a squared triumphal arch which rested upon a low plinth.[54] On each façade of the building there were semi-circular niches; above the arches on blocks stood helmeted figures of Memmius, his father, and his grandfather, the dictator, Sulla. This monument, set up for the grandson of Sulla, who had damaged the city in 84 BC, dated to the late first century BC.[55]

On the southern side of the Upper Agora, the archaic necropolis which previously had occupied the south-eastern corner was no longer used in AD 104.[56] South-west of the old necropolis, however, a fountain from the Roman period called the Nympheion,[57] and still further west, the hydrekdochion of C. Laecanius Bassus, which featured statues of Triton, the Nymphs, and the Muses in the niches between its two tiers of columns, constructed by the proconsul of AD 80/81, no doubt served the needs of Ephesians in the year when Salutaris' procession began.[58]

As the procession traveled through the basilika of the Upper Agora, a peripteral temple, 15 m by 22 m, with 6 by 10 columns, which dated from the second half of the first century BC, would have been visible.[59] Artefacts found in the temple, which included a statue of Ammon, bells emblematic of the Egyptian goddess Isis, and a marble portrait of Mark Antony, indicate that the temple could have been dedicated originally to Isis, or perhaps Antony and Kleopatra.[60] Since both the Egyptian goddess and the Roman triumvir left a deep impression upon the city, either attribution is possible,[61] although recently, some scholars have argued that this is the temple of Augustus in the city itself, based upon an inscription of 27 BC which refers to 'the foundation of

Augustus and the dedication of the sanctuary'.[62]

Also on the left of the procession, near the western extremity of the basilika, stood the monument of C. Sextilius Pollio, dedicated to the builder of the basilika and aqueduct of the Marnas, apparently the earliest of the built aqueducts of Asia Minor, between AD 4 and 14.[63] The high arch of this fountain building supported a triangular pediment, and water flowed into its small pool from a semi-circular wall on the side of the agora. A bilingual inscription names Pollio's stepson Offilius Proculus as the dedicator.[64] Later, the proconsul of AD 92/93, Calvisius Ruso, expanded this monument into a fountain dedicated to Domitian,[65] with a statue group of Polyphemos and Odysseus brought from the Isis temple of the Upper Agora.

Finally, on the left of the procession, just west of the Upper Agora, lay a peripteral temple, previously dedicated to Domitian, but after AD 96 rededicated to Vespasian and the Flavian Gens, standing on terrain which had first been leveled and then terraced.[66] This rather modest prostyle temple (8 by 13 columns built on a podium of 24 m by 34 m) nevertheless housed a colossal statue of the emperor Domitian which measured over 7 m in height,[67] with the head alone measuring 118 cm.[68] This was the first imperial neokorate temple of Ephesos, although the dedicatory inscriptions of the building refer to it as 'the Ephesian temple of the Sebastoi'.[69] Since 1956 excavators have explored the foundations and krepidoma of the 'Niche Building', set within a small square opposite the Memmius Monument, in front of the north wall of the temple, which, on stylistic grounds, probably belonged to the era of Augustus.[70]

Therefore, after the procession left the temenos of Artemis, it crossed the Selinous and Marnas before it entered the city through the Magnesian Gate. This choice will be critical for my interpretation of the procession. It was at least open to Salutaris to enter the city through the Koressian Gate, perhaps an easier route for the procession to follow from the temple. I hope to clarify the reasons why Salutaris did not choose to enter the city through the Koressian Gate at the end of this chapter.

Once inside the Magnesian Gate, the procession first traversed an area of the city which had centered around an agora since the fourth century BC at least. However, out of twelve major monuments visible within this space to the participants in the procession beginning in AD 104 (basilika, chalcidicum, bouleuterion, temple of Dea Roma and Divus Iulius, prytaneion, Memmius Monument, hydrekdochion, temple of Isis or Augustus, monument of Pollio, fountain of Domitian, temple of Domitian, Niche Building) at least eight had been constructed or significantly renovated since the reign of Augustus (basilika, chalcidicum, Dea Roma, prytaneion, temple of Domitian, fountain of Domitian, Pollio Monument, hydrekdochion) and two others (the disputed temple of Isis and the Niche Building) may belong to the Augustan context as well. Important Roman citizens dedicated at least four of these monuments (basilika/Pollio, hydrekdochion/Bassus, Pollio Monument/Proculus, fountain of Domitian/Ruso), and at least six were dedicated to Roman citizens (Pollio Monument/Pollio, Memmius Monument/Memmius), emperors (fountain of Domitian/Domitian, temple of Domitian/ the Sebastoi), and divinities (temple of Dea Roma and Divus Iulius, temple of Augustus?).

Although the majority of these buildings belonged more (if not exclusively) within the architectural category of secular buildings according to the criterion of *primary* function (basilika, chalcidicum, bouleuterion, Memmius Monument, hydrekdochion, Pollio Monument, fountain of Domitian, Niche Building), at least three were the centers of cults – Roman cults (temple of Dea Roma and Divus Iulius, temple of Isis/Augustus, and temple of Domitian/Vespasian). Artistically as well, while themes drawn from the classical canon figured prominently in the case especially of the new fountains (Tritons, Nymphs and Muses on the hydrekdochion, Odysseus and Polyphemos on the fountain of Pollio/ Domitian), nevertheless imperial images dominated the representational art of the Upper Agora to such an extent that one distinguished art historian has concluded that this space comprised a new urban center which grew up around the foundation of the imperial cult and the imperial image.[71] In truth, the transformation of this space began when Timon paved the agora in 66 BC, picked up momentum when Augustus allowed the resident Romans at Ephesos to dedicate a temple to Dea Roma and Divus Iulius, and culminated in the construction of the neokorate temple of Domitian or the Sebastoi. After the dedication of that temple, which completely dominated the south-western side of the agora, no one could ignore, or doubt, the fact that the upper city of Ephesos had been transformed completely out of its late Hellenistic shape. The simultaneous construction of four major

water installations within this civic space probably does not
indicate the need for an increased water supply, due to population
growth, but to new ideas about the desirability of having plenty
of running water and fountains within cities, which urban
historians have seen as being characteristic of Roman city
planning, and status competition among Italian elites.[72] The
Upper Agora of Ephesos had become the center of a small Roman
city, complete with all the basic amenities of Italian urban life.
Within this transformed space, a cluster of Roman images at the
very front of the procession would have been particularly
evocative of Roman influence over the lives of Ephesians.

THE ROMAN IMAGES

We know all too little about the imperial images in the procession;
the silver image of Trajan weighed at least 3 ounces, and that of
Plotina, at least three pounds. These images were no doubt copies
from originals, but we can only speculate about quality.
Surprisingly few representations of Trajan and Plotina from
Ephesos, whether sculpted or on coins, survive.[73]

However, Salutaris' endowment of these imperial images does
conform to the general pattern of local impetus in the sponsorship
of imperial portraits at Ephesos.[74] Salutaris' reasons for dedicating
these imperial images along with the type-statues, the other silver
images and donations are outlined in the letter of the proconsul
Proculus: '. . . to the honor of the most present and mighty
goddess Artemis and the imperial family and your city'.[75] In
procession, these images were substitutes for the presence of the
emperor and his wife.

The silver image of the Roman Senate is lost and its
iconography is not described. While other personifications of the
Senate did exist in the city, none have survived.[76] The
inscriptional record at Ephesos helps to suggest how the Senate
and its members may have been perceived by Ephesians.
Important members of the order of both sexes set up honorary
inscriptions for friends and local notables, and also received such
inscriptions.[77] Salutaris himself set up an honorary inscription for
his friend M. Arruntius Claudianus, who had been adlected into
the Senate.[78] Ephesians also recited prayers on behalf of the Senate
up to the third century AD.[79]

Most importantly, the Ephesians consistently perceived the

Senate as one of the centers of political and legal power in the Roman world. Ambassadors, such as the famous P. Vedius Antoninus, frequently went to the Senate to plead on behalf of the city 'about the great issues' during the second century AD.[80] The Senate also awarded such titles as 'neokorate' to Ephesos,[81] and therefore played a key role in the Ephesians' intense rivalries with the other Greek cities of Asia Minor. Senatorial decrees thus influenced both international and inter-city affairs.

The reality of the Senate's power to create legislation which affected the everyday lives of Ephesians reinforced this perception: a letter of a governor, probably from the tetrarchic period, makes clear that *senatus consulta* were regarded as sources of law by the Ephesians. Ancient precedence in the city was based upon 'the laws and the imperial constitutions and decrees of the sacred Senate'.[82]

Thus, the presence of senators living at Ephesos, their inscriptions scattered throughout the city, and the published decrees of the Senate no doubt created the perception that the Roman Senate played a central role in the lives of Ephesians. Asia was, after all, a province governed by proconsuls of the senatorial order selected by lot, and a representation of the personified Senate is to be expected there. Salutaris intended the silver image of the Senate, which followed the images of Trajan and Plotina through the Augustan basilika, to focus reflection upon the body which was at the center of political and legal authority in Rome.

The silver image of the Ephesian boule formed a conscious counterpoint to the image of the Roman Senate. One surviving representation of the boule at Ephesos from the Antonine Altar has been considered the art-historical equivalent of the Roman Genius Senatus.[83] Elsewhere in Asia Minor, boulai often were represented in statuary form.[84] At Ephesos, no actions can be associated with the now lost representation of the boule. But the real Ephesian boule existed for all to see, and such a body, filled with rich men who constantly voted on proposals brought before them, might appear to be a provincial mirror of the Roman Senate. Salutaris matched the images of the Roman Senate and the Ephesian boule in this first cluster of representations.

The silver image which represented the Roman demos obviously paralleled the silver image of the Ephesian demos and probably appeared as a representation of the Genius Populi Romani.[85] Unfortunately no such representations of the Genius of the

Roman people can be identified securely on coins or statuary at Ephesos; however, the inscriptional record of the city offers at least one significant piece of evidence for the perception of the influence of the demos of Rome over the lives of the Ephesians. A decree from Rome, which probably belongs to the period soon after 133 BC, but which was re-engraved during the Sullan era, after the destruction of the original location of the inscription, the temple of Jupiter Capitolinus on 6 July 83 BC, expressed the thanks of the people of Ephesos to the Roman people for the gift of *libertas*.[86] This decree shows that in the eyes of the Ephesians, at the time of the formation of the province, the Populus Romanus was seen as the ultimate source of administrative authority for the province of Asia, and the sovereign power at Rome.[87]

The silver image of the equestrian order is also lost and no other personifications of the order at Ephesos survive. Therefore, we cannot attribute any specific actions associated with the image alone. Salutaris himself was a member of the order and an element of self-advertisement should not be excluded. Certainly other members of the order were much in evidence at Ephesos from the early second century through the third century AD.[88] Equestrians such as the agoranomos L. Cornelius Philoserapis and the archiatros Aur. Apolaustos held many important offices in the city,[89] and others were connected with some of the most powerful families in the city, including the Vedia, whose equestrian father clearly was related to the great family of the Vedii Antonii.[90] In general terms therefore, Salutaris' silver image probably was intended to focus reflection upon Roman military and financial influence, rich representatives of which, including the donor himself, were active in Ephesos, holding important civic posts in AD 104.

The text of the foundation does not provide specific iconographic details about the silver image of Augustus, but the image of the first emperor was certainly well known in the city. Augustus and Livia appeared together on coins, and a bare-headed Augustus can be seen on the obverse of a coin from the city as well.[91] A larger-than-life seated statue of Augustus, with arms and legs covered by a cloak, probably with a statue of Livia next to the emperor, which dated from the late Augustan period, indicates that the Ephesians were focusing upon the imperial family.[92] Excavators found both statues in the eastern part of the basilika of the Upper Agora. Salutaris' procession of statues probably passed beneath the feet of the first imperial couple.

What other associations Salutaris intended the image of Augustus to hold is difficult to reconstruct. Within the city, the silver image may have evoked reflection upon the very origins of the imperial cult, since the impetus in 29 BC came from the provincials themselves.[93] If the Ephesians read the inscriptions on the stone monuments of their city, Augustus might have been associated with renovations in the city, such as the wall which surrounded the temple of Artemis and the Augusteum,[94] the erection of sacred boundary pillars along the roads and water-courses,[95] the restoration of the revenues of the goddess,[96] and the confirmation of the orders of the proconsuls.[97] His freedmen lived in the city,[98] and his procurators were honored there.[99] A statue of the first emperor stood in the middle of the Upper Agora and a tribe in the city, Sebaste, was named after him.[100] Finally, his birthday, 23 September, was celebrated as the beginning of the year throughout the province.[101]

In short, the epigraphical record reveals that Augustus had a deep and pervasive influence over the lives of Ephesians at the beginning of the second century AD. Salutaris' silver image of Augustus, moving through an Augustan basilika, past statues of the first emperor, on days devoted to the imperial cult, must have focused some reflection upon that continuing influence.

The association of Augustus' image with the silver image of the tribe Sebaste, the final Roman image in this first cluster of representations, no doubt reinforced reflection upon the legacy of Augustus. This choice shows a consciousness of the social history of the city, since the tribe clearly named for the first Roman emperor became the second tribe at Ephesos in order of precedence by the middle of the first century AD.[102] Thus Augustus marched along with his tribe near the front of Salutaris' procession. The Roman character of this cluster of images is highlighted by the fact that the image of tribe Sebaste appeared first of all the tribal images in the procession – even though the much older tribe of the Ephesians traditionally came first. Apparently, the influence of Augustus' image pulled his tribe ahead.

The first discernible cluster of images in Salutaris' procession perfectly matched the first space the procession marched through in the city. As the long procession moved through the upper city, it must have been as if Trajan, Plotina, the Senate and the people, the equestrian order, Augustus and his tribe were strolling over familiar streets, past their own stoas, fountains and temples, greeted by their own friends and relatives during their own festivals. Within the walls of the Greek city, the first road travelled by the procession was, in fact, a metaphorical Roman road.

THE EMBOLOS

From the Upper Agora the procession of statues probably turned at an oblique angle to the north-west, on to a street now called the street of the Kuretes, but named the Embolos in antiquity.[103] Covered colonnades, offering protection from the sun and the rain, flanked this street, which had been paved by the polis at the time of Domitian.[104] On plinths, in front of the colonnades, stood statues of the men and women honored by the city: senators and proconsuls such as Stephanos,[105] priests and priestesses such as Claudia Caninia Severa,[106] poets, philosophers and doctors such as Alexandros, whose now headless statue at the very beginning of the street near the later Herakles' Gate still begs for the fleeting attention of pedestrians.[107] Other citizens dedicated Nike statues to their 'most sweet fatherland' in the shadow of the same colonnades,[108] while, still later, Byzantine proconsuls would use the Embolos as a gallery for their learned epigrams.[109]

As the procession walked down the Embolos, it would have passed first the fountain of Trajan on the northern side of the street.[110] Tiberius Claudius Aristio, three times an asiarch and neokoros, along with Iulia Lydia Laterane, dedicated this fountain to Artemis, the emperor Trajan, and his native land between AD 102 and 104.[111] This fountain featured a rectangular pool surrounded on three sides by a two-storeyed colonnade. On two levels, niches or tabernacles, formed by the projections and inlets of the building, offered spaces for statues; it is known that there was one of Dionysos,[112] another of a Satyr, Aphrodite, and members of the imperial family. Within the central niche, a giant statue of Trajan depicted as the conqueror of the Dacians stood (later) with water flowing at his feet into the pool below.[113] Salutaris' silver image of Trajan no doubt passed in front of this fountain many times during the second century.

Next on the northern side of the Embolos came baths,[114]

originally built around AD 100 by P. Quintilius Valens Varius, but later destroyed by a strong earthquake in the fourth century. A pious and very wise Christian lady named Scholastikia then provided a great sum of gold 'for constructing the part of the [buildings] here that had fallen down' perhaps at the very beginning of the fifth century AD.[115] In AD 104, however, that renovation was far off. At the time of Salutaris' procession, water flowed through the baths for the first time.

Nor was work on the so-called 'temple of Hadrian' along the Embolos even begun. Work on this exquisite temple, eventually dedicated not only to Hadrian, but to Artemis, and to the demos of Ephesos as well, by P. Quintilius Valens Varius, with his wife, and his daughter, Varilla, was not finished until AD 117/118 or 118/119.[116]

At the end of the street on the northern side lay a complex of rooms, often called a mansion.[117] It was probably built at the end of the first century AD, and an inscription found in the adjoining public lavatory may indicate that the central building, dedicated, once again by Varius, with his wife, and daughter Varilla, was used as a brothel.[118] Behind this building, on the south-west slope of Panayir-Daǧ, stood a round building, built on a quadrangular plinth of two storeys. The lower storey had Doric half-columns, and a Doric architrave, while the upper storey had full Ionic columns, capitals, and architrave.[119] The construction date of this somewhat curious building has been fixed at any time between 409 BC, and the second century AD, but perhaps has been most convincingly attributed to the time of Caesar, based upon the comparative stylistic analysis of Alzinger among others.[120]

On the southern side of the Embolos the procession passed along the area which the stoa of the Alytarchs, named for the anonymous official of the Olympic Games who endowed the mosaic floor during the fourth century, would later fill up.[121] Behind the later stoa lay twelve shops on two levels where Ephesians both worked and lived from the first century AD.[122] The procession also passed beneath the terrace houses which served as residences both for individuals and families from the time of Augustus until the seventh century.[123] Built directly upon the slopes of Bülbül-Daǧ, these peristyle houses were set one behind another and one above another following almost identical floor plans. An interior courtyard surrounded by columns on three or four sides formed the core of each house, whether they were small, 80 by 100 sq. m, or luxurious, 600 by 1,000 sq. m. Except for the marble impluvia, the floors of these houses were covered with mosaics. Eventually, residence no. I of terrace house 2 included a 'theatre room', probably a reception salon, decorated with frescoes on the west wall which depicted scenes from Euripides' *Orestes* and Menander's *Sikyonioi*,[124] as well as heating and bath areas.[125] Residence II of terrace house 2, which surrounded a significantly larger peristyle than residence I, featured a large mosaic (2.87m by 1.39m) in front of its tablinum on which Poseidon was abducting Amphitrite on Hippokampos; on the ceiling of the tablinum itself there was a glass mosaic portraying heaven, various fruits and plants, a cock, a peacock, Eros, and, in the middle, the heads of Dionysos and Ariadne.[126] The house also boasted a latrine decorated with frescoes of philosophers, including Solon, Thales, and Chilon, complete with a Greek inscription advising users to wait for 'a convenient time or die',[127] as well as an exquisite ivory relief of the emperor Trajan in front of a group of Roman soldiers, meeting defeated barbarians.[128] Other less opulent houses included sitting rooms, dining rooms, bedrooms, kitchens, toilets, heating rooms and cellars, all set around inner courtyards. The larger houses were built on two and even three storeys linked by a stairway. Bedrooms usually were on the upper level. The inference must be that a good number of wealthy Ephesians lived within the city walls during the early empire, although Salutaris' procession, a conspicuous display of *philotimia*, would perhaps only have seen the plain exteriors of the houses, and their red-tiled roofs.

On the same side of the street, opposite the baths of Scholastikia were three heroa, including an octagonal one in the center,[129] on three levels: plinth, a main level which included an inner frieze with bulls' heads and garlands in relief all the way around, surrounded by eight Corinthian columns and capitals,[130] and, covering the entire structure, a pyramid made of steps.[131] The monument was erected during the early Augustan period, and in 1929 the undecorated sarcophagus of the vault yielded the bones of a woman of about eighteen years of age. The tomb to the west of the octagon[132] dated from the Julio-Claudian era, and was transformed during the Byzantine period into the pool of a fountain.[133] Above these monuments on the north slope of Bülbül-Dağ excavators discovered yet another tomb in 1955.[134] A dome constructed of rough-cut stones faced with marble covered the tomb chamber. Scholars have dated the monument to the period after AD 10 on stylistic grounds.[135]

As the procession passed these heroa and tombs, a right-hand turn due north was necessary to reach the theatre. At this corner, on the south side of the intersection, there was a monumental door, probably dating to the Hadrianic period, and an altar.[136] Beneath the pavement of the intersection lay another archaic necropolis, a hidden reminder of the days when the city was clustered around the Artemision.[137] In AD 92/93, at the same intersection, L. Veratius Felix dedicated a Dionysian statue group, apparently to remind spectators of the veneration of Dionysos at the yearly Katagogia, which included a procession along the Embolos.[138] The statue group should also remind us that there were other claims on the theological interests of the Ephesians, other festivals, and other processions, which, in some sense, offered alternative ways of experiencing time and space in the city. Finally, on the western side of the intersection, there was a heroon, which the extraordinary library of Celsus, built as a heroon by Tiberius Iulius Aquila for his father Tiberius Iulius Celsus Polemaeanus, eventually supplanted, probably by AD 120.[139]

Thus the procession marked off as significant the Embolos, perhaps the most luxurious section of the city during the early empire. Expensive private dwellings on both sides of the road dominated the space visually, and a forest of statues of emperors, proconsuls, and local aristocrats looked down upon Salutaris' procession. Out of twelve major monuments visible to the participants in the procession from the Embolos, at least nine dated since the reign of Augustus (fountain of Trajan, Varius baths, brothel, shops, terrace house 1, terrace house 2, the octagon, heroon (Fountain), the round Tomb), and the northern side of the street in particular was completely remade just before the date of the Salutaris foundation (fountain of Trajan/AD 104, varius baths/AD 100, brothel/end of first century AD). The Embolos, which also was paved during the last decade of the first century AD, exhibited just as stark an architectural and visual transformation in AD 104 as the Upper Agora did – a transformation so complete that some scholars have claimed that the Embolos constituted a second urban center of the city by the end of the first century AD.[140]

Yet the functional character of the architectural transformation of the Embolos was somewhat different from what had occurred in the Upper Agora. Whereas the Upper Agora by AD 104 had become the center of public monuments dedicated by Roman citizens to Roman gods, goddesses and emperors, focused upon the imperial cult, the monuments of the Embolos built during the first century AD (of which we know the dedicators in only two cases, fountain of Trajan/Pollio and Laterane, baths of Varius/ Varius) gave that street a character which belonged more to the sphere of private, secular life (the terrace houses, the brothel, the shops, the fountains). When the function of the monuments included cult activities (the round building, heroon, octagon, heroon/fountain, round tomb), the emphasis was upon individual display and local cult, rather than international cult. The dedication of the 'temple of Hadrian' would soon bring the public celebration of the imperial cult down from the Upper Agora into the heart of the Embolos; in AD 104, however, the Embolos retained its more individual, and local atmosphere. Just as the Upper Agora radiated public Roman influence, power, and city planning, the Embolos gushed forth aristocratic achievement and display, regardless of gender. The burial of the fallen heroes and heroines of the city along and above the Embolos perfectly symbolizes the heroic character of this urban space. Within such a visual context, the silver image of Lysimachos may have been particularly evocative of such heroic achievement. Indeed the Hellenistic ruler left a deep and lasting imprint upon the city after his death at Koroupedion in 281 BC.[141]

First, perhaps in 289 BC, Lysimachos had moved the inhabitants of the Hellenistic city to a new site on the hill near the river Kaystros, some distance below the original settlement, where a harbor could be constructed behind the end of a long ridge.[142] He had increased the population of the city by forcibly removing some of the inhabitants of the Ionian cities of Kolophon and Lebedos to the new city,[143] and renamed the new city Arsinoe in honor of his Egyptian princess wife.[144] Lysimachos also had strengthened the defenses of the city by the construction of a wall which followed the summits of the city,[145] replaced the Ephesian democracy with an oligarchical government dominated by the gerousia and the epikletoi,[146] and reorganized the celebration of the mysteries of Artemis.[147]

Amidst the crowd of statues along the Embolos, where even deified emperors would someday beg humble strangers to stop for a few moments, to read how they conquered the barbarians of Dacia and Parthia, where the mansions of the rich and the heroa of the famous cast long shadows over pedestrians, the silver image of Lysimachos might focus reflection upon one who had outstripped all of these suitors of public honor. Lysimachos had renamed the city after his wife, wrapped that city in a strong wall, and rewritten the story of Artemis' birth. Lysimachos, a man of the Hellenistic world, was the second founder of Ephesos; no Roman, however beautiful his temple, however ornate his honorary inscription, however large his mansion along the Embolos, could make such a claim.

THE MARBLE STREET

A northern turn at the intersection would have brought the procession onto the marble street, one of the longest thorough-fares in the city.[148] Along the entire western length of this street, a gallery of columns, 4m high, with undecorated capitals, supported a ceiling in Doric style. Built between AD 54 and 59, this elegant structure, now called the Doric Stoa, provided shade for pedestrians.[149] There was also a columned portico all along the eastern side of the street. At the end of the fifth century AD Eutropius repaved the entire street in marble.[150]

As the procession moved along the marble street, the Ephebes and the other escorts probably saw the gate of Mazaeus and Mithridates, which linked the Embolos to the lower (Tetragonos) Agora.[151] Mazaeus and Mithridates, freedmen of Augustus, dedicated this gate, composed of three blocks with three passages, to their patrons Augustus and Livia, Agrippa and Iulia in a Latin inscription, and, in a Greek inscription, to their patrons and to the demos in 4/3 BC.[152] The layout of this impressive gate, crowned with statues of members of the imperial family such as Lucius Caesar, the son of Agrippa and Iulia adopted by Augustus,[153] had the architectural outline of a traditional Roman triumphal arch, but the decorative elements of the arch were adapted to independent artistic traditions as well, an adaptation which can be seen most clearly by the example of the so-called Syrian architrave.

This gate led to the Tetragonos Agora, which was 111.89 m by 111.39 m.[154] Some form of this agora may have dated at least to the Hellenistic period (third century BC), but the archaeological evidence gathered so far shows that there were significant additions begun during the first century BC, which were completed only during the reign of Nero,[155] and this was the expanded agora the procession would have seen. Halls with double naves formed the periphery of the agora, and behind these were vaulted shops and warehouses. Goods brought into this agora from all over the Mediterranean made it the commercial center of early imperial Ephesos.[156] Merchants and craftsmen from all the different guilds of Ephesos bought and sold goods brought into the harbor which gave Ephesos its wealth;[157] the silversmiths' riot which the Apostle Paul started probably originated in one of the stalls of the agora.[158] No doubt Salutaris' procession would have aroused at least some interest among the shopkeepers and shoppers from Ephesos and the surrounding cities as they haggled over their wares.

The west gate of the agora led to the west street, a square 160 m by 24 m.[159] The gate itself was a columned portal with protruding wings and a stairway between, built by 20 BC and renovated by Ischyrion, a tax-exempt sacred victor from Alexandria, at the time of Domitian.[160] South of the west street lay the Serapeion, probably not constructed until, at the earliest, the reign of Hadrian.[161]

The procession then turned northward along the marble street until it reached the small Hellenistic fountain house, fed by the waters of the Marnas,[162] and the Great Theatre of Ephesos,[163] overlooked on Panayir-Dağ by what has often been called the residence of the proconsul – the only complication being that no residence of a proconsul in Ephesos has ever been securely identified.[164] The theatre was oriented almost due east and could have been seen from far out to sea.[165] The first form of this building, which eventually seated 24,000, was constructed at the time of Lysimachos; the prytanis Hieron Aristogiton provided his own money for the work on the entrance to the theatre around AD 30,[166] and, closest to the date of the foundation, both the north and south analemmas had been repaired between AD 92 and 112.[167] By AD 104 a large canopy protected spectators from the sun, and the public was seated on three different levels, each with 22 rows of seats. A colonnade set above the last row crowned the whole structure. The ekklesia of the city met here regularly during the imperial period, and the general public also watched various dramas and contests from the stone seats of the theatre.

At the theatre, the procession made its first and only stop. The Ephebes of the city filed into the theatre,[168] and placed the silver and gold type-statues and images dedicated by Salutaris 'in groups of three on nine pedestals according to the sectors',[169] on all the occasions stipulated in the foundation. The bases for statues of four of the tribes endowed in the foundation, found in the orchestra of the theatre, prove conclusively that the procession did in fact take place exactly as Salutaris planned it.[170] Lest the demos of the city forget Salutaris' generosity, his statues quite literally sat with the citizens of Ephesos at the meetings of their assembly, perhaps above the seating areas specified for the members of the boule, the gerousia, the ephebeia, and the tribes,[171] facing the magnificent scene building, which was decorated with various reliefs of Erotes on a lion hunt, carrying a slain deer and boar in a wagon drawn by a horse, and with a dead stag on their shoulders.[172]

The pattern of architectural and visual transformation continued along the marble street between the Mazaeus–Mithridates Gate and the Great Theatre. Four of the monuments visible to the procession in this space (the Doric Stoa, Mazaeus and Mithridates Gate, west gate, the 'residence of the proconsul') were built during, or after, the reign of Augustus, and the theatre was renovated constantly during the first century AD, right up to the time of the foundation. Roman freedmen (Mazaeus, Mithridates) and an archiereus (T. Flavius Montanus[173]) dedicated these monuments to the imperial family, Artemis, Domitian, and Trajan.

But if the general pattern of transformation remained constant in this space, the specific form of the change along the marble street was quite different from what had occurred in the Upper Agora and the Embolos, and no doubt can be explained by the proximity of the marble street to the harbor. The primary functions of the Doric Stoa (shade for pedestrian traffic), the Mazaeus and Mithridates Gate (access to and from the Tetragonos Agora), the west gate (access to and from the Tetragonos Agora), and the theatre fountain (water for pedestrians and those entering or exiting the theatre), were all related to public, economic activity, focused upon the harbor. Only the 'residence of the proconsul' could be understood as a private space, and, apart from its splendid view of the lower city, the symbolism of its position (if it was where the proconsul resided when he was visiting the city) looming over the theatre where the ekklesia met, probably was not lost upon Ephesians. The marble street provided access to the commercial and entertainment center of early imperial Ephesos, and was essentially connected to the harbor, which, when not filled with silt, brought Ephesos its wealth.

From the theatre on the very same day,[174] the procession proceeded further northward on what became the stadium street.[175] As the procession of statues marched out of the theatre at the end of the assemblies and contests, it would have faced the street gate on the western side of the road.[176] This street gate, which resembled a triumphal arch, led down the Arcadian Way, as it was named later after Arcadius (AD 395–408), the son of the emperor Theodosius, who restored it.[177] This massive street (500 m long by 11 m wide), which was originally laid out during the first century BC, linked the harbor to the theatre, and later had fifty lanterns along its two colonnades 'up to the statue of the boar',[178] probably a depiction of the boar slain by the city founder Androklos. These lanterns allowed the Ephesians to enjoy artificial light at night, a benefit shared only by the citizens of Rome and Antioch to our knowledge.

At the end of the street was the massive harbor gate, with its three passages perhaps built during the Julio-Claudian period,[179] which was the point of entry to the city for visitors such as proconsuls and emperors. It was also the point of exit from Ephesos, and indeed Asia Minor, for travellers from the east, who ended their journeys along the ancient Royal Road of the Persians underneath its Ionic capitals. Salutaris did not choose to have his procession march down this handsome avenue, perhaps because there was no way to proceed further northward, unless they simply retraced their steps. Salutaris specifically excluded the harbor.

Proceeding along the stadium street, the procession would have passed the space where the large theatre–gymnasium complex on the western side of the street was later constructed, perhaps as early as the end of the second century AD.[180] Therefore, the participants in the procession during the first half of the second century probably saw the halls now named after C. Claudius Verulanus Marcellus, who, along with his wife and son, wainscoted them around AD 130/31.[181] Behind these halls lay the harbor baths and gymnasium, from which there emerged in 1896 the marvellous bronze statue of the athlete cleaning off the strigil he has just used.[182] The original halls, with covered aisles which served as racetracks, were built by 18 September AD 96, when Apollonius of Tyana perhaps lectured in them, and had his simultaneous vision of the emperor Domitian's assassination by the freedman Stephanos.[183] Tiberius Claudius Aristio built the palaestra while he was prytanis, perhaps by the reign of Domitian, and certainly by the reign of Trajan,[184] from the south-west corner of which the excavators uncovered a fine roaring lion,[185] but the harbor baths probably were completed before L. Claudius Frugianus was gymnasiarch,[186] and certainly before P. Calvisius Ruso was proconsul in AD 92/93.[187] Further to the west of the gymnasium complex lay the two harbor warehouses, well out of sight of the procession on the stadium street.[188]

Still further down on the western side of the stadium street stood the market basilika (260 m by 29.5 m), which certainly was a substantial building already during the Hadrianic period.[189] The whole complex, which was later converted into the church of Mary, was suited for commercial purposes, with its naves and niches perhaps used as shops along its considerable length.[190] An Asklepieion may have been located a few steps further down the road on the left of the processional route,[191] and just ahead on the western side of the sacred road lay what was perhaps the palace (70 m by 50 m at a later date) of a wealthy man; the wall paintings of this house, which was eventually converted into a Byzantine bath, have been dated to the last years of Augustus' reign.[192] An Olympieion, which some scholars have dated and connected to the reign of Hadrian, may have been situated still further along on the western side of the street,[193] and, in the distance to the north-west, an unexcavated temple of Apollo according to J. Keil, which dated to the classical period, was probably visible to the Ephebes in the procession.[194] According to Kreophylos, quoted by Athenaeus, a temple of Pythian Apollo was located near the harbor of Ephesos.[195]

The final monument on the western side of the street passed by the procession was a heroon in the form of a circular building surrounded by a squared colonnade.[196] This monument was previously thought to be the tomb of Androklos, but more recently opinion has favored the stoa of Servilius, whose 'hemp–workers' reserved four places in the city latrine, a detail which probably gives this stoa a more commercial character.[197] The stoa itself was perhaps named after P. Servilius Isauricus, consul together with Caesar in 48 BC, and proconsul of Asia from 46–44, whose hero cult was very much alive in the city during the second century AD.[198]

The procession therefore set off the western space of the city along the stadium street as significant for the participants and the spectators. Within this space, out of eleven major monuments, only five (middle harbor gate, halls of Verulanus, harbor gymnasium, harbor baths, and the palace) can be dated to the period between Augustus and AD 104 with any degree of probability. At least two of the monuments (Asklepieion, temple of Apollo) may belong to the very early history of the city – and indeed signify that the procession was entering one of the sections of the Roman city most identified monumentally with the Ionian past. While that section did undergo considerable architectural changes during the first century, those changes were not as considerable as those affecting the Upper Agora and the Embolos.

The functional character of the stadium street, however, continued the basic trend we have perceived along the western side of the marble street. The harbor warehouses, the market basilika, the halls of Verulanus, and the stoa of Servilius (perhaps) all served as points of intense public economic activity in the city at the beginning of the second century AD, and grew up naturally around the harbor (as did the harbor gymnasium and baths at the time of Domitian). The point at which the harbor street or later Arkadiane met the stadium street – the street gate – was perhaps the spatial linchpin of the early imperial city: it was the place where the political and economic reality of the city's dependence upon Roman fiat and the chances of international trade met the social and even theological ideal of a free city with its assembly sitting in the Great Theatre amidst Salutaris' golden statues of Artemis. It was where the demos of the Ephesians greeted financial commissioners, proconsuls, emperors, and gods sent out from Rome.

Thus commercial and agonistic monuments filled this space, which was connected to a harbor that the procession skirted, but did not visit. Salutaris found no role for the harbor in his script. Within this space, the procession did establish a possible first link with the Ionian foundation myth of the city. The route of the procession brought the ephebes of the city within sight of the temple of Pythian Apollo – an old temple just inside the wall of Lysimachos for the god (Apollo of Delphi) who had supplied the oracle essential to the founding of the city: 'wheresoe'r a fish shall show them and a wild boar shall lead the way'.[199] Just before the final turn to leave the security of the city walls, the procession could see in the distance the first monument directly relevant to the Greek foundation myth of the city.

THE KORESSIAN GATE

After the stadium street, the procession turned eastward on to the road which led to their point of exit from the city. On the southern side of the street, the stadium (230 m by 30 m) was situated on the north-western slope of Panayir-Daǧ.[200] The first stadium was begun at the time of Lysimachos, and a major renovation took place during Nero's reign, thanks to the generosity of Stertinius Orpex and his daughter Stertinia Marina.[201] At the end of this street stood the Koressian Gate.[202] The name of this gate, which has not been excavated, commemorated various stories of the Greek city foundation which dated back to the time of Ephoros at least, including the crucial account of Kreophylos.

> Kreophylos, in his *Chronicles of the Ephesians* says that the founders of Ephesos, after suffering many hardships because of the difficulties of the region, finally sent to the oracle of the god and asked where they should place their city. And he declared to them that they should build a city 'wheresoe'r a fish shall show them and a wild boar shall lead the way'. It is said, accordingly, that some fishermen were eating their noonday-meal in the place where are the spring today called Oily and the sacred lake. One of the fish popped out with a live coal and fell into some straw, and a thicket in which a wild boar happened to be was set on fire by the fish. The boar, frightened by the fire, ran up a great distance on the mountain which is called Trecheia [rough], and when brought by a javelin fell where today stands the temple of Athena. So the Ephesians crossed over from the island after living there twenty years, and for the second time settled Trecheia and the regions on the slopes of Koressos; they also built a temple of Artemis overlooking the market-place, and a temple of the Pythian Apollo at the harbour.[203]

The name of this Gate must have recalled to the Ephesians the story of Androklos and the boar, and the foundation of the Greek city. The very last monument in the city which the procession visited before it left the city was the architectural focal point of the Greek foundation legend in the city. This legend was also the representational focal point of the second significant cluster of images in the procession of statues. The images of Androklos, Euonumos, Pion, and the five original tribes of Ephesos all had strong connections with the Ionian foundation story.

THE IONIAN IMAGES

R. Merkelbach restored the name of the mythical founder of Ephesos in a lacuna of the foundation text, and no scholar has challenged this restoration.[204] If Salutaris included an image of Androklos in his procession, he will have intended the image to focus reflection upon the Ionian founder. In fact, the image of the city founder was present throughout the city during the imperial period. Ephesians saw Androklos represented in statuary form, with his hunting dog, in armor and in scenes with the boar,[205] and on coins carrying a spear or charging the boar.[206] Around the middle of the second century, a large statue of Androklos (196 cm) was perhaps placed in the Vedius gymnasium, the head of which probably was a portrait of Antinoos, the favorite of Hadrian.[207]

Inscriptions from the period also indicate that the image of Androklos could be seen on a mosaic from the south side of the agora, and on a relief from the theatre.[208] The Ephesians celebrated a special day in honor of Androklos throughout the city each year,[209] after the second neokorate of the city, and probably named one of the divisions of one of the tribes after him as well.[210] His name has been found carved on to an architrave fragment from terrace house I along the Embolos,[211] and the Ephesians further preserved his memory in various honorary epigrams: one inscribed into a wall near the theatre,[212] another from the Artemision, in an inscription for the rhetorician Soteros, where the members of the boule were called Androklidai,[213] and in an epigram from the fourth century AD, where Messalinus, the proconsul of Asia, is called a founder of conspicuous Ephesos, superior to Androklos.[214] Finally, a corporation of tradesmen, who may have worked in the east hall of the agora, named themselves the Androklidai, again after the second neokorate (post AD 132) of the city.[215]

The evidence of these representations and allusions spread throughout the city suggests that Androklos experienced a revival of sorts under the empire, since none of these references date even to the late Hellenistic period. The silver image of Androklos, if carried about through the streets of the city in AD 104, would not have seemed extraordinary to Ephesians. In fact, the city founder would be shown bringing down the boar with his javelin all over the city until the fourth century AD.

The silver image of Euonumos was intended to recall the legend of the son of Kephisos or Uranos and Ge who gave his name to one of the original tribes of Ephesos, composed of the first Attic settlers.[216] Unfortunately no representations of Euonumos from Ephesos survive. The silver image of Pion, the mountain god, was another reference to the Greek foundation story.[217]

According to Kreophylos, the Ephesians settled Trecheia and the regions upon Koressos where the javelin brought down the boar.[218] After the discovery of the Salutaris endowment, some scholars concluded that, since the Koressian Gate was to be found at the northern exit of the city, the area called Koressos was located on the slopes of Panayir-Daǧ, not on Bülbül-Daǧ.[219] Following J. Keil, W. Alzinger has suggested that Androklos was understood to have slain the boar on Mt Pion, modern Panayir-Daǧ, in the region called Koressos.[220] Support for this view now comes first from the epigram of Claudia Trophime, the prytanis of AD 92/93, in which the description of Mt Pion, 'drinking in the rain from the sky', best suits the external characteristics of Panayir-Daǧ, and second, from an inscription which mentions a street in Koressos.[221] The latter inscription would seem to imply that Koressos was a region inside the city walls. Coins from the period also show the god of the mountain associated with the rock Trecheia, and a boar pierced by a javelin, both obvious allusions to the foundation story.[222]

All of the tribal images in the procession, except the representation of tribe Sebaste, also related to the Ionian foundation. The image of the tribe called Epheseis represented the original inhabitants whom the Attic colonists found on the land according to Ephoros.[223] This tribe occupied the first position in the order of tribal precedence at Ephesos until the late first century AD, and a complete list of its chiliastyes can be reconstructed.[224]

The tribe of the Karenaeans took its name from the settlers brought from Karene by the Ephesians to help during the struggle with the children of Androklos after the death of the founder.[225] The image of the tribe of the Teians constituted another reference to the early history of Ephesos. The Ephesians also brought the Teians into the city to help fight the sons of Androklos, and the new settlers gave their name to the tribe.[226] The tribe of the Euonumoi was named after the previously discussed Euonumos. The silver image of the tribe of the Bembinaeans may have recalled some rather subtle nuances within the story of the Ionian foundation. For while the Bembinaeans made up one of the original five tribes of the city,[227] the name itself may indicate that a significant non-Attic element accompanied the settlers from Athens. Bembina, in fact, was a village in the Argolid 2 miles from the Nemean temple, and in any case, Herodotus asserted that, with the possible exception of Miletos, large numbers of non-Attic settlers were included in all of the Ionian colonies.[228] Two of the tribes' chiliastyes, or sub-divisions of a thousand, Pelasgios and Aigoteos, possibly derived from the name of the Arcadian city destroyed by Sparta, recalled the Peloponnesos even during the imperial period.[229]

Thus the images of Androklos, Euonumos, Pion, the five original tribes of Ephesos, and possibly even the silver type-statue of Artemis 'resembling the one in Kastalia', which was a fountain on Mt Pion,[230] were meant to focus reflection upon the Ionian foundation of the city.

In truth, Salutaris assembled all the major characters of the story in the very setting in the city which was most evocative architecturally of the Ionian foundation myth. The ancient temple of Pythian Apollo, who produced the enigmatic oracle which directed the foundation, stood only a few hundred meters away. Androklos himself moved past the thickets of Koressos, ready to bring down that unfortunate boar with his javelin. At his side, the five original tribes of Ephesos returned to the area of the city which would have been associated automatically with the Ionian settlement, and prepared to fight for the succession. Above that settlement, the mountain god Pion drank from the same rains which fed the fountain of Kastalia. Protected by the wall of a second city founder, the last place the procession of statues visited within the city was precisely the spot where monumental remains show that the Ephesians believed the Greek city was born.

It was also at this time that the ephebes of the city left the procession, before the guards, the two neopoioi, the beadle, the chrysophoroi, and Musaios ventured to carry the type-statues and images out through the Koressian Gate.

THE TEMPLE OF ARTEMIS

After the guards, the neopoioi, the chrysophoroi, and Musaios left the Koressian Gate, they again marched along the sacred road, across the space which mediated between the city and the temple of Artemis. Once they reached the temple, they put all of the type-statues and images except those of Trajan and Plotina (kept in Salutaris' possession while he was alive) back into the pronaos of the temple. Since it would have taken the procession approximately thirty-five minutes to reach the temple from the theatre through the Koressian Gate, we can estimate the time necessary for completion of the route to be not less than ninety minutes.

The completion of the circular procession was thus signified by returning the dominant symbolic representation – Artemis – to her home outside the walls of the city. Nine out of the thirty-one statues in the procession depicted the goddess in her various forms. Golden Artemis with her stags led all the groups of statues in the procession, and at least five other type-statues of the goddess (nos. 6, 9, 12, 21, and 27) contained strong allusions to the celebration of the mysteries of Artemis.

The stag was the symbol most associated with the goddess Artemis, and appeared with her on an electrum coin from before 500 BC.[231] Coins which depicted Artemis flanked by two stags also were produced throughout the Roman period.[232] The same iconographic association can be seen on a cult statue which has survived,[233] and on a gem from the Roman period.[234] Therefore Salutaris chose a conventional representation of the goddess to lead his procession, one which was deeply rooted in the art-historical past of the city. The temple of Artemis, which produced privileged patterns of divine representations, generated such conventional prototypes.[235]

But if the temple limited Salutaris' iconographic choices, his personal selection of material was certainly free and highly significant. As a material for statues, gold had overt divine associations in the Greek world. The virtual indestructibility of the metal symbolized the immortality of the gods.[236] For this reason the use of solid gold was reserved for statues of emperors and gods alone during this period.[237]

Nevertheless, even golden Artemis with her ever-present stags did not dominate the procession visually. Rather, it was Artemis carrying a torch which was the dominant representation in the entire procession.[238] Such a representation would immediately evoke the spectacle of the celebration of her mysteries, which were probably performed at night.[239] The association of a female deity with torches may ultimately be connected with chthonic symbolism at Ephesos; certainly there was also a procession of torches at the celebration of the mysteries of Cybele, the native Anatolian goddess, on the night of the resurrection of Attis.[240] If the celebration of the mysteries of Artemis was essentially a spring festival, centered upon the re-enactment of Artemis' birth, the torchlight procession in it was perhaps borrowed from the rites of the ancient Anatolian goddess, where torches were used symbolically to rekindle the forces of the earth.[241] Certainly torches remained a popular iconographic symbol on coins connected with Artemis until the Severan period,[242] and a statue of Artemis, probably holding a bow in her right hand and a large torch in her left proves an association from the early Hellenistic era.[243] Finally, the epigraphical record reveals the existence of a female chief torch-bearer at festivals.[244]

Both on procession, and when back in the pronaos of the temple of Artemis, the statue of golden Artemis evoked her immortality, and Artemis with her torch recalled her birth and her mysteries. Together these representations dominated the procession numerically, visually, and symbolically.

CONCLUSION

Salutaris' procession of statues was a repeated civic ritual which did not involve any sacrifices. Salutaris himself conceived the procession, but the entire city ratified his conception and the Roman governors confirmed it. We can see how the procession dramatized a historical identity of the city, which was explicitly intended to be performed in front of the koinon, understandable both to Ephesians and outsiders, based upon a synthesis of the type-statues and images, the timing, the logistics, and the route of this public spectacle. When we superimpose the procession upon a topographical map of Ephesos in AD 104, we can distinguish five distinct scenes in this drama: the Roman road, the Embolos, the marble street, the Koressian Gate, and the temple of Artemis, each one essentially connected to one of the foundation legends of the city. The narrative theme of this drama, which we might entitle 'The Map of Foundations', was the successive foundation legends of Ephesos, walked in reverse chronological order by the procession. The lesson of this drama, acted out through the streets of Ephesos, was that, in AD 104, Androklos and ultimately Artemis gave the Ephesians their essential civic identity.

Based upon the structure of this drama, we may conclude that the *primary* purpose of this public ritual was to help acculturate the ephebes, who both acted and watched this drama, into their fathers' reconstruction of the past. This primary purpose does not exclude other social functions which the performance of the procession may have fulfilled. When the ephebes carried the statues into the theatre, and acted out the history of the city, they also advertised the *philotimia* of Salutaris, held up that *philotimia* as worthy of imitation by rival benefactors, and entertained the spectators in the streets of the city. These various social functions (and no doubt more) intergraded and reinforced each other through the medium of the repeated performance.

The actual performance of the procession was not, of course, the exact same phenomenon as the creation of the structure of the procession. Nevertheless, the themes and lesson of the procession, however they may have changed subtly from performance to performance over the years, and however they may have been presented and received as acculturation, education, advertisement, competitiveness, or entertainment on the day, must have always reflected the essential structure of the Map of Foundations, as long as the terms of the foundation itself were followed.

The physical map of the procession was circular; it began and ended at the temple of Artemis, a sacred space cut off from the walled city of Lysimachos. Within this space, the type-statues of Artemis, which dominated the procession numerically, would be particularly evocative. The golden type-statue of Artemis with her stags evoked her immortality. Artemis with her burning torch, however, was the thread which ran through the entire procession, and no doubt was intended to evoke the mysteries of Ortygia and Solmissos, the annual re-enactment of Artemis' birth. Ephesian civic identity began with this event, an event which predated the existence of the Greek city. The birth of Artemis at Ephesos remained central to the Ephesians' sense of their place in the world of AD 104.

After the procession left the sacred temenos of Artemis, which both Hellenistic dynasts and Roman potentates had adjusted several times, it followed the road to the Magnesian, rather than to the closer Koressian Gate. The choice was highly significant: in the narrative of Ephesian historical identity acted out over space, the Roman foundation came first, not the Ionian. Proceeding then through a boundary fixed by Lysimachos nearly four hundred years before, the procession entered the city into a space topographically, architecturally, and visually transformed by a gradual Roman building program. The Augustan basilika of C. Sextilius Pollio, the temple of Dea Roma and Divus Iulius, the Memmius Monument, the fountain of Sextilius Pollio, and, above all, the neokorate temple of Domitian/Vespasian – buildings of Romans, for Romans, by Romans – dominated the visual character of the Upper Agora in AD 104. Through a well-integrated building program, which centered upon the construction of Roman temples and fountains, the upper city of Ephesos had essentially been refounded since the reign of emperor Augustus. The architectural and visual character of this space perfectly matched the first cluster of images in the procession. Seven out of fourteen images at the front of the procession represented the imperial family (Trajan and Plotina), the political and legal authority of Rome (the Senate), the importance of Rome in the formation and administration of the province (the Roman demos), Roman military and financial power (the equestrian order), and the continuing influence of Augustus over the organization of the civic calendar, the spatial boundaries of the city, and the law and social structure of the city (Augustus and tribe Sebaste). The images of the Ephesian boule and the demos in the first five groups of statues were civic mirrors of Roman counterparts. The image of the gerousia of Ephesos lacked an exact Roman counterpart, but the gerousia had strong connections to the imperial cult, and Roman proconsuls scrutinized their financial affairs. The procession also marched to a Roman clock: each year on 1 January when the high priest of the common temple of Asia in Ephesos took office, and during the Sebasteia as well.

Augustus never refounded Ephesos. There was no need. The

Ephesians themselves refounded their upper city in his image. Salutaris' procession, full of Roman images at the front, marching first through an Augustan basilika in the city, on days devoted to the celebration of the imperial cult, validated the Roman contribution to Ephesian historical identity. Augustus was the star of the first scene of the procession within the city; but this was only the most recent mask of Ephesian identity.

The cluster of images at the heart of the procession – where the meaning and purpose of the center of society are most often displayed[245] – linked the narrative theme of Roman, Hellenistic, and Ionian foundations. Lysimachos reorganized the government of the city, changed its location, built the defensive wall, and even renamed the city. His image evoked an era when the radius of individual will was far greater. On the stage of the Embolos, amidst a whole gallery of leading men and women from the city's past, Lysimachos stood out like Lear amidst a host of pretenders: he openly refounded the city, although his name for it, Arsinoe, was destined to join the long list of names for the city – Alopes, Ortygia, Morges, Smyrna, Trachea, Samornium, Ptelea, Ephesos, Ephesus, Afasus, Efes – each of which reflected another layer in the rich history of the site.

Lysimachos did not need a heroon along the Embolos; the walls of the city, which finally did not keep out the Goths and the Turks, who had their own name for the city of the greatest goddess Artemis, nevertheless did furnish the finest of memorials for the dynast, one which neither invader nor time has been able to destroy. In AD 104 Lysimachos represented a heroic, if dangerous, Hellenistic past.

The cluster of images which revolved around the Ionian foundation was far more substantial – Androklos, Euonumos, Pion, Kastalian Artemis, and the five original tribes of Ephesos – and perfectly suited the topographical context where the temple of Apollo and the Koressian Gate still stood in AD 104. The procession left the city through the space most associated with the Ionian foundation legend of the city. The procession also marched during the celebration of the great Pan-Ionian festival, the Great Ephesia. All other latter-day Ionians would have witnessed the assertion of the Ionian identity of the city on days devoted to the celebration of a common Ionian past. The narrative of Ephesian identity moved backward over space and time within the city.

At the Koressian Gate the ephebes stopped. They remained at

the Koressian Gate, and did not escort the type-statues and images back to the pronaos of the temple of Artemis, the completion of the circular 'Map of Foundations'. That role was reserved for adults. The ephebes, about to become full-time citizens of Ephesos, halted on the very spot which commemorated in stone where Androklos slew the boar, fulfilled the oracle, and founded the city. The unique role of the ephebes in the procession, since it was repeated so many times over the course of a year during gymnastic and athletic competitions, no doubt involving members of the ephebeia, along with Salutaris' dedication of images of the ephebeia and Athena Pammousos, implies that the entire spectacle was intended to help draw the ephebes into the very map of historical foundations they so frequently walked.

That processional map first validated the implicit Roman refounding of the upper city, and also confirmed Lysimachos' Hellenistic refounding. But the heart of the procession affirmed the Ionian past of Ephesos above all. Historical identity began with Androklos, who, with his javelin in hand, chasing after that frightened boar in the thickets of Koressos, was the human protagonist of this drama.

Yet a stronger sense of identity, somehow outside of time, encircled these historical foundations told in reverse chronological order. The route of the procession led back to the temple of Artemis outside all walls built by human hands, and outside the map of historical foundations. Artemis with her torch lit the way to the Ephesians' ultimate sense of identity – and stole both the first and last scenes of the procession.

It hardly surprises, then or now, that Artemis should steal the first and last scenes of Salutaris' procession. The Ephesians believed, after all, that the goddess was born well before the Roman emperor, before Lysimachos, or even Androklos. More surprising, at first, is the procession's strong affirmation of the Hellenistic and Ionian past of the city in AD 104. Why the fathers of Ephesos chose to affirm their connection with that distant past, a full millennium after the Greek foundation of the city, I hope to clarify in Chapter 5, 'The Sacred Identity of Ephesos'.

NOTES

1. For bibliography and analysis of some processions related to the imperial cult see Price (1985) 110–12; also, for the Greek world in

general, W. Burkert, *Greek Religion* (Cambridge 1985) 99–102; 387–8.

2. Rice (1983) 26.
3. Rice (1983) 192.
4. For the procession of the Deipnophoroi at Ephesos see *IE*, 221.6, perhaps during the reign of Pius; 1577, from at least the time of Marcus Aurelius; and probably 26.11, definitely under Commodus; for other foundations from Asia Minor during the Hellenistic and imperial periods concerned with the creation or revision of processions see Appendix II.

   From the endowment of P. Aelius Menekrates from the village of Almoura outside Ephesos (*IE*, 3252; for commentary, see Pleket (1970) 61–74), we learn that men were assigned by lot to take part in the kalathos processions which preceded the celebration of the mysteries of Demeter, and that a silver standard dedicated by Menekrates was carried ahead of the procession which took place before the celebration of the mysteries of Mēn. These tantalizing, but small glimpses of one procession inside the city, and another in a village nearby, should remind us of just how little we know about the hundreds of processions of different types which must have taken place at Ephesos during the year. As the evidence stands, however, only one procession was memorialized by a vast display of writing on some of the most visible surfaces in the city. This memorialization should speak for the relative importance of Salutaris' procession in comparison to other civic processions in the city.

5. For a particularly vivid and elaborate example from Montpellier in 1768 see R. Darnton, *The Great Cat Massacre and Other Episodes in French Cultural History* (New York 1984) 107–43.
6. Muir (1981) 185–211; Davis (1981) 40–70; Trexler (1974) 200–64; (1983) 125–44.
7. Muir (1981) 211.
8. See Davis (1981) 57f.; privileged here means marked as significant by the procession for social, economic, political, or religious reasons.
9. Davis (1981) 57.
10. Trexler (1974) 233.
11. For the idea that different types of material culture can be analysed in terms of structural oppositions, a concept which can also be applied productively to social acts, see C. Tilley, 'Interpreting Material Culture', in *The Meanings of Things*, ed. I. Hodder (London 1989) 190.
12. For 'type-statues' see Hicks (1890) 481; Oliver (1941) 70; ἀπεικόνισμα generally seems to describe a copy of a recognized type, such as a representation of Artemis based upon a well-known statue.
13. See Merkelbach (1979) 157–62.
14. Artemis with two stags, *IE*, 27.158–9 was the silver type–statue overlaid with gold.

15. For εἰκών see Hicks (1890) 135 who argued that the term eikon is used for the representation of abstract ideas where more was left to the invention of the artist, as in the representations of the boule and demos, etc., or of Athena Pammousos as the patroness of the general education of the young. This conclusion is unsupported by the list of images including Trajan, Plotina, Augustus, Lysimachos, Euonumos, and Pion, clearly not representations of purely abstract ideas. Rather, an eikon was usually an honorific image placed in a square or other public place, but also could be associated with the agalma of the main deity of a temple; see also L. Robert, *REA* (1964) 316–24, who argued that an eikon was an honorific 'likeness' of a mortal, such as a living emperor or a local official; Price (1985) 177; K. Koonce, *AJP*, 109 (1988) 108–10; Salutaris' eikones included ones of Augustus and Athena Pammousos. Therefore Robert's definition may need adjustment.

16. Augustus from *IE*, 27.174–5; Androklos suggested by Merkelbach at line 183; Lysimachos, restored to line 187 from *IE*, 29.9, 18; Euonumos, a restoration at line 191; and the mountain god Pion at line 195, restored by Heberdey from *IE*, 38.8.

17. *IE*, 27.52–3, 203–4. The archieratic year at Ephesos began on 1 January, see *RE*, I (1913) 233.

18. *IE*, 27.53–4, 203, 468–9 (regular assemblies); 157, 207, 420 (assemblies); 476, 557–8 (every assembly).

19. Such as the one for C. Iulius Caesar held once every four years, *IE*, 251.7; cf. 205.

20. See *IE*, 27.55–6 note on 174; also Thucydides, *History of the Peloponnesian War*, 3.104; Diodorus, *World History*, 15.49; for the festival during the imperial period see *IE*, 22.42–3 (at the time of Pius); also 859a; 1106, for the kitharodos Tiberius Claudius Epigonos, a victor at the 517th penteteric Great Ephesia in AD 170.

21. *IE*, 27.213, 553–9, 213–14.

22. *IE*, 7Ib.6 from 98/97 or 94/93 BC.

23. *IE*, 924a; 1605.15; 1615.11.

24. *IE*, 27.268–73.

25. *IE*, 27.49, 90–3, 207–9, 270–3.

26. *IE*, 27.419–23, 438.

27. *IE*, 27.210.

28. *IE*, 27.49, 90–3, 207–9, 270–3.

29. The temple is no. 1 on the chart of 'The Procession of Statues and The Plan of Ephesos in AD 104' on p. 128.

30. Pliny, *Natural History*, 36.95–6; A. Bammer, *Die Architektur des jüngeren Artemision von Ephesos* (Wiesbaden 1972); for the dimensions of the temple see J. B. Ward-Perkins, *Roman Imperial Architecture* (London 1983) 117.

31. See Strabo, *Geography*, 14.1.23 for Augustus' nullification of Antony's extension of the temenos; also *IE*, 3501; 3502; 3503; 3506; 3507; 3508; 3509; 3510 for the temenos at the time of Domitian; 3511; 3512 under Trajan.

32. The Marnas is present-day Dervend Dere. The Marnas was depicted

on a coin from the time of Domitian, see Head (1964) Ephesus 218. For the Marnas as a water source see *IE*, 414; 415; 416; 417; 1530; 4105.

33. No. 4 on the chart of the procession: on 9 August 1988, I walked this section of the processional route in approximately 30 minutes; for the Magnesian Gate see *RE*, XII (1970) 1599; also *Anz. Wien*, 121 (1984) 209–32.

34. See *IE*, 27.50–1 (partially restored), 211 (restored), 424, 564–5; 2121 (restored).

35. No. 5 on the chart of the procession, the wall of Lysimachos wrapped around the city for 4.5 km; for the wall of Lysimachos, see Seiterle, *JÖAI*, 47 (1964–5) 8–11.

36. *IE*, 27.49–52, 210–13, 423–5.

37. The building on the site today, built by the famous sophist Flavius Damianus at the same time as repairs to the sacred road, dates from the mid-second century AD. See *RE*, Suppl. XII (1970) 1613–15; *Anz. Wien*, 119 (1982) 137–68; A. Farrington, 'Imperial Bath Buildings in South-West Asia Minor', in *RAGW* (1987) 50–1.

38. Chart, no. 6; see *RE*, XII (1970) 1676–7.

39. Chart, no. 7; for the building inscription see *IE*, 424A.

40. Chart, no. 8; *FiE*, III (1923) 1–168; *RE*, XII (1970) 1600–1601; Alzinger (1974) 49–51.

41. *IE*, 3004.

42. Chart, no. 9; for the basilika see Alzinger (1974) 24–37; E. Fossel-Peschl, *Die Basilika am Staatsmarkt in Ephesos* (Graz 1982); it would have taken the procession approximately 10 minutes to reach the basilika from the Magnesian Gate.

43. Chart, no. 10; for the building inscription, *IE*, 410.

44. *IE*, 404.

45. For one example see Ephesos Museum inv. no. 1, 1635; also Selçuk Museum inv. no. 1621.

46. For the statue of Augustus from the eastern hall of the basilika see W. Alzinger, *JÖAI*, 56 (1985) 61–3; and *JÖAI*, 53 (1981–2) 135, no. 144; *SEG*, 33 (1983) 934 for a statue of Drusus Caesar, the son of Tiberius, also in the basilika.

47. Chart, no. 11.

48. *IE*, 460.

49. Chart, no. 12; for the cults see Cassius Dio, *Roman History*, 51.20.6.

50. See *RE*, XII (1970) 1648–9; Alzinger (1974) 55–6; *IE*, 902; for the foundations of the temple see now, M. Waelkens, 'The Adoption of Roman Building Techniques in the Architecture of Asia Minor', in *RAGW* (1987) 96.

51. City plan, no. 13; *JÖAI*, 43 (1956–8) 33; see also *ANRW*, VII, 2 (1980) 817–18; R. Merkelbach, 'Der Kult der Hestia im Prytaneion der griechischen Städte', *ZPE*, 37 (1980) 77–92; and H. Engelmann, 'Die Bauinschriften des Prytaneions in Ephesos', in *Lebendige Altertumswissenschaft. Festschrift zur Vollendung des 70. Lebensjahres von Hermann Vetters dargebracht von Freunden, Schülern und Kollegen* (Wien 1985) 155–7, who argues on the basis of *IE*, 10.25–30 that there was

a temple of Demeter Karpophoros in the pre-Lysimachean prytaneion.

52. See *IE*, 437; 462; 528 (time of Trajan).
53. *IE*, 1001f.; also *FiE*, IX/1/1 (1981) 13–69, 75–6.
54. Chart, no. 14; see *FiE*, VII (1971); A. Bammer, 'Die politische Symbolik des Memmiusbaues', *JÖAI*, 50 (1972–3) 220–2; W. Alzinger (1974) 17.
55. For the building inscription see *IE*, 403. According to A. Bammer, *Ephesos* (Graz 1988) Table 2, before 30 BC.
56. Chart, no. 15.
57. No. 16 on the chart; for the building see *JÖAI*, 15 (1912) 173; the inscription of the second-century building, *IE*, 414; during the fourth century, *IE*, 1316; 1317.
58. Chart, no. 17; see *IE*, 695 and *RE*, XII (1970) 1606 for the fountain of Bassus; also E. Fossel and G. Langmann, 'Das Nymphaeum des C. Laecanius Bassus in Ephesos', *Antike Welt*, 14.3 (1983) 53–5.
59. Chart, no. 18; see E. Fossel, 'Zum Tempel auf dem Staatsmarkt in Ephesos', *JÖAI*, 50 (1972–3) 212–19; D. Knibbe, 'Ephesos-Nicht nur die Stadt der Artemis', *Studien zur Religion und Kultur Kleinasiens. Festschrift für Friedrich Karl Dörner zum 65. Geburtstag am 28. Februar 1976*, ed. S. Şahin, E. Schwertheim, J. Wagner (Leiden 1978) 501.
60. See *RE*, XII (1970) 1601; *ANRW*, VII 2 (1980) 814.
61. For dedications to Isis at Ephesos see *IE*, 1213; 1231; 1245; 1503.
62. *IE*, 902; Price (1985) 254.
63. Chart, no. 19; *RE*, XII (1970) 1676; A. Bammer, 'Das Denkmal des C. Sextilius Pollio in Ephesos', *JÖAI*, 51 (1976–7) 77–92; based upon the visibility of the mouldings, the entablature, and the long inscription, J. Coulton, 'Roman Aqueducts in Asia Minor', in *RAGW* (1987) 73 has concluded that the aqueduct was meant to be seen.
64. *IE*, 405; 406.
65. *IE*, 413; 415; 416; 419.
66. No. 20 on the chart; *RE*, XII (1970) 1649–50; H. Vetters, 'Domitianterrasse und Domitiangasse', *JÖAI*, 50 (1972–5) 311–30; Price (1985) 255: the terrace measured 50 m × 100 m on the south side of the square; on the design of the temple see M. Lyttelton, 'The Design and Planning of Temples and Sanctuaries in the Roman Imperial Period', in *RAGW* (1987) 44.
67. See R. Meriç in *Kenner*, II (1985) 239–41.
68. Izmir Museum inv. no. 670.
69. *IE*, 232; 232A; 233; 234; 235; 236; 237; 238; 239; 240; 241; 242; 1498; 2048; See also *ANRW*, VII 2 (1980) 772–3; Price (1985) 255; it would have taken the procession no more than three minutes to make it from the entrance of the Augustan basilika to the temple of Domitian/Vespasian.
70. Alzinger (1974) 44f.
71. P. Zanker, *The Power of Images in the Age of Augustus* (Michigan 1988) 298.

72. On this point see J. Coulton, *Anatolian Studies*, 36 (1986) 55.
73. Excavators found a marble head of Trajan in the kryptoporticus of the terrace of Domitian from the second century AD, now in the Ephesos Museum, inv. no. 11/37/72; Trajan may be depicted mounting the quadriga of torch-bearing Helios on slabs I and K of the 'profectio of Divus Traianus', from the Antonine Altar, with Plotina as Artemis/Selene, see Vermeule (1968) 107–9, 116; for Trajan on coins of Ephesos see Head (1964) Ephesus, 221, 222, 223.
74. A recent survey of all the epigraphical evidence shows that out of more than 50 imperial statues in the city, Roman officials set up three; local sponsors accounted for the rest. See *IE*, 251–304; 1500–1505; Price (1985) 174.
75. *IE*, 27.342–6.
76. See *IE*, 1499 for an inscription on a statue base which must have supported a personification of the Senate, set up by Pedanius Fuscus Salinator, proconsul of Asia in AD 98/99; for artistic personifications of the Senate in the Greek world during the imperial period see R. Talbert, *The Senate of Imperial Rome* (Princeton 1984) 217–18.
77. *IE*, 47; 502; 611a; 620; 635b; 637; 678; 709; 710b; 801; 810; 823; 864; 980; 1145; 3038; 3062; 3072; 3079; 3219; 3802; 4110; 4113.
78. *IE*, 620.
79. *IE*, 10.15–16.
80. *IE*, 728.18–20; cf. *IE*, 2069 for Cn. Pompeius Hermippus, sent as an ambassador, 'to the emperors and to the Senate'.
81. *IE*, 625; 740; 834; 2040; 3001.
82. *IE*, 217.4; cf. F. Millar, *The Emperor in the Roman World* (London 1977) 364 n.6; 392 n.41; also Millar in *JRS*, 76 (1986) 279–80.
83. Vermeule (1968) 114.
84. See T. Pekáry, 'Statuen in kleinasiatischen Inschriften', in Dorner, II (1978) 739.
85. See Vermeule (1968) 122–3.
86. *IE*, 1394; for the most recent discussion of the decree see A. Lintott, *ZPE*, 30 (1978) 137–44.
87. Thus this inscription, no. 1394, lends support to F. Millar's view, explicated most recently in *Ancient World*, 20 (1989) 93–7, that the provinciae belonged to the Populus Romanus. The Roman people, not the Senate, was perceived as being responsible for the administration of the provinces, both before the triumviral period, and after the settlement of 27 BC.
88. *IE*, 680; 743; 816; 845; 1540; 1553; 3015; 3055; 3071; 3072.
89. *IE*, 3015; 3055.
90. *IE*, 3072.
91. See Head (1964) Ephesus 195; cf. 196; 197.
92. Ü. Önen, *Ephesus Ruins and Museum* (Izmir 1983) inv. no. 1957; 1/10/75.
93. Cassius Dio, *Roman History*, 51.20.19.
94. *IE*, 1522.
95. *IE*, 1523; cf. 1524.

96. *IE*, 18b.4–6.
97. *IE*, 18c.10–11.
98. *IE*, 859.
99. *IE*, 3041.
100. *IE*, 902 for the statue; 1578a for the tribe.
101. *IE*, 26.19; 1393.3; see Merkelbach, *ZPE*, 36 (1979) 158.
102. A list of neopoioi gives the Ephesian tribes in order, with Sebaste second: *IE*, 1578a.
103. Chart, no. 22; *IE*, 1300.3; 3008; 3059; see W. Jobst, 'Embolosforschungen I. Archäologische Untersuchungen östlich der Celsusbibliothek in Ephesos', *JÖAI*, 54 (1983) 149–250.
104. *IE*, 3008.
105. *IE*, 1310.
106. *IE*, 635c.
107. *IE*, 1320.
108. *IE*, 521; 522–5; 525A–26; 1153.
109. *IE*, 1302; 1304; 1307; 1308; 1309; 1310.
110. Chart, no. 23; *RE*, XII (1970) 1605–7.
111. *IE*, 424.
112. See R. Fleischer, in *Kenner*, I (1985) 123–7.
113. See Keil (1955) 116–18; *JÖAI*, 50 (1972–5) 395–8.
114. Chart, no. 24; see *IE*, 500.
115. *IE*, 453; trans. M. Lefkowitz and M. Fant, *Women's Life in Greece and Rome* (Baltimore 1985) 159.
116. For the controversial dedication see E. Bowie, *ZPE*, 8 (1971) 137f.; also M. Wörrle, *Arch. Anz.* (1973) 470–7.
117. Chart, no. 25; *RE*, XII (1970) 1641.
118. *IE*, 455; for the building, see Miltner, *JÖAI*, 51 (1956) 20; Jobst, *JÖAI*, 51 (1976–7) 61–84; the interpretation of the function of the room turns on the meaning of παιδισκήοις (line 3), for which see the comments of Knibbe at the end of *IE*, 455, about why Miltner and Keil were (wrongly) sceptical that a brothel was meant.
119. For an Ionic capital, and the upper architrave of the monument, see Ephesos Museum inv. nos. 1, 1634 F4/5; 1, 1634 G1/2.
120. Chart, no. 26; Alzinger (1974) 37ff.
121. *IE*, 447; the stoa itself perhaps dated to the second half of the fourth century BC; see *FiE*, VIII/1 (1977) 13.
122. Chart, no. 27; *FiE*, VIII/1 (1977) 13.
123. Chart, nos. 28 (Hanghaus II) and 29 (Hanghaus I); for these houses see W. Jobst, 'Römische Mosaiken aus Ephesos I: Die Hanghäuser in Ephesos', *FiE*, VIII/2 (1977); V. Strocka, 'Die Wandmalerei der Hanghäuser in Ephesos', *FiE*, VIII/1 (1977); esp. 12–28 for Vetters' building history of the tetrace houses.
124. See V. Strocka, 'Die Wandmalerei der Hanghäuser in Ephesos', *FiE*, VIII/1 (1977) 53–5; the theatre room is H2SR6 on H. Vetters' provisional plan.
125. H2SR3 on H. Vetters' provisional plan of terrace houses I and II at the end of *FiE*, VIII/1 (1977).
126. H2SR22 on H. Vetters' provisional plan.

127. *FiE*, VIII/1 (1977) 87–90; *IE*, 561.
128. Selçuk Museum inv. no. 6–11/4/75; see also *JÖAI*, 50 (1972–5) 545ff.
129. Chart, nos. 31, 31a, 32; *RE*, XII (1970) 1674.
130. For two of the capitals see Ephesos Museum inv. nos. 1, 1633 E and 1633 C.
131. Keil (1955) 113f.; Alzinger (1974) 40–3 for the dating of the monument.
132. Chart, no. 32.
133. *RE*, XII (1970) 1574.
134. Chart, no. 33; *JÖAI*, 43 (1956–8) 49ff.
135. Alzinger (1974) 57–8.
136. Chart, no. 34; *RE*, XII (1970) 1598.
137. Chart, no. 35.
138. For the dedication, see *IE*, 507; for discussion of the placement of the statue group, see H. Engelmann in *Römische Geschichte, Altertumskunde und Epigraphik. Festschrift für A. Betz*, ed. E. Weber and G. Dobesch (Wien 1985) 249–55.
139. See *FiE*, V/1 (1953); V.M. Strocka, *Proceedings of the Xth International Congress of Classical Archaeology*, ed. E. Akurgal, II (1978) 893–900; to march from the Herakles Gate down to the corner of the marble street would have taken the procession less than 3 minutes.
140. See F. Hueber, 'Der Embolos, ein urbanes Zentrum von Ephesos', *Antike Welt*, 15.4 (1984) 1–23.
141. For a sketch of the history of the city after the death of Alexander see D. Knibbe, *RE*, XII (1970) 254–6.
142. Strabo, *Geography*, 14.1.20; Bülbül-Daǧ is the present name of the ridge.
143. Pausanias, *Description of Greece*, 1.9.7; 7.3.4.
144. Strabo, *Geography*, 14.1.21; cf. *IE*, 1381 for Ephesos as Arsinoe.
145. Strabo, *Geography*, 14.1.21; see *IE*, 1441, a citizenship decree for Athemis from Kyzikos, the architect of Lysimachos' wall.
146. Strabo, *Geography*, 14.1.21; for a decree of the gerousia and epikletoi see *IE*, 1470.3–4.
147. *IE*, 26.1–6.
148. Chart, no. 36; *RE*, XII (1970) 1598.
149. *IE*, 3003; *RE*, XII (1970) 1603.
150. *IE*, 1304.
151. No. 37 on the chart; see *FiE*, III (1923) 40f.; *RE*, XII (1970) 1602; Alzinger (1974) 9–16.
152. *IE*, 3006.
153. *IE*, 3007, the base for the statue of L. Caesar.
154. Chart, no. 38; for the name of the agora, Tetragonos, see *IE*, 3005; 4123.
155. *RE*, XII (1970) 1601–4; Alzinger (1974) 48–9.
156. Keil (1955) 94–8.
157. Strabo, *Geography*, 14.1.23.
158. *Acts*, 19.23–41.
159. Chart, nos. 39 and 40; *RE*, XII (1970) 1600; 1602.
160. *RE*, XII (1970) 1602; Alzinger (1974) 45–8; see *IE*, 3005 for

Ischyrion's financing of an access way from the stoa to the agora in the area of the west gate.

161. *RE*, XII (1970) 1652–4; apparently a prostyle, Corinthian temple based upon the imperial fora in Rome; see M. Lyttelton, 'The Design and Planning of Temples and Sanctuaries in Asia Minor in the Roman Imperial Period', in *RAGW* (1987) 46–7.

162. Chart, no.41; see *RE*, XII (1970) 1604; for the water source see *IE*, 417.

163. Chart, no. 42.

164. Chart, no. 43; *RE*, XII (1970) 1639–40; for doubts that proconsuls actually owned residences at Ephesos (or anywhere else in Asia for that matter) see F. Millar in, 'Introduction', *RAGW* (1987) xi.

165. For the theatre see *FiE*, II (1912).

166. *IE*, 2033.

167. For work on the north analemma in AD 92 see *IE*, 2035; for work on the south analemma between AD 102 and 112 see 2037.

168. *IE*, 27.49–52, 210–13, 423–5; from the corner of the marble street to the entrance into the theatre would have taken perhaps 3 minutes to walk.

169. *IE*, 27.204–6.

170. *IE*, 28–31. Two other inscriptions relating to Salutaris are now visible in the theatre: *IE*, 33, the statue base of the paides from AD 104, on the left at the top of the stairs on the southern side of the stage terrace, and 36D, a base for a statue of Artemis, and perhaps the imperial family, from AD 107/108 and 109/110, now resting on the northern section of the orchestra.

171. This is possibly the implication of lines 202f., if the eikones of Artemis dedicated to the various civic groups mentioned were placed on pedestals directly above real seating blocks which were in order. If this was the case, it might mean that the boule sat in the assembly at Ephesos on certain occasions, and perhaps recommended measures for ratification during meetings of the full assembly, possibly after passing measures itself. This hypothesis would be one way of accounting for the usual formulaic prescript of Ephesian public decrees in which measures are passed first by the boule.

172. Ephesos Museum inv. nos 1, 821, 820 (lion hunt); 1, 819 (wagon with boar and deer); 1, 1538 (stag); for the reliefs, see *JÖAI*, 43 (1956–8) 15ff.

173. For Montanus, see R. Kearsley, 'A Leading Family of Cibyra and Some Asiarchs of the First Century', *Anatolian Studies*, 38 (1988) 43–5, although it is not correct to state that, 'The scope of his [Montanus'] benefactions is hard to equal among the many other honorific inscriptions so far published from the city' (p. 45). Salutaris' many benefactions to the city, as well as those of Stertinius Orpex (*IE*, 4123), easily equalled those of Montanus both in terms of money spent and social significance.

174. *IE*, 27.270–3.

175. Chart, no. 44.

176. Chart, no. 45; *RE*, XII (1970) 1597.

177. Chart, no. 46; *FiE*, I (1906) 132–40.
178. *IE*, 557.
179. Chart, no. 47; *RE*, XII (1970) 1597; Alzinger (1974) 60–1.
180. *RE*, XII (1970) 1613.
181. Chart, no. 48; see *IE*, 430.
182. Chart, nos. 49 and 50; for the statue, which stands 192 cm. high, now in the Ephesos Museum, see inv. no. VI, 3168.
183. Philostratus, *Life of Apollonius*, 8.26.
184. *IE*, 427.
185. Kunsthistorisches Museum Vienna inv. no I, 824.
186. *IE*, 1128, 1129, 1129A.
187. *IE*, 508.
188. Chart, no. 51.
189. Chart, nos. 52 and 53; for the building and its various phases, see S. Karwiese, *Die Marienkirche in Ephesos* (Wien 1989) esp. 9–27.
190. 260m by 29.5m; *RE*, XII (1970) 1636–7.
191. Chart, no. 54; see *RE*, XII (1970) 1644; *IE*, 105 which implies a sanctuary of Asklepios.
192. Chart, no.55; *RE*, XII (1970) 1642; Alzinger (1974) 59.
193. Chart, no. 56; *Anz. Wien*, 121 (1984) 209–32; C. P. Jones has pointed out to me, however, that the connection of the Olympieion with Hadrian has no basis in the text of Pausanias, *Description of Greece, Achaia*, 7.2.9.
194. No. 57 on the chart; see *RE*, XII (1970) 1646.
195. Athenaeus, *Deipnosophistae*, 8.361c.
196. Chart, no. 58; *RE*, XII (1970) 1645.
197. See *IE*, 454b; 445; *RE*, XII (1970) 1645; Pausanias, 7.2.9 puts the tomb of Androklos between the Artemision and the Magnesian Gate, and Wood thought he had discovered the substructure of the monument 700m from the gate (Wood (1877) 126–7), but this attribution was considered highly uncertain by J. Keil, *JÖAI*, 21–2 (1922–4) 110 and n. 30. Until more evidence is produced, which confirms or refutes the attribution, the location of the tomb of Androklos – and thus where the procession might have passed it – must remain uncertain.
198. See L. Robert, *BE* (1948) 38.
199. Athenaeus, *Deipnosophistae*, 8.361.
200. No. 59 on the chart; see Alzinger (1974) 146.
201. *IE*, 411.
202. Chart, no. 60; on Koressos see *FiE* I (1906) 65; *JÖAI* 21–2 (1922–4) 96–112; L. Robert, *Hellenica* XI/XII (1960) 139–44; Bammer, *JÖAI*, 46 (1961–3) 136–7, who argued that Koressos was on Ayasuluk; Alzinger, 'Koressos', *Festschrift für Fritz Eichler zum achtizigsten Geburtstag* (Wien 1967) 1–9; *BE* (1969) 509; G. Lehmann, *ZPE*, 26 (1977) 189; Alzinger, 'Ephesiaca', *JÖAI*, 56 (1985) 59–64; S. Karwiese, 'Koressos – Ein fast vergessener Stadtteil von Ephesos', in *Kenner*, II (1985) 214–25; almost a century of scholarship has been unable to establish whether 'Koressos' during the early empire designated a mountain, a quarter of the city, or a neighborhood.

Although I will go on to argue that Koressos should be located on modern Panayir-Dağ, the eventual identification of Koressos in no way will alter my argument about the significance of the procession leaving the city through the Koressian Gate. Whatever Koressos was (and it remains to be securely located), there is no real doubt about where the Koressian Gate itself was placed. Nor can there be any doubts about its historical and symbolic associations with the Ionian foundation myth.

203. Athenaeus, *Deipnosophistae*, 8.361.
204. *IE*, 27.183 p. 181.
205. See Ü. Önen, *Ephesus Ruins and Museum* (Izmir 1983) inv. no. 773/1–2, a second-century AD statue from the corner of the west wall of the fountain of Trajan which depicted Androklos standing with a cloak attached to his right shoulder, falling over a tree stump, with a dog looking up at him; also inv. no. 1016, a relief from AD 170 from east of the bouleuterion in front of a fountain, the fifth plate from the Antonine Altar which shows an armored figure who may be Androklos; inv. no. 713, a relief from Block A of the frieze from the 'temple of Hadrian', which depicted Androklos pursuing the boar; see also *IE*, 501, an inscription on a base for a statue of Androklos, the city-founder, from the area of the so-called Auditorium in front of the library of Celsus.
206. Head (1964) Ephesus 232, on the reverse of a coin with Antinous on the obverse, a naked Androklos advancing with a spear over his left shoulder, a boar on his right; 315, on the reverse of a coin with Severus Alexander on the obverse, a naked Androklos charging the boar with a spear; 316, also under Severus Alexander; 375, under Gallienus; see also *FiE*, I (1906) 53–6.
207. Izmir Museum inv. no. 45.
208. *IE*, 501A; 557A.
209. *IE*, 644.12.
210. See *SEG*, 33 (1983) 890.
211. *IE*, 1943, a partial restoration.
212. *IE*, 1064.
213. This inscription is dated to the late second century AD, *IE*, 1548.20.
214. *IE*, 2044.
215. *IE*, 3079.13–14.
216. See Stephen of Byzantium s.v. Εὐωνύμεια; also Aulis; *RE*, VI (1907) 1156. Euonumos was also a well-known Attic deme.
217. R. Heberdey restored the genitive form 'Pionos', in line 195 on the analogy of *IE*, 31.8 P[ion]os, another partial restoration.
218. Quoted in Athenaeus, *Deipnosophistae*, 8.361.
219. References to the Koressian Gate in the Salutaris foundation at lines 425, 566–7; for the identification of Koressos on Panayir-Dağ see Alzinger (1962) 105.
220. Alzinger (1962) 104–5.
221. On the epigram see *IE*, 1062; also H. Engelmann, *ZPE*, 36 (1979) 90; R. Merkelbach, *ZPE*, 37 (1980) 90; for the street, see *IE*, 3013.
222. Head (1964) Ephesus 237.

223. See Stephen of Byzantium s.v. Βέννα.
224. *IE*, 1578a; *RE*, XII (1970) 275–8.
225. Stephen of Byzantium s.v. Βέννα; according to Herodotus, *Histories*, 8.42, Karene was a town of Mysia, north of Atarneus, not far from the coast.
226. Stephen of Byzantium s.v. Βέννα.
227. Stephen of Byzantium s.v. Βέννα.
228. Herodotus, *Histories*, 1.46.
229. See Hicks (1890) 69, 71.
230. Heberdey proposed this restoration for lines 194–5; see *IE*, 27.194–5.
231. See C. Kraay, *Archaic and Classical Greek Coins* (Berkeley 1979) 20f.
232. Head (1964) Ephesus 244; 257; 258; 263; 264; 327.
233. Selçuk Museum inv. no. 712, Artemis with stags from the late second century AD from the prytaneion.
234. W. Oberleitner, *Funde aus Ephesos und Samothrake* (Wien 1978) inv. no. IXB337.
235. See R. L. Gordon, 'The Real and the Imaginary: Production and Religion in the Graeco-Roman World', *Art History*, 2 (1979) 22.
236. See K. Scott, 'The Significance of Statues in Precious Metals in Emperor Worship', *TAPA*, 62 (1931) 101–23; J.E.G. Whitehorne, 'Golden Statues in Greek and Latin Literature', *Greece and Rome* 22, 2 (1975) 109–19.
237. Price (1985) 187.
238. *IE*, 27.164–5, 168, 173 (restored), 186–7, 196 (restored).
239. Picard (1922) 297.
240. See H. Graillot, *Le Culte de Cybèle* (Paris 1912) 130–1.
241. Picard (1922) 297 n.2.
242. Head (1964) Ephesus, 201; 392; 397.
243. Selçuk Museum inv. no. 1572.
244. *IE*, 3068.8–9; cf. 1138.5; 2446.
245. See C. Geertz, 'Centers, Kings and Charisma: Reflections upon the Symbolics of Power', in *Culture and its Creators: Essays in Honor of Edward Shils*, ed. J. Ben-David and T. Clark (Chicago 1977) 159.

4
THE CITY PLAN OF EPHESOS

THE PROCESSION OF STATUES AND THE PLAN OF EPHESOS IN AD 104

I Temple of Artemis to the Magnesian Gate

Plan	Building	Builder	Date	Renovated	Renovator	Date	Reference
1	Temple of Artemis	–	4th C. BC	–	–	–	–
		–	–	temenos	Augustus	–	*IE*, 3501
							IE, 3502
							IE, 3513
		–	–	temenos	Domitian	–	*IE*, 3506
							IE, 3507
		–	–	temenos	Domitian	–	*IE*, 3508
							IE, 3509
		–	–	temenos	Domitian	AD 87/88	*IE*, 3510
		–	–	temenos	Trajan	AD 111/112	*IE*, 3511
					Trajan	–	*IE*, 3512
2	Altar of Temple	–	–	–	–	–	Bammer (1984) 130–9
3	Shrine of Mother Goddess	–	–	–	–	–	*JÖAI*, 18 (1915) 66–78

II Magnesian Gate and Upper Agora

Plan	Building	Builder	Date	Renovated	Renovator	Date	Reference
4	Magnesian Gate	–	3rd C. BC	–	–	–	–
						AD 69–79	*Anz. Wien*, 121 (1984) 209–32

5	Wall of Lysimachos	–	3rd C. BC	–	–	–	–	JÖAI, 47 (1964–5) Grab. 1966, 8–11
6	Heroon (Luke Tomb)	–	1st C. BC	–	–	–	–	JÖAI, 15 (1912) 177f.
7	Street Fountain	Aristio, Laterane	AD 102–117	–	–	–	–	IE, 424A
8	Upper Agora –	– –	4th C. BC –	plaster, portico	– Timon	– 66 BC	– IE, 3004
9	Basilika	Pollio, Bassa, Proculus, children	AD 4–14	–	–	–	–	IE, 404
10	Chalcidicum of Basilika	–	Neronian	–	–	–	–	IE, 410
11	Bouleuterion –	– –	1st C. BC –	– –	– Vedius, Flavia	– AD 140–60	– IE, 460
12	Temple of Dea Roma and Divus Iulius	–	29 BC	–	–	–	–	Dio, 51.20.6 JÖAI, 51 (1976–7) 57–8

Plan	Building	Builder	Date	Renovated	Renovator	Date	Reference
13	Prytaneion	–	Augustan	–	–	–	*FIE*, IX/I/I (1981) 75–6
		–	–	forecourt, etc	–	1st C. AD	*IE*, 437
		–	–	floor, etc.	–	1st C. AD	*IE*, 462
		–	–	columns, etc.	Montanus?	AD 102–16	*IE*, 528
		–	–	–	Dionysodorus	AD 104+	*IE*, 1024
14	Memmius Monument	–	before 30 BC	–	–	–	*IE*, 403
15	Nekropolis	–	archaic	–	–	–	–
16	Nympheion (Fountain)	–	2nd C. AD	–	–	–	*JÖAI*, 15 (1912) 173
		–	–	–	Montius	AD 337–50	*IE*, 1316, 1317
17	Hydrekdochion of C. Laecanius Bassus	Bassus	AD 80/81	–	–	–	*JÖAI*, 50 (1972–5) Beib. 300–11 *IE*, 695
18	Temple of Isis? or Augustus	–	2nd half of 1st C. BC	–	–	after 27 BC	*JÖAI*, 50 (1972–5) 212–19 *IE*, 902 *Ist. Mitt.*, 30 (1980) 241–60

No.	Building		Date				References
19	Monument of Pollio & Fountain of Domitian	Proculus	AD 4–14	—	—	—	*IE*, 405, 406 *JÖAI*, 51 (1976–7) 77–92
		—	—	Fountain	polis	AD 93	*IE*, 413
		—	—	—	demos	AD 92/93	*IE*, 415, 416
		—	—	—	—	AD 92/93	*IE*, 419
20	Temple of Domitian	—	after AD 81	—	—	—	*IE*, 232–42, 1498, 2048 *JÖAI*, 50 (1972–5) 311–30
21	Niche Building	—	Augustan?	—	—	—	*JÖAI*, 45 (1960) 21f.

III The Embolos

No.	Building		Date				References
22	The Embolos	—	—	—	—	—	*IE*, 1300, 3059
		—	—	paved	polis	AD 94/95	*IE*, 3008
23	Fountain of Trajan	Aristio, Laterane	AD 102–104	—	—	—	*IE*, 424
24	Baths of Varius	Varius	AD 100	—	—	—	*IE*, 500
		—	—	baths	Scholastikia	end of 4th C. AD	*IE*, 453
25	Private Residence (Brothel)	—	end of 1st C. AD	—	—	—	*IE*, 455 *JÖAI*, 51 (1976–7) 61–84

Plan	Building	Builder	Date	Renovated	Renovator	Date	Reference
26	Round Building	–	mid 1st C. BC	–	–	–	*FiE*, I (1906) 143f.
27	Shops	–	1st C. AD	–	–	–	*FiE*, VIII/1 (1977) 13
		–	–	shops 9–12	–	Byzantine	*FiE*, VIII/1 (1977) 13
28	Terrace House I	–	after AD 17	–	–	1st–7th C. AD	*FiE*, VIII/1 (1977) 12–19 Alzinger (1974) 58
29	Terrace House II	–	Augustan	–	–	2nd–early 7th C. AD	*FiE*, VIII/1 (1977) 19–28
30	Terrace Alley	–	1st C. AD	–	–	–	*FiE*, VIII/1 (1977) 12
31	Octagon	–	early Augustan?	–	–	–	Alzinger (1974) 40f.
31a	Heroon	–	–	–	–	–	*RE*, XII (1970) 1675
32	Heroon (Fountain)	–	Julio-Claudian?	–	–	–	*RE*, XII (1970) 1674–5
33	Round Tomb	–	after AD 10	–	–	–	*JÖAI*, 43 (1956–8) 49f.
34	Door, Altar	–	–	–	–	–	*RE*, XII (1970) 1598

IV The Marble Street

35	Nekropolis	—	—	—	—	—	—
36	The Marble Street	—	paved	Eutropius	end of 5th C. AD		RE, XII (1970) 1598; IE, 1304
36a	Doric Stoa	—	Neronian	—	—	—	IE, 3003
37	Mazaeus Mithridates Gate	Mazaeus Mithridates	4/3 BC	—	—	—	IE, 3006
38	Tetragonos Agora	—	Hellenistic?	—	—	—	JÖAI, 58 (1988) Grab. 9
39	West Gate of Agora	—	early Augustan?	—	—	—	JÖAI, 25 (1929) 22f.
	—	—	—	access from Stoa to Agora	Ischyrion	Domitian	IE, 3005
40	West Street	—	—	—	—	—	RE, XII (1970) 1600
41	Fountain House	—	Hellenistic	—	—	—	IE, 417
42	Palace of the Proconsul?	—	early imperial	—	—	—	JÖAI, 27 (1932) Beib. 8f.
43	Theatre	—	Hellenistic	—	—	—	FiE, II (1912); RE, XII (1970) 1625–9

Plan	Building	Builder	Date	Renovated	Renovator	Date	Reference
—	—	—	—	north & south analemma	—	AD 92, 102–12	IE, 2035, 2037
V The Stadium Street							
44	Stadium Street	—	—	—	—	—	RE, XII (1970) 1596
45	Street Gate	—	—	—	—	—	RE, XII (1970) 1597
46	Harbor Street (Arkadiane)	—	1st C. BC	—	—	—	FiE, I (1906) 132–40
—	—	—	—	street	Arcadius	AD 395–408	IE, 557
47	Harbor Gate	—	Julio-Claudian	—	—	—	FiE, III (1923) 189f.
48	Halls of Verulanus	—	before AD 96	—	—	—	Philostratus, Life of Apollonius, 8.26
—	—	—	—	—	Verulanus	AD 130	IE, 430 JÖAI, 28 (1933) 22
49	Harbor Baths	—	Domitian	—	—	—	IE, 508, 1128, 1129, 1129A
50	Harbor Gymnasium	Aristio	Domitian	—	—	—	IE, 427

No.	Name		Date				Reference
51	Harbor Warehouses	—	—	—	—	—	—
52 53	Market Basilika	—	2nd C. AD?	—	—	—	JÖAI, 18 (1915) 279
54	Asklepieion?	—	—	—	—	—	IE, 105 JÖAI, 28 (1933) 23f. Dörner, II (1978) 493
55	Palace?	—	late	—	—	—	JÖAI, 44 (1959) Beib. 243f.
56	Olympieion?	—	—	—	—	—	Kenner, II (1985) 220–1; JÖAI 56 (1985) 105
57	Temple of Apollo	—	classical	—	—	—	Dörner, II (1978) 493–4
58	Stoa of Servilius?	—	2nd C. AD	—	—	—	IE, 454b, 445 JÖAI, 56 (1985) 39f.

VI The Koressian Gate

No.	Name		Date				Reference
59	The Stadium	—	3rd C. BC	—	—	—	JÖAI, 15 (1912) 180f. IE, 411
—	—	—	—	—	Orpex, Marina	Neronian	—
60	Koressian Gate	—	Hellenistic	—	—	—	Kenner, II (1985) 219

5

THE SACRED IDENTITY OF EPHESOS

REVIEW

The foundation of C. Vibius Salutaris was a sacred public act embodied in law and displayed on stone. This public act created two civic rituals which the whole demos ratified and the Roman governors confirmed. Through the repeated performance of these civic rituals, the Ephesians established and maintained the sacred identity of their city: as we shall see, the birth of the goddess Artemis *at Ephesos* defined that sacred identity, and also empowered those adult male Greeks who celebrated it. I will argue that in AD 104 the Ephesians affirmed their sacred identity at least partially in response to the implicit Roman refoundation of their upper city.

The first civic ritual involved individuals and civic bodies in a scheme of lotteries and distributions of cash doled out inside the temple of Artemis each year during the mysteries. The second ritual included the ephebes in a procession of thirty-one gold and silver type-statues and images along a circular route from the temple of Artemis at least once every two weeks during the year.

Behind the performance of these two rituals lay conceptual blueprints of a contemporary social hierarchy and a version of the history of Ephesos. Salutaris and the fathers of the city intended the paides and ephebes of the city to learn about the social hierarchy and history of Ephesos through physical participation in these civic rituals, but, except for slaves and foreigners, virtually the whole adult male population of Ephesos either took part in or watched these public rituals.

The social hierarchy implied in the scheme of lotteries and distributions stressed the importance of membership in the tribes, the boule, and the gerousia of Ephesos above all other possible social or institutional affiliations which might confer status upon individuals in the city. The oldest of these predominantly adult male civic institutions, the five original tribes of Ephesos, traced their origins back to the time of the Ionian foundation. The boule and the gerousia dated to the classical period at the very latest.

When the young men of the city joined in the scheme of the lotteries and distributions, they learned that the institutional roles they would play in the public life of Ephesos, which began when they officially entered into the tribes, and even the order in which they would play those roles, were fixed at the time of the Ionian foundation of the city. The ephebes also could not have failed to recognize that adult males of local Greek birth filled most of those institutional roles in AD 104. Thus the Ionian foundation established the institutional framework within which the ephebes of AD 104 would soon operate, and into which all non-natives had to be brought to have any sort of social or institutional status in the city. In other words, the men of Ephesos used the Ionian foundation as an institutional charter to bestow positions of social and political power upon individuals in the city.

The social hierarchy of the city was grounded in the same ancient, but still human, event which also presupposed the reconstruction of the past woven into the procession of the statues. A thousand years after that boar led the Ionian colonists to the thickets of Koressos, Salutaris' procession still drew upon the Ionian foundation story for its narrative theme of successive foundations. The foundation on Koressos also provided the historical background against which all new founders and their foundations could be understood, accommodated, given meaning and, finally, limited.

We may recall that Lysimachos had forced the Ephesians to change their homes, surrounded the city with a wall, and even renamed the city. The city of Arsinoe, however, became Ephesos again shortly after the death of Lysimachos at Koroupedion. For his efforts, the Hellenistic refounder earned a place among the heroes and heroines of the Embolos, half-way between the Romans of the upper city, and the Ionians of Koressos on the map of foundations.

Roman citizens transformed the upper city architecturally and visually. The colonnaded basilikas, imperial temples and elaborate fountains in this space, embedded in that concrete-like rubble mass which Italian architects had developed in Italy, spoke an architectural vocabulary foreign to the native Ionian dialect. These buildings were designed to make a Roman businessman, pro-consul, emperor, or god feel at home. But the procession did not even pause in the upper city on its way to the Embolos and Koressos. On the map of historical foundations, the first road the ephebes walked within the city walls was not the most memorable; it was only the most recent. The image of the emperor, accompanied by those of the Senate, the equestrian order, and the Roman people, ultimately paled in the reflected brilliance of the Ionian images at the very heart of the procession, where Androklos still hunted, at least artistically, along the ridges of Koressos, not for space to begin a modern building program, but for a wild boar, and a site for a Greek city. The Ionian foundation still gave the Ephesians their bed-rock sense of historical identity in AD 104, and provided a tradition against which new founders might be measured first, and then cut down to size.

The procession demonstrated finally that the Ephesians' recre-ation of the past was founded upon one non-human event, the birth of the goddess Artemis at Ephesos. The image of Artemis with her torch, which Salutaris and the demos intended to evoke the story of her birth, dominated the procession numerically and symbolically. Furthermore, the procession itself began and ended at the temple of Artemis. On the circular map of foundations, the temple of Artemis came both before and after the historical Roman, Hellenistic, and Ionian foundations; Artemis somehow preceded and followed even the events of Koressos in the minds of the Ephesians. Just as the social hierarchy of the city required a specific form of the Ionian foundation story, so, in turn, the Ionian foundation necessitated the birth of the Greek goddess Artemis at Ephesos. The foundation of the Greek city demanded the existence of a patron deity with impeccable Greek divine credentials.

THE SIGNIFICANCE OF THE FOUNDATION

What then is the significance of the discovery that the demos of Ephesos encoded a version of its historical and sacred past into two civic rituals long after the 'events' themselves, which both justified and shaped their social world in AD 104? Certainly, in the context of modern Middle Eastern history, Bernard Lewis has shown brilliantly how ancient events, such as the story of the siege and suicide of the Jewish defenders at Masada, have been recovered and reinterpreted during the twentieth century, for a variety of reasons, most typically perhaps, to foster a sense of national identity.[1] In the case of Ephesos, the discovery reveals at the very least that the men of Ephesos who ratified this foundation re-examined the past in AD 104 in a much more serious and systematic way than any historian has yet realized. The creation of these rituals entailed not only an inquiry into the story of Artemis' birth, the Ionian foundation, the refoundation of Lysimachos, and the transformation of the upper city, but also necessitated from the organizers considerable thought about how to arrange those stories in the most persuasive educational form possible. Once the Ephesians chose the educational medium of a processional map of foundations – surely not the simplest, but perhaps one of the most vivid ways to dramatize the past – they had to relate the foundation stories of the city to its changing architecture and topography.

The intellectual process of relating the history of the city to the physical context of the city, or more precisely, relating *one version* of the history of the city to another version of the physical context, clearly was a complicated task.[2] At first, such an intellectual process, which challenged the Ephesians to find a congruence between a symbolic representation of their history and their city, might be seen as part of a broader trend within the Greek cities of the eastern Roman empire during the second century AD, a trend characterized by a predilection for antiquity and archaism which was so general that one scholar has written of 'cultural archaism' when describing the activities of upper-class Greeks during the cultural renaissance known as the Second Sophistic.[3]

As my interpretation of the Salutaris foundation suggests however, far more than mere reflection upon the past took place at Ephesos in AD 104. The past was more than a treasury of learned allusions, stylistic flourishes, or even moral exemplars from the golden age between Athens and Alexander to be trotted out by famous sophists for use in polished speeches before weary emperors. For the majority of Ephesians, the past, which included the birth of Artemis and the refoundation of Lysimachos, events which lay well outside the usual time parameters of the sophistic thematic canon, was a present source, and framework of power, used, first, to give order, point, and direction to the lives of the young men of Ephesos, and second, to justify the positions of authority held by the fathers of the city. The past was a *present* source and framework of power because that was precisely when, and, I will argue shortly, why that past had been constructed the way it was in AD 104.

Since the past was a source and framework of power to be used in AD 104 by the men of the city, arguably the most important city in the richest province of the eastern Roman empire, perhaps we need to reconsider generally the relationship between the Greeks – not just the various aristocracies – and their own complex pasts at the beginning of the second century AD. Salutaris' educational procession, which 'starred' a city founder well past his thousandth birthday, cannot be considered solely an example of cultural archaism, if, by that term, a purely reflective or passive relationship to the past is implied on the part of the Greeks of Ephesos. On the contrary, in the real, visible world of public action and shared meaning, the Ephesians did not merely reflect upon the past or resort to it as an alternative to a politically unsatisfactory present; rather, the past was a source of power wielded by the men of Ephesos over the young, over new founders, and, at last, over new gods.

THE ORIGINS OF THE FOUNDATION

If the past was a source of power in AD 104, what then stimulated its use in the form, peculiar perhaps only to us, of two civic rituals, based upon the Ionian foundation of the city and the birth of the goddess Artemis at Ephesos? The sudden appearance of these civic rituals certainly cannot be interpreted as an overt response to any discernible political, military, or economic crisis. In fact, I believe that my interpretation of the foundation itself has already supplied the most plausible answer to this difficult question.

I believe the Ephesians' remaking of the past in AD 104 was only part of a long, drawn-out social process, during which the city as a whole gradually asserted a particular civic identity in the face of what had once been primarily a military and political threat, but, by the end of the first century AD, had settled down into a much more diffuse and subtle social and theological challenge to the Ephesians' sense of the basic Greek character of their city.

As my discussion of the list of beneficiaries of the foundation has clarified already, Roman citizens, officials, and governors, although no doubt comparatively few in number within the city itself in AD 104, nevertheless became extremely visible and powerful in all areas of everyday life, especially if the epigraphical evidence does not present a distorted picture, toward the end of the first century, particularly during the reign of the emperor Domitian. They stood out perhaps most conspicuously within those traditional areas of contact between Romans and all provincials, the systems of taxation and the administration of justice, but also served frequently within various civic institutions, guilds, professional organizations, and colleges of priests. The percentage of Roman citizens within any one of these social groups is impossible to discover, but, as we have seen, Roman citizens certainly transformed the upper city architecturally and spatially, changed the calendar of the city, took control over the celebration of major festivals, and celebrated the cult of a new god – the emperor. In short, it is extremely difficult to find even one area of Ephesian institutional or social life documented in the huge epigraphical corpus of the city in which the Roman presence – and that presence embraced not only officials of the Roman government, but also Latin-speaking immigrants or visitors, Greeks from other cities who were Roman citizens and, of course, many Ephesians – was not pervasive or persistent by the end of the first century AD. Finally, within a few short years, a Roman emperor, Hadrian, would officially become a new founder of the city.[4] In such a context, simply being 'Greek' or 'Roman' was ethnically, socially, and even economically ambiguous.

We have also seen how Roman citizens and philo-Roman Ephesians such as Tiberius Claudius Aristio, the man Pliny called 'princeps Ephesiorum, homo munificus et innoxie popularis',[5] C. Laecanius Bassus, and C. Sextilius Pollio, the visible leaders of the Ephesian aristocracy, utterly transformed the architectural and visual character of the city through their building projects between the reign of Augustus, and the time of Domitian. Scholars have documented this transformation in great detail for the reign of the emperor Augustus, and have argued that these donors made the Upper Agora of Ephesos in particular a new urban center clustered around the temples of the imperial cult.

The architectural changes which took place during the reign of the emperor Domitian have been less noticed – although the trouble the Ephesians took to erase Domitian's name from *all* of the public buildings dedicated to him should have alerted historians to his profound impact upon the development of the city. Salutaris and the demos of Ephesos, like Tacitus, the greatest of Roman historians, had flourished under Domitian. In fact, out of the sixty major monuments, streets and agoras in the city which were probably visible to the procession in AD 104, not less than eleven were built or heavily renovated during the reign of Domitian, and these monuments especially came to dominate two important areas of the imperial city: the space between the Upper Agora and the Embolos, and the harbor.

Therefore, I would like to suggest that this deep penetration of influence into the social fabric of Ephesos, into the topographical layout of the city, and into its architectural and visual character, especially during the last two decades of the first century AD, may eventually have created, if not a kind of social identity crisis among Greek Ephesians by AD 104, certainly a social situation in which the need to assert some social, historical, and theological definitions and boundaries may have developed. For by AD 104, some Ephesians at least may have forgotten precisely what differentiated Ephesians from Romans socially, historically, and theologically.

This is not to say that any attitudinal conflict between Greek Ephesians and Roman citizens existed or developed in the city; only that, in every area of city life we know about where the two cultures met – and, of course, they frequently met in the same person, such as the founder Salutaris himself – a process of mutual self-definition, adjustment, and accommodation must have taken place, even hundreds of years after the first Roman set foot in Ephesos, and maybe because of that long relationship. No historian should assume that time alone erases the periodic need for a challenged culture to assert its social, political, and theological boundaries. When we hold the Salutaris foundation under the microscope of research, and focus upon that fixed moment when these civic rituals were created, we see, not only the familiar Romanization of Greeks, but, more sharply, the Hellenization of Romans.

Thus, at the beginning of the second century AD, the Ephesians consciously framed that Roman presence within the institutional, historical, and sacral structures of the city. The status which Romans, and, for that matter, all other outsiders, had for Ephesians depended almost totally upon how and where they were brought into that local context. In other words, the idea of a new founder during the second century AD only had, or could be given, meaning within the historical context of previous Greek founders at Ephesos. New citizens, new founders, and new gods at Ephesos lived upon borrowed power. At exactly the time when the kind of political autonomy enjoyed by the city states of the classical era was finally and irrevocably out of the question for Ephesos, the recreation of a past traced to the birth of Artemis furnished an undiminished source of tangible, useful power. Is it purely an accident that we find such a creative use of the Ionian and sacred past of Ephesos just a few short years before the city reached its economic, cultural, and especially architectural apogee under the patronage of the Vedii Antonini, which culminated in the construction of the library of Celsus and, finally, the exquisite temple on the Embolos, dedicated to Artemis, Hadrian, and the demos? While scholars have argued over the exact significance of the dedication,[6] no one has doubted that it is Androklos that we see on the frieze of the temple, on horseback, ready to kill that poor boar once again.[7] At the turn of the century, Androklos was the historical star of the city which would lead the Greeks of Asia Minor into their renaissance.

The past then, in which successive founders occupied center stage, perhaps had always been, but became more overtly, the central arena of self-definition between two very familiar cultures at the beginning of the second century AD at Ephesos. My interpretation of this process of self-definition almost purely from the Ephesian point of view is admittedly based upon the one outline of the past which the foundation presents. That outline, however, refers to a series of rather more detailed stories preserved in literary sources which, when taken together, and analyzed from the point of view of how they might have played before an audience of second-century Ephesians, may have some important implications for our understanding of why the Ephesians answered the social challenge of what amounted to the Roman refoundation of their city, with the affirmation of a sacred identity.

THE SACRED IDENTITY OF EPHESOS

As we have already discovered, Androklos, who led the Ionians against Ephesos, a town named after the son of the river Kaystros,[8] was really an invader, who, according to Strabo, had to drive out the Carians and the Leleges,[9] and, according to Pausanias, the Lydians from the upper city as well.[10] Accompanied by a mixed lot of settlers,[11] Androklos founded the city where he slew the boar, and fulfilled the terms of the oracle of Pythian Apollo. Later, the Ionian colonists were forced to bring over additional colonists from Teos and Karene to strengthen the colony. After the death of Androklos, according to Pausanias, in a battle helping the people of Priene against the Karians,[12] the Ephesians fought succession wars against the sons of Androklos. Thus the Ionian foundation story available to the Ephesians in the primary literary sources during the second century AD hardly gives a picture of tranquility and stability; in its full narrative form, however the details may have varied from account to account, the basic Ionian foundation tale probably could not have been used to cement social cohesion.

The complete story of Lysimachos' Hellenistic refoundation of Ephesos was also filled with indications of discord. According to Strabo, Lysimachos first built a wall around the city, but the Ephesians had no desire to change their abodes. Lysimachos then waited for a heavy rainfall, stopped up the sewers of the old city, and flooded the Ephesians out.[13] Thus Lysimachos forced the refoundation of the city upon the Ephesians against their collective will. The story shows that the refoundation of the city, so far from promoting civic unity, was associated by the first century AD with upheaval and social tension between the city and the new founder.

The Ionian and Hellenistic foundations constituted the Ephesians' collective historical experience of foundations. If neither story could serve as a civic paradigm of anything except violence, conflict, and ethnic heterogeneity, hardly suitable material for the formation of a civic consensus, what paradigm could hold together such a city, with its glorious, but dangerous past, unsatisfactory present, and uncertain future? Only the story of an event which preceded even the Ionian colonization, an event fraught with tension and violence to be sure, but, most importantly, a sacred event in which those proto-Ephesians, the

Kuretes, played a vital role: the story of Artemis' birth at Ephesos.

We have already seen how, according to the myth found in the primary first-century source, Hera tried to spy upon Leto when she was giving birth in the grove of Ortygia.[14] The Kuretes, stationed on Mt Solmissos, frightened Hera out of her wits with the din of their arms when she was spying upon Leto, and then helped Leto to conceal the birth of her children from Hera.

In fact, the myth of Artemis' birth at Ephesos was not only the theological blueprint behind the structure of Salutaris' foundation. The Ephesians also acted out that blueprint every year in the grove of Ortygia from at least the time of Lysimachos, until the reign of the emperor Commodus, at the mysteries of Artemis. The birth of Artemis was not just a story told to Ephesian children by their parents; it was the event of the Ephesian year, performed by generations of Ephesians, at the most important religious festival in the city.[15]

Unlike the stories of the historical foundations, or the other sacred legends from the past of the city, such as the tale of Apollo fleeing to Ortygia to avoid the anger of Zeus after slaying the Kyklops, or Dionysos pardoning the suppliant Amazons who had gathered around the shrine,[16] the myth of Artemis' birth did provide a model for the creation of a city unified behind a sacred event. In Strabo's account of the myth at least, only the willingness of the Kuretes to take up arms and then conceal the birth of Leto's children from Hera ensured the successful birth of Artemis (and Apollo). Since there could be no Greek city at the site of Ephesos without the prior condition of Artemis' birth in the grove of Ortygia, and there could be no birth of Artemis without the Kuretes, the Kuretes could reasonably claim that, without them, the Greek city of Ephesos would not exist. In other words, when the Ephesians, dressed as Kuretes each year at the celebration of the mysteries, re-enacted their role in the birth of Artemis, they did far more than take part in the biggest birthday party of the city; rather, they reaffirmed their vital contribution not only to Artemis' birth, but to the very existence of the Greek city itself. It was this dual contribution which established the theological claim of the Kuretes in the city, and consequently empowered the select group of adult male Ephesians who composed the college.

Thus Artemis gave the city its sacred identity as the birthplace of one of the original Olympian deities; but the Ephesians themselves, as the Kuretes, also had a major role in creating that sacred identity, a corporate role which defined the Ephesians for all time as Artemis' protectors and defenders against hostile and jealous deities. Her birth at Ephesos functioned for the Ephesians as a model of civic unity, especially in the absence of binding historical paradigms, conferred power upon the Kuretes, and, perhaps most importantly, established a pattern of response to other deities, particularly new and jealous ones. A Roman emperor who became *another* god could easily be fitted into the Ephesians' theological framework, and did not threaten their role as Artemis' defenders; but a god who was exclusive, universalist, and intolerant, struck at the very heart of the Ephesians' essentially polytheistic framework of belief, and was destined to bring the Kuretes back to Mt Solmissos with their arms, as first the Jews, and then later the Christians of Ephesos found out.[17] Artemis' birth gave the Ephesians their essential sense of civic identity in AD 104, and empowered the group in society who celebrated that birth to act for ever as the protectors of that sacred identity of the city.

The civic rituals in which all of these social, historical, and theological layers of meaning unfolded at Ephesos had just as much political significance as meetings of the assembly or the boule. Ephesian politics did not die with the loss of 'political' autonomy at Ephesos; rather the focus of politics has been misperceived by scholars, who have imposed their own anachronistic conceptual split between the performance of rituals and the exercise of power upon the Ephesians. But as the Salutaris foundation demonstrates (and the foundation accurately represents thousands of other inscriptions from the city), the Ephesians themselves did not make such a firm distinction in theory or practice between religious or political acts.

As we have seen, the creation and execution of Salutaris' foundation was imbued with equal measures of piety and pragmatism. Instead of re-inventing our present into their past, if we recognize that the Ephesians were culturally different from us in this critical respect, we can begin to see Ephesos as the Ephesians apparently perceived their own city – as a place where neither politics, nor religion could be, or now can be, understood in isolation. The power to shape the lives of young men in the city, and to mould new founders and new gods into pre-existing casts, derived from a story about the sacred past of Ephesos, which the fathers of Ephesos sustained and celebrated, both because they believed in that story, and because the story legitimated the positions they held in the city. Thus power was located in many different spheres of life in the city at once, but was perhaps endowed with special authority in the field of the divine, where the story of the birth of Artemis at Ortygia provided a cultural template of unique human agency. But in every sphere of life, including the sacred, power depended vitally upon a set of shared beliefs, a consensus about reality, which the elite of the city may have shaped, but the demos itself ultimately ratified, by its decrees and its acts.

Through the medium of the foundation we see the demos of Ephesos presenting itself to the world essentially as a sacred community. Within that sacred community, individuals were bound together and defined in relation to the institutional roles they played in the great drama of the sacred past of Ephesos, which was performed each year during the celebration of the mysteries of Artemis. The institutional roles of that great drama had been written at the time of the birth of the goddess. It was possible for selected outsiders to take part in the drama, but only within the overall script of the drama, and the institutional roles that it established. Alternative dramas of the past were written and performed, but none were acted out as often, over so many centuries, by so many, as the drama of the nativity.

What are the broader implications of the discovery that the demos of Ephesos saw itself as a sacred community in AD 104, responsible for the maintenance of a sacred framework of reference, into which new citizens, new founders, and new gods had to be fitted to have any sort of social significance? There are perhaps two of importance for our understanding of the history of the Greek city within the Roman empire, and possibly even one for our understanding of our own world.

First of all, the emphatic insistence of the demos that it be identified as a sacred community shows that the gods at Ephesos were not dying, indeed had not begun to die, in the imaginations of the Ephesians at the beginning of the second century. If anything, the gods were multiplying in the city, a fact of great inconvenience for those who would wish to see a decline in pagan piety at Ephesos during this period. An atmosphere of heightened *pagan* piety in the city from the middle to the late first century may also make better historical sense out of both the sometimes violent pagan reaction to figures such as Paul, with his mission specifically to the Gentile population of the city, and the ultimate success of the Christian proselytizers at Ephesos, than a model of Christian growth, which depends upon the pagans of Ephesos beginning to lose interest in their gods somewhere in the middle of the second century. A general rise in the religious temperature at the end of the first century may have turned some Ephesians into the defenders of the pagan past, and others into the prophets of the Christian future.

Second, if the demos was responsible for that sacred framework in which the place of outsiders of various origins was negotiated, it is impossible to speak of Ephesian and Roman relations only in terms of relations between Ephesian and Roman elites. Too often the history of relations between Ephesos and Rome has been written, not as *Hamlet* without the prince, but as *Hamlet* without Denmark – that is, without the demos of Ephesos playing any role whatsoever. The Salutaris foundation shows that, at least in the omnipresent area of civic rituals, the demos of Ephesos played a vital, if not *the* vital role, in that mutual process of Romanization and Hellenization.

Finally, the Ephesians' use of their sacred past to justify their social hierarchy, and give meaning to their lives at a time of social change perhaps has some close, but limited analogies in the modern world. Today, prophets of various sacred identities have arisen in countries experiencing social conflicts due to rapid modernization in the wake of colonialism and imperialism. These spokesmen preach conflicting versions of the same sacred past, which are being used to justify absolute claims to authority, to privilege, and even to land. The reinstatement of sacred history once again has tied national identity to religious ideology. Believers, in search of simple answers to complex questions, march where their prophets lead them.

In the case of Ephesos, we have seen how the sacred identity of the city empowered those adult male Ephesians who celebrated the mysteries in the face of a broad social and theological challenge from abroad which was centuries old. I hope I have shown that, in the creation of that sacred identity, the Ephesians, whether by choice or compulsion – it hardly matters – left social room for foreigners, historical room for founders, and theological room for new gods. This room, even though it too had its boundaries, was probably the secret to the vitality of the city of Ephesos – and, to a certain extent, classical civilization itself as well.

Those barefooted pilgrims at Ephesos, the followers of the Star, the Cross, and the Crescent, whom we left tending those well-kept graves, may someday wish to pause, lay aside faith, and cast their eyes upon a series of fragmentary Greek inscriptions. With some effort, those pilgrims too might learn, before it is too late, how the men of Ephesos could imagine truths other than their own, at the same time that they found in their sacred past a relatively flexible source of inspiration, power, and, at last, compromise, in an equally complex and dangerous world.

NOTES

1. B. Lewis, *History – Remembered, Recovered, Invented* (Princeton 1975) 3–41.
2. No doubt individuals, and other social and economic groups at Ephesos attempted to encode other versions of the past of the city into other civic rituals. As we have seen in Chapters 2 and 3, there certainly *were* other major distributions of money, and large processions in the city, where competitive myths of the social structure and history of the city could have been acted out. I think we have to imagine a dynamic social context in which various old and new civic rituals, performed throughout the year according to a set schedule, fulfilled a great many social needs and desires, including the socialization of the youth of the city. Nor did all Ephesians have to participate in all the rituals, or understand them, in order for the rituals themselves to be culturally significant. Different rituals may have answered the needs or goals of different social groups in the city on a competitive basis.

   It may also have been the case that revisions of certain rituals or the creation of altogether new rituals, such as Salutaris' distributions and procession, were intended to challenge the traditional pattern of Ephesian civic rituals. The Ephesian assembly was probably not the only, or even the most important place, where the struggle for the hearts and minds of the demos was fought out. Although we know very little about the performance of other rituals at Ephesos, I would argue only that Salutaris' version of the past, which was proposed by a wealthy individual, supported by powerful officials of the city, ratified by the assembly, confirmed by agents of the imperial government, and concerned with the birth of the goddess Artemis, was the dominant, and preferred one performed in AD 104.
3. E. Bowie, 'Greeks and their Past during the Second Sophistic', *Past and Present*, 46 (1970) 3–41 and in *Studies in Ancient Society*, ed. M.I. Finley (London 1974) 166–209.

4. *IE*, 274.8.
5. Pliny, *Letters*, 6.31.3.
6. Price (1985) 149–50, 255–6.
7. R. Fleischer, 'Der Fries des Hadrianstempels in Ephesos', *Festschrift für Fritz Eichler zum achtzigsten Geburtstag* (Wien 1967) 23–71.
8. Pausanias, *Description of Greece, Achaia*, 7. 2.7.
9. Strabo, *Geography*, 14.1.21.
10. Pausanias, *Description of Greece, Achaia*, 2.8.
11. Herodotus, *Histories*, 1.146.
12. Pausanias, *Description of Greece, Achaia*, 2.9.
13. Strabo, *Geography*, 14.1.21.
14. Strabo, *Geography*, 14.1.20.
15. While it is impossible to write a complete history of this important festival, we can at least reconstruct certain aspects of the celebration of the mysteries from the time of Lysimachos until the reign of Commodus. The primary evidence for the festival at the time of Lysimachos comes from a decree of the Ephesian gerousia during the reign of Commodus (*IE*, 26) in which an old banquet and sacrifice to Artemis, originally ordered by Lysimachos in connection with mysteries and sacrifices, was re-endowed by Tiberius Claudius Nikomedes. The sources for the mysteries from the Hellenistic and early Roman periods include the Kuretes' lists brought together and studied by D. Knibbe in *FiE*, IX/1/1 (1981), and the passage of Strabo, *Geography*, 14.1.20 cited in Chapter 2. From these sources, it would appear that the festival became particularly important for the youth association known as the neoi by the end of the first century BC, and that control over the celebration of the mysteries was increasingly in the hands of the Kuretes, who were attached directly to the Augustan prytaneion. As we have seen, the Salutaris inscription sheds some light on how other civic rituals could be timed to coincide with the celebration of the mysteries at the beginning of the second century, and thereby partake of the atmosphere of the festival, although the foundation tells us very little about the mysteries themselves. Finally, the decree of the gerousia from the time of Commodus cited above does add one potentially very significant element to our knowledge of what took place at the same time as, if not as part of, the celebration of the mysteries. The decree informs us that, since sufficient means were raised again through Tiberius Claudius Nikomedes, the gerousia returned to its ancient custom of reverencing and sacrificing both to Artemis and to the emperor Commodus, the annual sacrifice each year on behalf of his eternal continuance (lines 7–10). While this may not necessarily mean that the sacrifices given to the emperor were equal to those of Artemis, or actually at the celebration of the mysteries at all, it should mean, at some level, and in some concrete context during the festival probably, that it was deemed appropriate for one of the most important civic institutions of Ephesos to treat the patron deity of the city and the emperor both as deities on a nearly equal footing. The key difference apparently was that the sacrifice was on behalf of *his*

eternal continuance. This was perhaps a way of distinguishing one deity (Artemis) from another (Commodus). Artemis would not appear to need sacrifices for her eternal continuance. For the ambiguous nature of this formula, see Price (1985) 216.

16. Tacitus, *Annals*, 3.61.
17. Jews had settled in Ephesos by the reign of Antiochus II Theos (262–46 BC) according to Josephus (*Against Apion*, 2.39; *Jewish Antiquities*, 12.125) and there had been conflicts in the city between the Greeks and the Jews since at least 14 BC when M. Vipsanius Agrippa wrote to the city officials in Ephesos ordering the safe conduct of the temple tax to Jerusalem and, further, that no one should compel the Jews to appear in court on the Sabbath (*Jewish Antiquities*, 16.167–8).

In a separate, and perhaps subsequent dispute, between the Greek city authorities and the Jews of the Ionian cities, the Greeks petitioned Agrippa that they alone might enjoy citizenship, and claimed that if the Jews were to be their fellow citizens, 'they should worship the Ionians' gods' (*Jewish Antiquities*, 16.58–9; 12.125–6).

For evidence of the conflict among Jews, Christians, and Greeks precisely focused upon the question of Artemis' divinity, see *Acts of the Apostles*, 19.23–41; R. Oster, 'The Ephesian Artemis as an Opponent of Early Christianity', *Jahrbuch für Antike und Christentum*, 19 (1976) 24–44; and G.M. Rogers, 'Demetrios of Ephesos: Silversmith and Neopoios?' *Belleten* (1987) 877–82.

Appendix I

THE GREEK TEXT AND THE
ENGLISH TRANSLATION

THE GREEK TEXT

ἐπὶ π[ρυτ]άνεω[ς]

[τ]ιβ. Κλ. Ἀντιπάτρου Ἰουλ[ι]ανοῦ μην[ὸς]

Ποσειδεῶνος ς΄ ἱσταμένου.

4 [ἔ]δοξε τῇ βουλῇ καὶ τῷ νεωκόρῳ δήμῳ φ[ι]λοσεβάστῳ.

[πε]ρὶ ὧν ἐνεφάνισαν Τιβ. Κλ., Τιβ. Κλ. Ἀλεξά[νδρ]ου υἱός, [Κυρ(είνα),

[Ἰ]ουλιανό]ς, φιλόπατρις καὶ φιλοσέβαστο[ς, ἀγν]ός, εὐσεβής,

[γραμματεὺς το]ῦ δήμου το β΄, καὶ οἱ στρατηγοὶ τῆ[ς] πό[λ]εως φιλοσέ-

8 [βαστοι. ἐπειδὴ τοὺς] φιλοτείμους ἄνδρας περὶ τὴν [πόλ]ιν καὶ κατὰ

[πάντα ἀποδειξαμένοι]ς στοργὴν γνησίων πολει[τῶν ἀ]μοιβαί-

[ων χρὴ τυχεῖν τειμῶν πρὸς] τὸ ἀπολαύειν μὲν τοὺς εὖ [ποι]ήσαν-

[τας ἤδη τὴν πόλιν, ἀποκεῖσθαι δὲ τοῖς βο]υλομένοις περ[ὶ τὰ]

12 ὅμοια ἀμι[λλᾶσθαι, ἅμα δὲ τοὺς] ἐσπουδα[κ]ότας τὴν μεγίστην θε-

ὸν Ἄρτεμιν [τειμᾶν, παρ' ἧς γ]είνεται πᾶσιν τ[ὰ] κάλλιστα, καθήκε[ι]

παρὰ τῇ πόλε[ι εὐδοκιμεῖν, Γάιός] τε Οὐίβι[ος Σαλο]υτάριος, ἀ-

νὴρ ἱππικῆς τά[ξε]ος, γένει καὶ ἀξίᾳ διάσημος, στρατείαις τε καὶ

16 ἐπιτροπαῖς ἀ[πὸ] τοῦ κυρίου ἡμῶν αὐτοκράτορος κεκοσμημένος,

πολείτης ἡ[μέτε]ρος καὶ τοῦ βουλευτικοῦ συνεδρίου, πρὸς πα[τρός]

[τε ἀγ]αθῇ χρώμ[ενος δι]αθέσι, ὡς καὶ τὰς ἀπὸ τῆς τύχης ἐπὶ τὸ κρε[ῖσ-]

[σον] προκοπὰς κοσ[μεῖν τῇ] τῶν ἠθῶν σεμνότητι, εὐσεβῶν μὲν φιλοτεί-

20 [μως] τὴν ἀρχηγέτιν πο[ικίλ]αις μὲν ἐπινοίαις ἐσπούδακεν περὶ τὴν θρησ-

[κείαν,] μεγαλοψύχο[ις δὲ] καθιερώσεσιν τὴν πόλιν κατὰ πᾶν τετε[ίμη-]

κεν, προσ[έτι δὲ καὶ νῦν προσελθ] ὼν εἰς τὴν ἐκκλησίαν ὑπέσχε[το ἐννέα

πεικονίσ[ματα καθιερώσειν,] ἓν μὲν χρύσεον, ἐν ᾧ καὶ ἀργ[υρεα]

24 ἐπίχρυσα, ἕτ[ερα δὲ ἀργύρεα] ἀπεικονίσματα ὀκτώ, εἰ[κόνας τε]

ἀργυρέας εἴ[κοσι, πέντε μὲν] τοῦ κ[υ]ρίου ἡμῶν αὐ[τοκράτορος]

Νέρουα Τραϊα[νοῦ Καίσαρος Σ]εβαστοῦ Γερμανικοῦ, Δ[ακικοῦ, καὶ]

τῆς ἱερωτάτ[ης γυναικὸς αὐτοῦ Πλ]ωτείνης καὶ τῆς ἱερ[ᾶς συνκλήτου]

28 καὶ τοῦ Ῥωμαίων ἱππικοῦ τάγμα]τος καὶ δήμου, [τούτων δὲ χω-]

ρὶς εἰκόν[ας δεκαπέντε Ἐφεσίω]ν τὴν πόλιν προσ[ωποποιούσας,]

[το]ῦ δήμ[ου καὶ τῶν ἓξ φυλῶν κα]ὶ βου[λῆ]ς καὶ γερ[ουσίας καὶ ἐφη-]

31 βεία[ς   ]στου [. . . .]νκ[   ]

THE ENGLISH TRANSLATION

(1) In the prytany of Tib. Cl. Antipater Iulianus, on the sixth day
of the month of Poseideon. It was resolved by the boule and the
neokorate loyal demos. About the things Tib. Cl. Iulianus, the
son of Tib. Cl. Alexander, from the tribe Quirina, a patriot and
loyal, pure, pious, secretary of the demos for the second time, and
the loyal generals of the city reported: Since men who are
munificent in the case of the city, and on every occasion show the
affection of genuine citizens, should have honors corresponding to
the enjoyment of those who have done well to the city in the past,
and is laid up for those who are wishing to rival them about
similar things, and corresponding at the same time to the
enjoyment of those who have been zealous to honor the greatest
goddess Artemis, from whom the most beautiful things come to
all, it is fitting for them to be honored by the city, and Caius
Vibius Salutaris, a man of the equestrian order, conspicuous by
birth and personal worth, and adorned with military commands
and procuratorships by our lord emperor, a citizen of our city and
a member of the bouleutic council, regulating his life well as his
father did, since, to crown his prosperity from fortune to the
better by the gravity of his morals, piously making donations he
has been zealous about the foundress with diverse plans about the
cult, and with generous dedications has honored the city in every
way, and further now coming forward in the assembly he has
promised to dedicate nine type-statues, one of gold, on which is
gold-gilded silver, and eight other type-statues, and twenty silver
images, five of our lord emperor Nerva Trajan Caesar Augustus
Germanicus Dacicus and his most revered wife Plotina and the
revered Senate and the Roman equestrian order and the Roman
people, and apart from these fifteen statues representing the city of
the Ephesians, of the demos and the six tribes and the boule and
the gerousia and the ephebeia [lines 31–47 missing]

48 [ὑπὸ τῶν φυλάκων, συνεπιμελουμένων καὶ] δύο νε[οποι-]
ῶν [καὶ σκηπτούχου, φέρηται καὶ] αὖ φ[έρη]ται, διαδ[εχομέ-]
νων [καὶ συμπροπεμπόντων τῶν] ἐφή[β]ων [ἀ]πὸ τῆς [Μαγνη-]
τικῆς [πύλης εἰς τὸ θέατρον κα]ὶ ἀπὸ τοῦ θε[άτρου κατὰ]
52 τὸν αὐ[τὸν τρόπον,] τῇ τε ν[ουμ]ηνίᾳ ἀρχ[ιερατικοῦ]
ἔτους θυσί[ᾳ καὶ ἐν τ]αῖς ι[β′ καθ′ ἕκαστο]ν μῆνα ἀ[θροιζο-]
μέναις ἱερα[ῖς τε κα]ὶ νομ[ίμοις ἐκκλ]ησίαις κα[ὶ ἐν ταῖς τῶν]
Σεβ[ασ]τείων [καὶ Σω]τηρίων [καὶ τῶν π]έντ[ετηρικῶν   ]
56 [   ]ω[ν ἑορταῖς   ]

----

62 μοτε[τῶν δὲ χρημάτων τῶν καθιε-]
ρωμένω[ν ὑπ′ αὐ]τ[οῦ 'Εφεσίων τῇ βουλῇ καὶ τῇ γερουσίᾳ]
64 καὶ πολ[είταις καὶ ἐ]φή[βοις καὶ παισὶν ὑπέσχετο αὐτὸς]
ἐπὶ τοῦ σ[ἐκδανιστὴς γενέσθαι]
καὶ [τε]λεῖν τόκ[ον δραχμιαῖον] ἀσσαριαῖον
[δι]αιρεθ[η]σόμενον κ[αθ′ ἕκαστον ἐ]νιαυτὸν κα-
68 [τὰ τ]ὴν διάταξιν αὐτοῦ τ[ῇ γεν]εσ[ίῳ τῇ]ς θεοῦ ἡ[μέρᾳ,]
[ἥτι]ς ἐστὶν τοῦ Θαργηλιῶ[ν]ος μηνὸς ἕκ[τ]η ἱσταμέ[νου]
70 [ὁ]μολογήσας ἀποδώσε[ι]ν τὰ χρήατ[α ἢ] ἑαυτὸν τὰ [κα-]
[θι]ερωμένα, ὅταν βουλη[θ]ῇ, ἢ τοὺς κληρονό[μους αὐ-]
72 [το]ῦ τῇ πόλει, κομιζομένων τῶν ἑκά[σ]του προ[σώ-]
[που π]ροϊσταμένων. περὶ [ὧν] ἁπάντων διάταξιν εἰσηγ[ησάμε-]
νος ἰδί[ᾳ ἡ[ξί]]ωσεν ἐπι[κυ]ρωθῆναι καὶ διὰ ψ[η]φίσμα[τος τῆς]
[βουλῆς καὶ τοῦ δήμου, καὶ νῦ]ν τῆς ἐπα[ρχ]είας [ἡγεμο-]
76 [νεύοντες ὁ κράτιστος ἀν]ὴρ καὶ εὐεργέ[τ]ης 'Ακο[υί]λλι-
[ος Πρόκλος, ὁ ἀνθύπατο]ς, καὶ 'Αφράνι[ο]ς Φλαουια-
[νός, ὁ πρεσβευτὴς καὶ ἀντ]ιστράτηγο[ς, ἀν]υπερβλήτῳ
[τῇ φιλανθρωπίᾳ καὶ] φιλοστορ[γί]ᾳ ἐ[πιγνό]ντες τὴν
80 τοῦ ἀνδρὸ[ς μεγαλοψ]υχίαν, ὡς γνή[σιοι] πολεῖται ἡ-
μῶν αὐτοί, κα[θ′ ἃ ἀντημεί]ψαντο αὐτῷ[ι κ]αὶ δι′ ἐπιστολῶν
[συ]νηδόμενο[ι ἀντέ]γραψαν, ἐ[πεκέλ]ευσαν, ὥστε δι′
[αὐτῶ]ν εἰσενε[νκεῖν π]ερὶ τῶν [καθιερώσ]εων αὐτ[οῦ.]

154

(48). . .by the guards, and two of the neopoioi attending and the beadle, to be brought and brought back, the ephebes receiving and escorting from the Magnesian Gate into the theatre, and from the theatre in the same manner during the first new moon's sacrifice of the archieratic year, and on the occasions of the twelve sacred gatherings and regular assemblies every month, and during the Sebasteia and the Soteria and the penteteric festivals . . . [5 lines missing]

(62). . . of the money dedicated by him to the boule of the Ephesians, and to the gerousia, and to the citizens, and to the ephebes, and to the paides he promised. . . . . to be the lender and to pay the interest at a rate of twelve asses per one hundred denarii, distributing every year according to his bequest on the birthday of the goddess, which is the sixth day of the month of Thargelion, he has agreed to give out the money dedicated, either himself, or his heirs, whenever it was wanted, to the city, and that the officers of each group would receive it. (73) Concerning all these things having privately proposed the bequest, he has asked that it be ratified by a decree of the boule and the demos, and now the governors of the province, the *vir clarissimus* and benefactor Aquillius Proculus, the proconsul, and Afranius Flavianus, the legatus pro praetore, with kindness not to be outdone and affection, recognizing the generosity of the man, as being our true citizens themselves, by the things they answered to him, and in letters rejoicing wrote, have ordered us to introduce with their sanction the motion concerning his dedications.

APPENDIX I

84 δ[εδόχθ]αι Γ[άϊον Οὐεί]βιον [Σαλουτάριον, ἄνδρα ε]ὐσεβῆ

[μὲν] πρὸς [τοὺς θεοὺ]ς, εἰς δὲ τ[ὴν πόλιν φι]λότειμον, τε-

[τει[μῆσ]θαι τ[αῖς κρ]ατίσταις τιμ[αῖς εἰκόν]ων τε ἀναστάσε-

σιν ἔν [τε τῷ] ἱερῷ τῆς 'Αρτέμιδο[ς καὶ ἐν τοῖ]ς ἐπισημοτάτοις

88 τόποις τῆς πόλεως, ἀναγορεῦσαι δὲ αὐ]τὸν καὶ χρυσέῳ

στεφάνῳ ἐν ταῖς ἐκκ[λησίαις ὡς σπουδά]ζοντα καὶ φιλάρ-

90 τεμιν. τὴν δὲ παρατή[ρησιν τῶν προγ]εγραμμένων ἱε-

ρῶν [εἰδ]ῶν καὶ τὴν πρὸ κοιν[οῦ ἀπὸ τοῦ ἱ]ερόῦ εἰς τὸ θέα-

92 τρον καὶ τὴν ἐκ τοῦ θεάτρου εἰ[ς τὸ ἱερὸν] τῆς 'Αρτέμιδος

[μετακομιδὴν ποιῆσαι κατὰ τὴν διάταξιν κ]αθ' ἕκαστον [ἔ-]

τος [ἐκ τῶν νεοποιῶν δύο καὶ σκηπτ]οῦχον καὶ τοὺ[ς]

95 φ[υλάκους   ]

----

104 [   ] τὸν ναὸν τῆς 'Αρ[τέμιδος   ]

[τ]ῶν καθηκόντω[ν   ]

[. τὴν δὲ διάταξιν αὐ]τοῦ κυρίαν ε̣ῖ̣ν̣[αι, ἀμετάθετον,]

[ἀκατάλυτον, ἀπαράλλακτ]ον εἰς τὸν [ἅπαντα χρόνον.]

108 [ἐὰν δέ τις εἴτε ἰδιωτῶν ε]ἴτε ἀρχό[ντων ἐπιψή]φίσῃ τ[ι πα-]

[ρὰ τὴν διάταξιν τὴν διὰ ψηφί]σμα[τος κυρωθη]σομένη[ν] ἢ

[ἀλλάξῃ, ἔστω ἄκυρον ἅπαν τὸ ἐναντίον τῇ διατάξ]ει, ὅ τε ποιή-

[σας τι τούτων ἢ εἰσηγησάμ]εν[ος ἀποτεισάτω εἰ]ς προ[σ]κόσ-

112 [μησιν τῆς κυρίας 'Αρτέμιδο]ς δ[ην. β'] μ(ύρια) [, ε καὶ εἰς τὸν] τοῦ

κ[υρ]ίου Κ[αί-]

[σαρος φίσκον ἄλλα] δην. [β'] μ(ύρια) ,ε , κ[αθάπερ οἱ κράτισ]το[ι ἡ-]

[γεμόνες 'Ακουίλλιος] Πρόκλο[ς, ὁ ἀνθύπατος, καὶ 'Αφράνι-]

[ος Φλαουιανός, ὁ πρεσβευ]τ[ὴς καὶ ἀντιστράτηγος, δι' ἐ-]

116 [πιστο]λῶν τὸ [προγεγραμμένον πρόστειμον ὥρισαν.]

[πρὸς δ]ὲ τὸ φαν[ερὰν γενέσθαι τήν τε πρὸς τὴν πό-]

[λιν μ]εγαλοψυχ[ίαν αὐτοῦ καὶ τὴν πρὸς τὴν θεὸν εὐσέβειαν]

[τὴν ὑπ' αὐτ]οῦ γεγ[ραμμένην καὶ διὰ τούτου τοῦ ψηφίσ]ματ[ος]

120 [τῆς βουλῆς καὶ τοῦ δήμου κεκυρωμένην διά]ταξιν, [ἀναγ]ραφ[ῆ-]

[ναι   ]θα[...]σ[..]

[   ]

[ca.10   ]ν ἐν μὲν τῷ θεάτρῳ [ἐπὶ τῷ τῆς νοτίας πα-]

124 [ρόδου τοίχῳ] αὐτοῦ μαρμαρίνῳ, ᾗ β[ούλεται αὐτός, ἐν δὲ]

[τῷ 'Αρτεμ]ισίῳ ἐν τόπῳ ἐπιτηδείῳ, θιλοτει[μίας ἕνεκα κ]αὶ

156

(84) It was resolved that: Caius Vibius Salutaris, a man pious toward the gods, munificent to the city, to be honored with the most senior honors, and with the setting up of statues in the temple of Artemis and in the most conspicuous places in the city, and to proclaim this man by a golden crown during the assemblies as being zealous and loving Artemis. The care of the afore-mentioned sacred images, and the conveyance before everyone, from the temple into the theatre, and from the theatre into the temple of Artemis, will be done according to the bequest every year by two of the neopoioi, and a beadle, and the guards [7 lines missing](104) [ ] the temple of Ar[temis](105) [ ] of the things fitting [ ](106) [his bequest] to be valid, unable to be changed, indissoluble, precisely similar for all time. If anyone, either of private citizens, or city officials, should put to the vote anything against the bequest which is ratified by this decree, or should change it, let the whole thing opposite to the bequest be invalid, and he, who does any of these things, or proposes any of these things is to pay toward the further adornment of lady Artemis 25,000 denarii, and to the fiscus of lord Caesar another 25,000 denarii, just as the excellent governors Aquillius Proculus, the proconsul, and Afranius Flavianus, the legatus pro praetore, through letters have determined the aforementioned penalty.

(117) That his generosity toward the city, and piety toward the goddess be clear, the bequest written by him and ratified by this decree of the boule and the demos, to be written up

(121) [ ]

(122) [ ]

(123) [ca.10] in the theatre, on the marble wall of its south parodos, wherever he wishes, and in the Artemision, in a suitable place, on account of his munificence and virtue. And concerning

APPENDIX I

[ἀρετῆς.] καὶ περὶ τῆ[ς δ]ιαμονῆς τῶν καθι[ερωμένων] ὑπ' αὐ-

[τοῦ χρ]ημάτων τῆ τε βουλῆ καὶ τῆ γερο[υσίᾳ καὶ πολείταις καὶ]

128 [ἐφήβ]οις ὑπέσχετο αὐτὸς κατὰ [τὴν διάταξιν   ]

[...]ι ἐκδανιστὴς γενέσθαι [   ]

130 [   ]

[   ]

132 [δεδόχθαι τῆι βουλῆι καὶ τῶι νεωκ]όρωι δήμωι θιλοσε[βάστωι]

[γενέσθαι, καθότι προγέγρα]πται.

(B)   Σέξτ[ῳ 'Αττίῳ]

Σουβουρανῷ τ[ὸ β´, Μάρκῳ 'Ασινίῳ]

136 Μα[ρκέλλῳ ὑπάτοις,   'Ιαν..]

[ἐπὶ πρύτάνεως Τιβ. Κλ. 'Αντιπάτρου 'Ιουλιανοῦ,]

[μηνὸς Ποσειδεῶνος . ´ ἱσταμένου.]

Γάιος [Οὐείβιος, Γ. υἱός, Οὐωφεντείνα, Σαλουτάριος διάτα-]

140 ξιν εἰ[σφέρει τῆ 'Εφεσίων βουλῆ φιλοσεβάστῳ καὶ τῷ νεοκόρῳ]

'Εφεσίω[ν δήμῳ φιλοσεβάστῳ, περὶ ὧν καθιέρωκεν ἐπὶ]

ταῖς ὑπ[ογεγραμμέναις οἰκονομίαις τῆ μεγίστη θεᾶ 'Εφεσίᾳ 'Αρ-]

τέμιδ[ι καὶ τῷ νεοκόρῳ 'Εφεσίων δήμῳ φιλοσεβάστῳ καὶ]

144 τῆ 'Εφ[εσίων βουλῆ φιλοσεβάστῳ καὶ τῆ 'Εφεσίων γερουσίᾳ]

φ[ιλοσεβάστῳ καὶ ταῖς ἒξ 'Εφεσίων φυλαῖς καὶ τοῖς κατ' ἐνιαυτὸν]

['Εφεσίων ἐφήβοις καὶ τοῖς θεολόγοις καὶ ὑμνῳδοῖς καὶ τοῖς νεο-]

[ποιοῖς καὶ σκηπτούχοις καὶ τοῖς αἰεὶ ἐσομένοις 'Εφεσίων]

148 [παισὶν καὶ παιδωνόμοις ἀπεικονισμάτων τῆς θεοῦ ἐννέα, ἑ-]

[νὸς μὲν χρυσέου, τῶν δὲ λοιπῶν ἀργυρέων, καὶ εἰκόνων ἀργυρέων]

[εἴκοσι καὶ δηναρίων δισμυρίων, ἐφ' ᾧ εἰκὼν ἀργυρέα τοῦ κυρίου]

[ἡμῶν αὐτοκράτορος Καίσαρος Νέρουα Τραϊαν]ο[ῦ Σεβαστοῦ, Γερ-]

152 [μανικοῦ, Δακικοῦ, ὁλκῆς λειτρῶν .´,] οὑνκιῶν γ´, καὶ εἰκὼν [ἀργυρέα]

[Πλ]ῳ[τείνης Σεβαστῆς, ὁλ]κῆς λειτρῶν γ´, νεοκορῶνται πα[ρ' αὐτῶι]

Σαλο[υταρίωι] τῶι κ[αθι]ερωκότι, μετὰ δὲ τὴν Σαλουταρίο[υ τελευτὴν]

ἀποδοθ[ῶ]σιν αἱ προδηλούμεναι εἰκόνες τῶι 'Εφεσίων γραμμ[ατεῖ ἐπι τῶι]

156 προγεγραμμένοι σταθμῶι ἀπὸ τῶν κληρονόμων αὐτοῦ, ὥ[στε καὶ αὐ-]

τὰς τίθε[σ]θαι ἐν ταῖς ἐκκλησίαις ἐπάνω τῆς σελίδος τῆς βουλ[ῆς μετὰ τῆς]

χρυσέας 'Αρτέμιδος καὶ τῶν ἄλλων εἰκόνων. "Αρτεμις δὲ χρυσ[έα, ὁλκῆς]

λειτρῶν τριῶν καὶ αἱ περὶ αὐτὴν ἀργύρεοι ἔλαφοι δύο καὶ τὰ λοιπ[ὰ

ἐπίχρυσα,]

the permanence of the money dedicated by him to the boule, and to the gerousia, and to the citizens, and ephebes he promised, according to the bequest to be the lender

(130) [ ]

(131) [ ]

(132) It was resolved by the boule and neokorate loyal demos to be inscribed above.

(134) When Sextus Attius Suburanus for the second time, and Marcus Asinius Marcellus were consuls on the . . . day of January.

During the prytany of Tib. Cl. Antipater Iulianus, on the . . . . . day of Poseideon. Caius Vibius Salutaris, the son of Caius, from the tribe Oufentina, proposes the bequest to the loyal boule of the Ephesians, and to the loyal neokorate demos of the Ephesians, concerning the things he dedicated on the conditions written below, to the greatest goddess Ephesian Artemis, and to the neokorate loyal demos of the Ephesians, and to the loyal boule of the Ephesians, and to the loyal gerousia of the Ephesians, and to the six tribes of the Ephesians, and to the annual ephebes of the Ephesians, and to the theologoi, and to the hymnodoi, and to the neopoioi, and to the beadles, and to the future paides of the Ephesians, and to the paidonomoi, nine type-statues of the goddess, one of gold, the remaining silver, and twenty silver images, and 20,000 denarii, on the condition that the silver image of our lord Emperor Caesar Nerva Trajan Augustus Germanicus Dacicus, weight of . . . . . pounds, 3 ounces, and a silver image of Plotina Augusta, weight of 3 pounds, to be cared for by Salutaris himself the dedicator, and after the death of Salutaris the aforesaid images to be delivered to the secretary of the Ephesians at the aforesaid weight by his heirs, that these be placed during the assemblies above the block of the boule among the golden Artemis, and the other images. A golden Artemis, weight of 3 pounds, and the two silver stags about her and the rest gold

160 ὁλκῆς λειτρῶν δύο, οὐνκιῶν δέκα, γραμμάτων πέντε, καὶ εἰ[κὼν ἀργυ-]
ρέ[α τῆ]ς ἱερᾶς συνκλῆτου, ὁλκῆς λειτρῶν δ´, οὐνκιῶν β´, καὶ εἰ[κὼν ἀργυ
ρ[έα τῆ]ς φιλοσεβάστου καὶ σεμνοτάτης Ἐφεσίων βουλῆς, ὁ[λκῆς λει-]
[τρῶ]ν δ´, γραμ‹μ›άτων θ´, τὰ καὶ αὐτὰ καθιερωμένα τῇ τε Ἀρτέμιδι [καὶ
τῇ φιλο-]
164 σ[εβ]άστῳ Ἐφεσίων βουλῇι. ὁμοίως καὶ ἀργυρέα Ἄρτεμις λα[μπαδηφό-]
ρ[ο]ς, ὁλκῆς λ ζ´, καὶ εἰκὼν ἀργυρέα τοῦ δήμου τοῦ Ῥωμαίων, [ὁλκῆς λ .´
καὶ εἰκὼν ἀργυρέα τῆς φιλοσεβάστου γερουσίας, ὁλκῆς λ [.´, τὰ καὶ]
αὐτὰ καθιερωμένα τῇ τε Ἀρτέμιδι καὶ τῇ Ἐφεσίων γερουσίᾳ.
168 ὁμοίως καὶ ἄλλη Ἄρτεμις ἀργυρέα λαμπαδηφόρος, ἐ[μφερὴς]
τῇ ἐν τῇ ἐξέδρᾳ τῶν ἐφήβων, ὁλκῆς λ ζ´, οὐνκιῶν ε´, γραμ[μάτων .´,]
καὶ εἰκὼν ἀργυρέα τοῦ ἱππικοῦ τάγματος, ὁλκῆς λ γ´, ἡ[μιουν-]
κίου, γραμμάτων γ´, καὶ ἄλλη εἰκὼν ἀργυρέα τῆς ἐφηβεία[ς, ὁλκῆς λ .´,]
172 τὰ καὶ αὐτὰ καθιερωμένα τῇ τε Ἀρτέμιδι καὶ τοῖς κατ´ ἐνιαυτὸ[ν οὖ-]
[σι]ν ἐφήβοις. ὁ[μοίως καὶ ἄλλη Ἄρτεμις ἀργυρέα λαμπαδηφόρος, ἔχου-]
174 [σα] φιάλην, ὁλκ[ῆς λ .´, οὐνκιῶν .´, γραμμάτων .´, καὶ εἰκὼν ἀργυρέα]
[θεο]ῦ Σεβαστοῦ, [ὁλκῆς λ .´, οὐνκιῶν .´, γραμμάτων .´, καὶ εἰκὼν
ἀργυρέα φυ-]
176 [λῆς Σε] βαστῆς, ὁ[λκῆς λ .´, τὰ καὶ αὐτὰ καθιερωμένα τῇ τε Ἀρτέμιδι καὶ
[τοῖς αἰεὶ ἐ]σομέν[οις πολείταις τῆς Σεβαστῆς φυλῆς. ὁμοίως καὶ ἄλλη]
[Ἄρτεμις ἀργυρέα   , ὁλκῆς λ .´,]
[καὶ εἰκὼν ἀργυρέα τοῦ φιλοσεβάστου Ἐφεσίων δήμου, ὁλκῆς λ .´,]
180 [καὶ εἰκὼν ἀργυρέα φυλῆς Ἐ]φ[εσέων, ὁλκῆς λ .´, τὰ καὶ αὐτὰ καθιερωμ-]
ἐν[α]
[τῇ τε Ἀρτέμιδι καὶ τοῖς αἰεὶ ἐ]σομέν[οις πολείταις τῆς Ἐφεσέων φυλῆς.
[ὁμοίως καὶ ἄλλη Ἄρτεμις] ἀργυρέα [χ]ειρὶ
[,ὁλκῆς λ .´, οὐνκιῶν] θ´, καὶ ε[ἰκὼν ἀργυρέα   ὁλκῆς
λ .´,] καὶ
184 [εἰκὼν ἀργυρέα φυλῆς Καρηναίων, ὁλκῆς λ .´, οὐνκιῶν .´, γραμμ]άτων γ´, τὰ
[καὶ αὐτὰ καθιερωμένα τῇ τε Ἀρτέμιδι καὶ τοῖς αἰεὶ ἐσομένοις πο]λείταις
[τῆς Καρηναίων φυλῆς. ὁμοίως καὶ ἄλλη Ἄρτεμις ἀργυρέα λαμπ]αδηφό-
[ρος   8-9   , ὁλκῆς λ .´, καὶ εἰκὼν ἀργυρέα Λυσιμάχου, ὁλκῆς λ .´,
γ]ρ(αμμάτων) γ´, καὶ εἰκὼν
188 [ἀργυρέα φυλῆς Τηΐων, ὁλκ]ῆς [λ .´, τὰ καὶ αὐτὰ καθιερωμένα τῇ τ]ε
Ἀρτέμιδι
[καὶ τοῖς αἰεὶ ἐσομένοις π]ολε[ίταις τῆς Τηΐων φυλῆς.] ὁμο[ίω]ς καὶ

gilded, weight of 2 pounds, 10 ounces, 5 grammes, and a silver image of the revered Senate, weight of 4 pounds, 2 ounces, and a silver image of the loyal and solemn boule of the Ephesians, weight of 4 pounds, 9 grammes, these same things dedicated to Artemis, and to the loyal boule of the Ephesians. Equally a silver Artemis the Torch-bearer, weight of 7 pounds, and a silver image of the demos of the Romans, weight of . . . . . pounds, and a silver image of the loyal gerousia, weight of . . . . . pounds, these same things dedicated to Artemis, and to the gerousia of the Ephesians.

(168) Equally another silver Artemis the Torch-bearer, similar to the one in the exedra of the ephebes, weight of 7 pounds, 5 ounces, ... grammes, and a silver image of the equestrian order, weight of 3 pounds, ½ ounce, 3 grammes, and another silver image of the ephebeia, weight of . . . . . pounds, these same things dedicated to Artemis and to the annual ephebes of each year. Equally another silver Artemis the Torch-bearer, holding a libation bowl, weight of . . . . . pounds, ... ounces, ... grammes, and a silver image of deified Augustus, weight of . . . . . pounds, ... ounces, ... grammes, and a silver image of the tribe Sebaste, weight of . . . . . pounds, these same things dedicated to Artemis and to whosoever shall be citizens of tribe Sebaste. Equally another silver Artemis [ ] weight of . . . . . pounds, and a silver image of the loyal demos of the Ephesians, weight of . . . . . pounds, and a silver image of the tribe of the Ephesians, weight of . . . . . pounds, these same things dedicated to Artemis and to whosoever shall be citizens of the tribe of the Ephesians.

(182) Equally another silver Artemis [ ]in hand, weight of . . . . . pounds, 9 ounces, and a silver image [of Androklos?] weight of . . . . . pounds, and a silver image of the tribe of the Karenaioi, weight of . . . . . pounds, ... ounces, 3 grammes, these same things dedicated to Artemis and to whosoever shall be citizens of the tribe of the Karenaioi. Equally another silver Artemis the Torch-bearer[. . . . .], weight of . . . . . pounds, and a silver image of Lysimachos, weight of . . . . . pounds, 3 grammes, and a silver image of the tribe of the Teioi, weight of . . . . . pounds, these same things dedicated to Artemis, and to whosoever shall be citizens of the tribe of the Teioi. Equally

APPENDIX I

ἄλλη Ἄρ-

[τεμις ἀργυρέα ἔχου]σα τὸ τ[5-6 , ὁλκῆς λ . ΄, οὐνκι]ῶν γ΄,

ἡμίσους γράμμα-

[τος, καὶ εἰκὼν ἀργ]υρέα Ξ[ὐωνύμου, ὁλκῆς λ . ΄, καὶ εἰκὼν ἀργυρ]έα

φυλῆς Εὐ-

192 [ωνύμων, ὁλκῆς λ] γ΄, ἡμ[ιουνκίου, γραμμάτων . ΄, τὰ καὶ αὐτὰ κ]αθιερωμέ-

[να τῇ τε ᾿Αρτέμιδι καὶ το]ῖς [αἰεὶ ἐσομένοις πολείταις τῆς

Εὐωνύμω]ν φυλῆς.

[ὁμοίως καὶ ἄλλη Ἄρτεμις ἀργυρέα λαμπαδηφόρος   Κα]σταλί-

[α   , ὁλκῆς λ . ΄, οὐνκιῶν . ΄, καὶ εἰκὼν ἀργυρέα Πίωνος, ὁλκῆς λ . ΄,

καὶ ε]ἰκὼν

196 [ἀργυρέα φυλῆς Βεμβειναίων, ὁλκῆς λ . ΄, τὰ καὶ αὐτὰ καθιερωμένα τῇ]

τε ᾿Α[ρ-]

[τέμιδι καὶ τοῖς αἰεὶ ἐσομένοις πολείταις τῆς Βεμβειναίων φυλῆ]ς.

[ὁ δὲ προγεγραμμένος σταθμὸς τῶν ἐννέα ἀπεικονισμάτω]ν τῆς θε-

[οῦ καὶ τῶν εἴκοσι εἰκόνων παρεστάθη Εὐμέ]νει Εὐμέν[ους τοῦ θεοφίλ]ου, τῶι

200 [καὶ αὐτῶι στρατηγῶι τῆς ᾿Εφεσίων πόλεως, δι]α τοῦ ζυγ[οστάτου ᾿Ερμίου,]

ἱεροῦ τῆς

[᾿Αρτέμιδος, συμπαραλαμβάνο]ντ[ος Μουσαί]ου, ἱεροῦ τ[ῆς ᾿Αρτέμιδος, τοῦ]

ἐπὶ τῶν

[παραθηκῶν. τὰ δὲ προγεγρ]αμμέ[να ἀπεικο]νίσματ[α ἀποτιθέσθω]σαν κατὰ

[πᾶσαν νόμιμον ἐκκλ]ησίαν κ[αὶ τῇ τῇ νέᾳ] νουμη[νίᾳ ἔτους ἀρ]χιερατι-

204 [κοῦ ἐπιτελουμένῃ θυσί]ᾳ ἐν τῶι [θεάτρωι ὑπ]ὸ τῶν κα[θηκόντων ἐπὶ τὰ]ς

κατὰ σε-

[λίδας τεθειμένας κ]αὶ ἐπιγεγ[ραμμένας] θ΄ βάσεις [ἀνὰ γ΄, ὡς ἡ ἐπὶ]

τοῖς βά-

[θροις καὶ ἡ ἐν τῇ δ]ιατάξει βο[υλῆς, γερου]σίας, ἐφη[βείας καὶ

φυλῆ]ς καθιέ-

[ρωσις. μετὰ δὲ τ]ὸ λυθῆν[αι τὰς ἐκκλησί]ας ἀποφ[ερέσθωσαν τὰ ἀπεικονίσ-

208 [ματα καὶ αἱ εἰκόνε]ς ε[ἰς τὸ ἱερὸν τῆς ᾿Αρτέμ]ιδος κα[ὶ παραδιδόσ-

θωσαν ὑπὸ]

[τῶν φυλάκων, συνεπιμελουμένων ἐκ] τῶν νεο[ποιῶν δύο καὶ σκηπτούχου,]

[Μουσαίῳ, ἱερῷ τῆς ᾿Αρτέμιδος τῷ ἐπὶ τῶν παρ]αθη[κῶν, διαδεχομένων

καὶ συμ-]

[προπεμπόντων καὶ τῶν ἐφήβων ἀπὸ τῆς Μαγνητικῆς πύλης εἰς τὸ θέα-]

212 [τρον καὶ ἀπὸ τοῦ θεάτρου μέχρι τῆς Κορησσικῆς πύλης μετὰ] πάσης [εὐπρε-

162

another silver Artemis having the t[. . . . .], weight of . . . . . pounds, 3 ounces, ½ gramme, and a silver image of Euonumos, weight of . . . . . pounds, and a silver image of the tribe of the Euonumoi, weight of 3 pounds, ½ ounce, ... grammes, these same things dedicated to Artemis, and to whosoever shall be citizens of the tribe of the Euonumoi. [Equally another silver Artemis carrying a torch . . . Ka]stalia weight of . . . . . pounds, ... ounces, and a silver image of Pion, weight of . . . . . pounds, and a silver image of the tribe of the Bembinaioi, weight of . . . . . pounds, these same things dedicated to Artemis, and to whosoever shall be the citizens of the tribe of the Bembinaioi.

(198) The aforementioned weight of the nine type-statues of the goddess, and of the twenty images to be entrusted to Eumenes, the son of Eumenes, the grandson of Theophilos, who is also a general of the city of the Ephesians, through the weight master Hermias, sacred slave of Artemis, receiving them Mousaios, sacred slave of Artemis, custodian of things deposited. The aforementioned type-statues should be placed during every regular assembly, and during the new moon's sacrifice of the archieratic year in the theatre by the fitting people on the nine inscribed bases in three groups over the blocks set out as the dedication on the bases and the dedication in the bequest for the boule, the gerousia, the ephebeia, and (each) tribe. After the assemblies have been dismissed, the type-statues and the images should be carried back to the sanctuary of Artemis and should be handed over by the guards, two of the neopoioi and a beadle attending, to Mousaios, sacred slave of Artemis, custodian of the things deposited, the ephebes receiving and escorting from the Magnesian Gate into the theatre, and from the theatre right to the Koressian Gate with all due dignity. In like manner (let it) be

[πείας. ὡσαύτως δὲ γενέσθαι καὶ ἐν πᾶσι τοῖς γυμνικοῖ]ς ἀγῶσιν κ[αὶ εἴ

τινες]

[ἔτεραι ὑπὸ τῆς βουλῆς καὶ τοῦ δήμου ὁρισθήσονται ἡμέραι. μηδ]ενὶ δὲ

ἐξ[έστω]

[μετοικονομῆσαι ἢ τὰ ἀπεικονίσματα τῆς θε]οῦ ἢ τὰς εἰκόνας πρὸς τὸ

216 [μετονομασθῆναι ἢ ἀναχωνευθῆναι ἢ ἄλλωι] τινὶ τρόπωι κακουργηθῆνα[ι,]

ἐπ(ε)ὶ

[ὁ ποιήσας τι τούτων ὑπεύθυνο]ς ἔστω ἱεροσυλίᾳ καὶ ἀσεβείᾳ καὶ οὐδὲν

218 [ἧσσον ὁ αὐτὸς ἐπιδεικνύσθω στα]θμὸς ἐν τοῖς προγεγραμμένοις ἀπεικονίσ-

[μασιν καὶ εἴκοσιν λειτρῶν] ρια', ἔχοντος τὴν περὶ τούτων ἐκδικίαν

ἐπ' ἀνάν-

220 [κη   .] τῶν δὲ καθιερωμένων ὑπὸ Σαλουτα-

[ρίου δην. β'] μ(υρίων) τ[ε]λέσει τόκον Σαλουτάριος δραχμιαῖον καθ'

ἕκαστον ἐνι-

[αυτὸν] τὰ γει[ν]όμενα δηνάρια χίλια ὀκτακόσια, ἀφ' ὧν δώσει τῷ γραμμα-

[τεῖ τῆς β]ουλῆς δηνάρια τετρακόσι[α π]εντήκοντα, ὅπως ἐπιτελεῖ διανομὴν

224 [τοῖς] βουλευταῖς ἐν τῷ ἱερῶι ἐν τ[ῶι πρ]ονάωι τῆι γενεσίωι τῆς

μεγίστης θεᾶς Ἀρ-

[τέμιδος,] ἥτις ἐστὶν μηνὸς Θαργη[λι]ῶνος ἕκτῃ ἱσταμένου, γεινομένης

τῆς διανο-

226 [μῆς ἤδη τῆ]ς πέμπτης, διδομένο[υ ἐ]κάστῳ τῶν παρόντων δηναρίου ἑνός,

[μὴ ἔχον]τος ἐξουσίαν τοῦ ἐπὶ τῆς διανομῆς ἀπόντι δοῦναι, ἐπεὶ ἀποτεισά-

228 [τω τῆι β]ουλῆι ὑπὲρ ἑκάστου ὀνόματος τοῦ μὴ παραγενομένου καὶ λαβόντος

[προστείμου δην. . . ἐὰν δὲ μείζω]ν γεί[νηται ὁ κόλλυβος, ὥστε]

[εἰς πλείονας χωρεῖν, ἐξέστ]ω καὶ [   ]

[   ]α ἀνὰ κυ[. . . .]ν. ὁμοίω[ς δώ-]

232 [σει τῷ τοῦ συνεδρίου τῆς] γερουσ[ίας γ]ραμματεῖ κ[ατ' ἐνι-]

[αυτὸν ἕκαστον ἀπὸ τοῦ προγεγραμμέν]ου τόκου δη. [τπβ']

[ἀσσάρια θ', ὅπως ἐπιτελῇ κλῆρον τῇ] γενεσίῳ τῆς θεο[ῦ]

[ἡμέρᾳ τοῖς τοῦ συνεδρίου μετέχουσι]ν εἰς ἄνδρας τθ' [ἀνὰ δη. α'. ἐὰν]

236 [δὲ μείζων ᾖ ὁ γενόμενος κόλλυβος,] ὥστε εἰς πλείο[νας]

[χωρεῖν, κληρώσει καὶ πλείονας, ἐκ]άστου τῶν λαχ[όν-]

[των ἀνὰ δηνάριον ἓν λαμβάνοντ]ος. διδόσθ[ω δὲ καὶ]

[τοῖς   τοῖς νεοκοροῦσι παρὰ] Σα[λ]ουταρίῳ τ[ῷ καθιερω-]

240 [κότι εἰς διανομὴν δη.   καὶ το]ῖς ἀσιαρχή[σασι] τοῖς

[ἀναγραψανένοις δη.   εἰς κλῆρον] ἀνὰ [δηνάρ]ια ια' ᾧ καὶ

during all athletic contests, and if any other days are determined by the boule and demos. Nor let it be possible for anyone to make changes in the administration either of the type-statues of the goddess, or the images with a view toward changing the names or melting down, or in any other way to do evil, since the one who does any of these things, let him be liable for sacrilege and impiety, and none the less let the same weight be shown in the aforementioned type-statues and images, 111 pounds, having the prosecution about these things by necessity [half-line missing]. (220) Of the 20,000 denarii dedicated by Salutaris, Salutaris will pay the interest at 9 per cent every year, amounting to 1,800 denarii, from which he will give to the secretary of the boule 450 denarii, that he carry out a distribution to the members of the boule in the sanctuary in the pronaos on the birthday of the greatest goddess Artemis, which is on the sixth of Thargelion, the distribution being already on the fifth, one denarius being given to each of those present, but the one in charge of the distribution not having the right to give to anyone absent, since (if he does) let him pay to the boule, on behalf of each person not there who has received something, a fine of . . . denarii. But if the exchange rate should be greater, so that he can distribute to more men, it is possible [ ]

Equally he will give to the secretary of the council of the gerousia every year from the aforementioned interest 382 denarii 9 asses, that he should complete a lottery on the birthday of the goddess for the regular members of the council, to 309 men at a rate of one denarius apiece. If the existing rate of exchange should be greater, so that he can distribute to more men, he will allot more portions, each of those winning the lottery taking at a rate of one denarius.

And let be given to the neokoroi in the house of Salutaris the dedicator, for distribution . . . . denarii, and to the former asiarchs who have registered, ... denarii for a lottery at a rate

APPENDIX I

[τὰ εἰς τὴν θυσίαν ἀγοράσουσιν,] τοῦ κλήρου γεινομένου

[τῆι πέμπτηι, μὴ ἔχοντος ἐ]ξουσίαν τοῦ γραμματέος τῆς

244 [γερουσίας τοῦ παριέναι τὴν δ]ιανομὴν ἢ ἀναγραφὴν μετὰ

[τὴν Σαλουταρίου τελευτή]ν, ἐπεὶ ἀποτεισάτω πρόστειμον

[τὸ ἐν τῇ διατάξει ὡρισ]μένον. ὁμοίως ἀπὸ τοῦ προγε-

[γραμμένου τόκου δώσει κατ' ἐ]νιαυ[τὸν ἔκ]αστον καὶ τοῖς ἕξ φυ-

248 [λάρχοις ἀνὰ δη. ρκε', ὅπ]ως ἐπ[ιτελῶ]σ[ι] κλῆρον τῆς προγεγραμ-

[μένης καθιερώσεως τῆς] θεοῦ ἐξ [ἑκάστη]ς φυλῆς εἰς ὀνόματα δι-

[ακαόσια πεντήκοντα, λα]μβανόν[των τ]ῶν ληξομένων ἀσσάρια θ'

[καθ' ἕκαστον. ἐὰν δὲ μείζων ᾖ ὁ γεν]όμενος κόλλυβος, ὑπὸ

252 [τῶν φυλάρχων ἐξέστω καὶ ἄλλους πολ]είτας κληροῦσθαι.

[ὁμοίως δώσει ἀπὸ τοῦ προγεγραμμένο]ν τόκου κατ' ἐνιαυτὸν

[ἕκαστον τῷ ἐφηβάρχῳ δην. ρκς', ὅπω]ς ἐπιτελῇ κλῆρον

[τῶν κατ' ἐνιαυτὸν ὄντων ἐφήβων τῇ γενεσίῳ τ]ῆς 'Αρτέμιδος

256 [εἰς ὀνόματα διακόσια πεντήκοντα, λαμβανόν]των τῶν ληξο-

[μένων ἀνὰ ἀσσάρια θ', λαμβανέτω δὲ] ὁ ἐφήβαρχος χω-

[ρὶς τούτων δη. α'. ὁμοίως δώσει ἀπὸ τ]οῦ προγεγραμμέ-

[νου τόκου καὶ τῷ ἀρχιερεῖ 'Ασίας τοῦ ἐν 'Εφέ]σῳ ναοῦ κοινοῦ

260 [τῆς 'Ασίας δη. κδ' ἀσ. ιγ' ἥμισυ] κατ' ἐνιαυτὸν ἕκασ-

[τον, ὅπως ἐξ αὐτῶν τῇ γενεσίῳ τῆς θ]εοῦ ἡμέρᾳ ἐπιτελεῖ

[κλῆρον τῶν θεολόγων ἐν τῷ ἱερῷ] τῆς 'Αρτέμιδος, λαμ-

[βάνοντος ἑκάστου τῶν παρ' αὐτῷ]ι ἀναγραψαμένων

264 [καὶ λαχόντων ἀνὰ δη. β' ἀσ. ιγ' ἥμισυ, γ]ει\νομένης τῆς ἀνα-

[γραφῆς τῇι πέμπτηι. ὁμοίως δώσ]ει ἀπὸ τοῦ προγεγραμ-

[μένου τόκου κατ' ἐνιαυτὸν ἕκαστον τ]ῇ ἱερείᾳ τῆς 'Αρτέμιδος

[ὑπὲρ τῶν ὑμνῳδῶν τῆς θεοῦ τῇι γενεσίω]ι τῆς 'Αρτέμιδος εἰς

268 [διανομὴν δηνάρια ιη'. ὁμοίως δώσε]ι ἀπὸ τοῦ π[ρ]ογεγραμ-

[μένου τόκου κατὰ πᾶσαν νόμιμον ἐκκλ]ησίαν δυσ[ὶ]ν νεοποι-

270 [οῖς καὶ σκηπτούχῳ ἀσ. δ' ἥμισυ, ὥστε φέρ]εσθαι ἐκ τοῦ προνάου

[εἰς τὸ θέατρον τὰ ἀπεικονίσματα τῆς] θεοῦ καὶ τὰς εἰκόνας καὶ

272 [πάλιν ἀναφέρεσθαι ἐκ τοῦ θεάτρο]ν εἰς τὸν πρόναον αὐθημε-

[ρὸν μετὰ τῶν φυλάκων. ὁμοίως δώ]σει ἀπὸ τοῦ προγεγραμμέ-

[νου τόκου κατ' ἐνιαυτὸν ἕκαστο]ν καὶ τοῖς παιδωνόμοις

[δη. ιε' ἀσ. ιγ' ἥμισυ, ὅπως τῇ γενε]σίῳ τῆς θεοῦ ἡμέρᾳ ἐπιτελέ-

276 [σωσι κλῆρον τῶν παίδων πάν]των εἰς ὀνόματα μθ', λαμβανόν-

[των τῶν ληξομένων ταύτ]ῃ τῇ ἡμέρᾳ ἐν τῷ ἱερῷ τῆς 'Αρτέμιδος

166

of eleven denarii, with which they will buy the things for sacrifice, the lottery being on the fifth, the secretary of the gerousia not having the right to halt the distribution or registration after the death of Salutaris, since (if he does) let him pay the fine determined in the bequest. Equally from the aforementioned interest he will give every year to the six phylarchs up to 125 denarii apiece, that they should complete a lottery of the aforementioned dedication of the goddess for 250 named individuals from each tribe, those taking part in the lottery getting 9 asses each. If the current rate of exchange should be greater, it is possible for other citizens to be allotted by the phylarchs.

(253) Equally he will give from the aforementioned interest every year 126 denarii to the ephebarchos, that he may carry out a lottery of the annual ephebes, on the birthday of Artemis, to 250 named individuals, those winning the lottery taking up to 9 asses, and let the ephebarchos apart from these take one denarius. Equally he will give from the aforementioned interest to the high priest of Asia of the common temple of Asia in Ephesos 24 denarii and 13½ asses every year, that from these on the birthday of the goddess he complete a lottery of the theologoi in the sanctuary of Artemis, each of those who have registered with him, and winning the lottery taking at a rate of 2 denarii 13½ asses, the registration being on the fifth. Equally he will give from the aforementioned interest each year to the priestess of Artemis 18 denarii on behalf of the hymnodoi of the goddess for distribution on the birthday of Artemis. Equally he will give from the aforementioned interest at each regular assembly to two neopoioi and to a beadle 4½ asses, to carry the type-statues of the goddess and the images, from the pronaos into the theatre, and to carry them back from the theatre into the pronaos on the same day along with the guards. Equally he will give from the afore-mentioned interest each year 15 denarii 13½ asses to the paidonomoi, that on the birthday of the goddess they may complete a lottery of all the paides to 49 named individuals, those winning the lottery taking on that same day in the sanctuary of Artemis 4½ asses apiece, and apart from these the paidonomoi

[ἀνὰ ἀσ. δ' ἥμισυ, λαμβανό]ντων καὶ τῶν παιδωνόμων χωρὶς

[τούτων ἀνὰ ἀσσάρια θ'. ὁ]μοίως δώσει ἀπὸ τοῦ προγεγραμ-

280 [μένου τόκου καθ' ἕκαστον ἐν]ιαυτὸν τῷ τὰ καθάρσια ποιοῦντι παρε-

[   ] τὰ λοιπὰ δη. τριάκοντα, ὥστε κα-

[θαρίζειν ἑκάστοτε, ὁπόταν εἰ]ς τὸ ἱερὸν ἀποφέρηται τὰ ἀπεικον-

[ίσματα τῆς θεοῦ, πρὶν ἀποθεῖν]αι αὐτὰ εἰς τὸν πρόναον τῆς Ἀρτέ-

284 [μιδος. ἐὰν μὲν οὖν ἕτερός τις κατ'] ἰδίαν προαίρεσιν ἀγοράσῃ

[τὴν κληρονομίαν ταύτην καὶ βουλ]ηθῇ δίδοσθαι καθ' ἕκαστον ἐνι-

286 [αυτὸν τὸν τόκον, διδότω ὁ ἀγορά]ζων τὰ προγεγραμμένα δη. χίλια

[ὀ]κτακό[σια, μὴ ἐξὸν παρὰ τὴ]ν διάταξιν εἰσε[ν]ενκεῖν μηδὲν

288 ἔλασσο[ν   , ἀ]λλὰ προσασφαλιζομένου.

ἐὰν δέ τι[ς ἀγοράσῃ αὐτήν, βουλ]ηθῇ δὲ ἀποδοῦναι τάχειον τὰ τῆς

καθιερώ[σεως ἀρχαῖα ἅπαντ]α, ἐξέσται αὐτῷ ἐπ' ἀνάνκη ληψομέ-

νῳ τ[ῷ ἐπὶ τῶν χρημάτω]ν τῆς βουλῆς τὰ γεινόμενα ὑπὲρ τῶν

292 κα[θ]ιερω[μένων τῇ βουλῇ] ἀρχαίου δη. πεντακισχίλια,

ὁμ[ο]ίως κα[ὶ τῷ ἐπὶ τῶν χρη]μάτων τῆς γερουσίας τὰ γεινόμενα

ὑπὲρ τῆς καθιερωμέ[ν]ων τῇ γερουσίᾳ δη. τετρακ[ι]σ[χ]ε[ί-]

λια τετρακόσια πεντήκοντα, ὁμοίως καὶ τοῖς θεολόγοις

296 καὶ ὑμνῳδοῖς τὰ γεινόμενα ὑπὲρ τῆς καθιέρωσεως ἀρχαίου

δη. διακός[ι]α πεντήκοντα πέντε, ὁμοίως τῷ γραμματεῖ

τοῦ δήμου τὰ λοιπὰ γεινόμενα τοῦ ἀρχαίου ὑπὲρ τῆς καθιερώ-

σεως τῶν εἰς τοὺς πολείτας κλήρων καὶ ἐφήβων καὶ νεο-

300 ποιῶν καὶ σκηπτούχων καὶ καθαρσίων δη. μύρια διακόσια

ἑβδομήκοντα πέντε, ὅπως ἐκδανίζωσιν αὐτὰ ἐπὶ τόκῳ

ἀσσαρίων δεκαδύο ἀργυρῶν ἀδιάπτωτα καὶ ἐπιτελῆ-

ται καθ' ἕκαστον ἐνιαυτὸν ἀπὸ τοῦ τόκου τὰ διατεταγμέ-

304 να ἀνυπερθέτως, ὡς προγέγραπται. ἐὰν δὲ πρὸ τοῦ ἀπο-

δοῦναι τὰ δισμύρια δη. ἢ διατάξεσθαι ἀπὸ προσόδου

χωρίων δίδοσθαι τὸν τόκον αὐτῶν {ἢ} τελευτήσει

Σαλουτάριος, ὑποκείσθωσαν οἱ κληρονόμοι αὐτοῦ τῇ εὐ-

308 λυτήσει τῶν καθιερωμένων δη. δισμυρίων καὶ τοῖς ἐπα-

κολουθήσασι τόκοις μέχρι τῆς εὐλυτήσεος, ὑποκει-

μένων αὐτῶν τῇ πράξει κατὰ τὰ ἱερὰ τῆς θεοῦ καὶ τὰ πα-

ρὰ τοῖς πρεσβυτέροις ἐκδανιστικὰ ἔνγραφα. ὑπέσχετο

312 δὲ Σαλουτάριος, ὥστε ἄρξ[α]σθαι τὴν φιλοτειμίαν αὐτοῦ

τῷ ἐνεστῶτι ἔτει, ἐν τῇ γενε[σί]ῳ τῆς θεοῦ ἡμέρᾳ δώσει[ν]

taking 9 asses apiece. Equally he will give from the aforementioned interest each year to the one who does the cleanings [ ] remaining 30 denarii, so as to clean on each occasion, when the type-statues of the goddess are carried back to the sanctuary, before they deposit them in the pronaos of Artemis. If anyone else buys this estate in accordance with [the donor's] own purpose, let the purchaser give regularly the aforementioned 1,800 denarii, and it shall not be permitted to pay any smaller amount contrary to the bequest [ ] but making it secure.

(289) But if anyone buys this, and wishes to pay out more quickly the sum total of the dedication, it will be permitted for him to hand it over to the one obligated to accept it, as follows: to the treasurer of the boule the 5,000 denarii capital sum for the things dedicated to the boule.

(293) Equally to the treasurer of the gerousia the 4,450 denarii sum for the things dedicated to the gerousia, equally to the theologoi and the hymnodoi the 255 denarii sum for the dedication, equally to the secretary of the demos the remaining 10,275 denarii sum for the dedication of the distributions to the citizens by lot among ephebes and neopoioi and beadles and for the cleanings: in order that they should lend these same (capital totals) on good security at 12 asses interest, and that the arrangements specified in the bequest, as has been described above, may be executed without delay. If, before he hands over the 20,000 denarii, or before he makes the arrangements that the interest on the sum be paid regularly from the revenue of his estates, Salutaris should die, let his heirs be liable for the discharge of the dedicated 20,000 denarii, and for the interest accruing up to the moment of the discharge, and let them be subject to the conditions of collection according to the sacred customs of the goddess and the regulations relating to loans deposited among the elders. Salutaris, in order to begin his munificence in the current year, promised to give 1,800 denarii for the aforementioned distributions and lotteries on the birthday of the goddess. Let it

δη. χείλια ὀκτακόσια εἰς τὰς προγεγραμμένας διανομὰς
καὶ κλήρους. μηδεν[ὶ] δὲ ἐξέστω ἄρχοντι ἢ ἐκδίκῳ ἢ ἰδιώ-
316 τῃ πε[ιρᾶ]σαί τι ἀλλάξαι ἢ μεταθεῖναι ἢ μετοικονομῆσαι ἢ μετα-
ψηφί[σ]ασθα[ι] τῶν καθιερωμένων ἀπεικονισμάτων ἢ τοῦ
ἀργυρίου ἢ τῆς [π]ροσόδου αὐτοῦ ἢ μεταθεῖναι εἰς ἕτερον πόρον
ἢ ἀνάλωμα ἢ ἄ[λ]ο τι ποῆσαι παρὰ τὰ προγεγραμμένα καὶ δια-
320 τετ[αγ]μένα, ἐπεὶ τὸ γενόμενον παρὰ ταῦτα ἔστω ἄκυρον.
ὁ δὲ πε[ι]ράσας ποιῆσαί τι ὑπεναντίον τῇ διατάξει ἢ τοῖς
ὑπὸ τ[ῆ]ς βου[λ]ῆς καὶ τοῦ δήμου ἐψηφισμένοις καὶ ἐπικεκυ-
ρωμέν[οις περὶ] ταύτης τῆς διατάξεως ἀποτεισάτω εἰς
324 προσκ[όσμημα τ]ῆς με[γίστ]ης θεᾶς 'Αρτέμιδος δη. δισμύρια
[π]ε[ν]τα[κισχείλια καὶ εἰς τὸν τοῦ Σε]βαστοῦ φίσκον ἄλλα δη.
β΄ μ(ύρια) ,ε.
[ἡ δὲ προγεγραμμένη διάταξις ἔσ]τω κυρία εἰς τὸν ἄπαντα χρό-
[νον   , καθάπερ 'Ακουίλλι]ος Πρόκλ[ος, ὁ ε]ὐ[ε]ρ[γ]έτης
328 [καὶ ἀνθύπατο]ς, καὶ 'Αφράνιος Φλαουιανός, ὁ κράτιστος πρεσβευτὴς
κα[ὶ ἀντιστ]ράτηγος, διὰ ἐπιστολῶν περὶ ταύτης τῆς διατάξεως ἐπεκύρωσαν καὶ ὥρισαν τὸ προγεγραμμένον π[ρ]όστειμον.
Γάϊος Οὐείβιος, Γαίου υἱός, 'Ωφεντείνα, Σαλουτάριος εἰ[σ]ενήνοχα
332 τὴν διάταξιν καὶ καθιέρωσα τὰ προγεγραμμένα.

not be permitted to anyone, either archon, or advocate, or private citizen, to try to alter or change anything, or to make different arrangements for the administration, or to transfer by decree any of the dedicated type-statues or the silver, or its revenue, or to divert it to any other source of revenue or to any other expense, or to do any other thing against the things written above and ordered, since the thing against these things will be invalid. Whoever tries to do anything contrary to the bequest, or to the articles decreed and ratified about the bequest by the boule and the demos, let him pay toward the further adornment of the greatest goddess Artemis 25,000 denarii, and into the fiscus of the emperor another 25,000 denarii.

(326) The aforementioned bequest should be valid for all time, just as Aquillius Proculus the benefactor and proconsul, and Afranius Flavianus, the legatus pro praetore, through letters about this bequest have confirmed and determined the aforementioned fine. Caius Vibius Salutaris, the son of Caius, from the tribe Oufentina, proposed the bequest, and dedicated the aforementioned things.

(C)   [ἐπὶ πρυτ]άνεως Τιβ.

       [Κλαυδίου ᾽Αντι]πάτρου ᾽Ιουλιανοῦ,

         [μηνὸς] Ποσειδεῶνος.

336 [᾽Ακουίλλιος Πρόκλος, ὁ λαμπρό]τατος, ᾽Εφεσ[ι]ων ἄρχ‹ο›υσι,

             [βουλῇ, δήμῳ] χαίρειν.

     [Οὐείβιον Σαλουτάριον ὄντ]α τοῖς τε ἄλ[λο]ις πᾶσι[ν]

     [πολείτην ἄριστον καὶ πρό]τερον ἐν πολλ[ο]ῖς τῆς ἑαυ-

340 [τοῦ φιλοτειμίας πολλά τε καὶ οὐ]χ ὡς ἔτυχεν π[αρε]σχημένον

     [παραδείγματα εἰδώς, ὥσπερ] ἦν ἄξιον, ἐν τοῖς [οἰκ]ειοτάτο[ι]ς

342 [ἡμῶν εἶχον φίλοις. νῦν δέ, ἐ]πεὶ τὴν μὲν πόλ[ιν προή]ρηται

     [μεγίστοις τε καὶ ἀξιολογω]τάτοις δώροι[ς κοσ]μῆσαι με-

344 [γαλοπρεπῶς εἰς τειμὴν τῆς] τε ἐπιφανε[στάτη]ς καὶ μεγισ-

     [της θεᾶς ᾽Αρτέμιδος καὶ το]ῦ οἴκου [τῶν Σεβασ]τῶν καὶ τῆς

     [ὑμετέρας πόλεως, τοῖς δὲ πολείταις εἰς διανο]μὰς καὶ κλή-

     [ρους καθιέρωκε δην. δισμύρια, νομίζω καὶ ὑμᾶς,] ἐφ᾽ οἷς ἤδη

348 [πεποίηκεν ὑμεῖν καὶ νῦν ἐπαγγέλλεται ἀγαθοῖ]ς, χρῆναι τῇ τε

     [φιλοτειμίᾳ αὐτοῦ ἀνταποδοῦναι καὶ τῇ εὐμεν]είᾳ, ἃ πρὸς

     [τειμὴν αὐτοῦ ἐψηφίσατε. συνήδομαι δ᾽ ὑμεῖν εἰς τὸ ἐπαι]νέσαι τε τὸν

     [ἄνδρα καὶ ἀξιῶσαι αὐτὸν δικαίας παρ᾽ ἡμεῖ]ν μαρτυρίας

352 [πρὸς τὸ καὶ πλείους γενέσθαι τοὺς κατὰ τὰ] δυνατὰ προ-

     [θυμουμένους εἰς τὰ ὅμοια. τὰ δὲ ὑπ᾽ αὐτοῦ καθιε]ρούμενα χρή-

     [ματα καὶ τὰ ἀπεικονίσματα τῆς θεοῦ καὶ τὰ]ς εἰκόνας η τισ

     [   ]

356 [. . . . .]χε[ca.12]αισ[   ]

     [.]εταιονδε[ca.10]εχρησ[   ]

     [.]ε οὐδένα β[ούλομαι νυ]νὶ τρόπ[ῳ οὐδενὶ οὔτε παρευρέσει οὐ]

     [δ]εμιᾷ μετ[αθεῖναι ἢ π]αραλλά[ξαι τι τῶν ὑπ᾽ αὐτοῦ διατεταγμέ-]

360 [ν]ων. εἰ δ[έ τις ἐπι]χειρήσει ἢ λῦσ[αι ἢ παραλλάξαι τι τῶν]

     [ὑ]φ᾽ ὑμῶ[ν διὰ το]ύτου τρ[ῦ ψηφίσματος κυρωθησομένων]

     [ἢ] εἰσ[ηγ]ήσασθαί τι τοιοῦτον [πειράσει, ὑποκείσθω εἰς προσ-]

     [κ]όσ[μ]ησιν τῆς κυρίας ᾽Αρτεμιδ[ος δη. β᾽ μ(υρίοις) ,ε καὶ εἰς τὸν ἱε-]

364 [ρ]ώτατον φίσκον ἄλλοις δη. [δισμυρίοις πεντακισχειλίοις καὶ]

     [οὐ]δὲν ἔλαττον ἔστω ἄκυρον ἅ[παν τὸ παρὰ τὴν] καθιέ[ρωσιν. συν-]

     [ή]δο{ι}μ‹α›ι δὲ αὐτῷ εἰς τὸ πᾶσιν [νῦν φανερὰν γενέ]σθαι τή[ν]

     [τ]ε πρὸς τὴν θεὸν εὐσέβειαν [καὶ τὴν πρὸς τοὺς Σ]εβαστοὺ[ς]

368 [κ]αὶ τὴν πρὸς τὴν πόλιν εὐ[μένειαν αὐτοῦ ἐν τ]ῷ θεάτρῳ.

                  ἔρρ[ωσθε.]

(333) In the prytany of Tib. Cl. Antipater Iulianus, the month of Poseideon. Aquillius Proculus, *vir clarissimus*, to the archons of the Ephesians, to the boule, to the demos, greetings. Knowing that Vibius Salutaris was an excellent citizen in all other respects and that he had previously furnished numerous and extraordinary examples of his munificence, I held him among my most intimate friends, as was proper. And now, since he has decided to adorn the city magnificently with the greatest and most remarkable gifts for the honor of the most manifest and greatest goddess Artemis, and of the house of the emperors, and of your city, and has dedicated 20,000 denarii to the citizens for distributions and lotteries, I think, for the good things he has already done for you and now announces, you are right to give, in return for his munificence and goodwill, the things you have voted in his honor. I congratulate you for having praised this man, and for having deemed him worthy of just commendation from us, with a view toward there being more who, according to capabilities, are enthusiastic for similar things. As for the money dedicated by him, and the type-statues of the goddess and the images

(355) [ ]
(356) [ ]
(357) [ ]
(358) I wish no one now in any way, or under any pretext, to alter, or to change any of the things arranged by him. And if anyone attempts either to rescind or change any of the things ratified by you through this decree, or tries to introduce any such thing, let him be liable for 25,000 denarii toward the further adornment of lady Artemis, and another 25,000 denarii to the most holy fiscus, and every act contrary to the dedication will be nonetheless invalid. May I congratulate him that his piety toward the goddess and the Augusti, and his goodwill toward the city in the theatre now become clear to all. Farewell.

(D) ἐπ[ὶ] πρυτάνεως Τ[ιβ. Κλ. ᾿Αντι]πάτ[ρου]

     ᾿Ιουλιανοῦ, μηνὸς [Ποσειδεῶνος.]

372 ᾿Αφράνιος Φλαουιανός, [πρεσβευτὴς καὶ ἀντι]στρά[τη-]

     γος, ᾿Εφεσίων ἄρχ[ουσι, βουλῇ, δήμῳ χα]ίρειν.

     Ουείβιος Σαλουτάρ[ιος, ὁ] φίλτα[τος ἡμεῖν, εὐγενέσ]τατος

     [μ]ὲν ἐκ τοῦ ἀξιώμ[ατος αὐτο]ῦ ὑπάρχ[ων, προσέτι δὲ κ]αὶ τοῦ ἀρίσ-

376 [το]υ ἤθου[ς ὤν, ὅτι ἐξ ἧς πρ]ὸς ἡμᾶς ἔχ[ει διαθέσε]ος, τῶν οἰκιο-

     [τ]ά[των καὶ ἀν]ανκα[ι]ο[τάτ]ων ἡμεῖν διεφ[άνη φί]λος, ἐν πολλοῖς

378 [ἐ]γ[νωρίσθη,] εἰ καὶ τοὺ[ς] πλείστους ἐλάγ[θανε]ν, ὡς ἔχει, πρὸς

     [ὑ]μ[ᾶς εὐνοία]ς τε καὶ προαιρέσεος. νῦν [δὲ ἤδ]η τὴν ἑαυτοῦ

380 [δι]απ[ρεπῆ φ]ιλοσ[τ]οργίαν, ἣν ἐξ ἀρχῆ[ς πρὸς τὴν πόλιν ἔχει,

     φαν[ερὰν πᾶσι] πεπο[ιη]μένου, οἰκεῖον [ἅμα καὶ] πρέπον τῷ

     τε β[ίῳ τῷ ἑαυτ]οῦ κ[αὶ] τῷ ἤθει ν[ομίζοντος τὸ] κοσμεῖ[ν]

     καὶ σ[εμνύνειν καὶ τὰ ἀγ]νὰ κ[αὶ] τὰ κοινὰ τ[ῆς μεγίστης] καὶ

384 ἐπισ[ημοτάτης ὑμῶν πόλεως, εἴ]ς τε τειμὴν καὶ εὐσέβ[ειαν τῆ]ς ἐπι-

     φανεσ[τάτης θεᾶς] ᾿Αρτέμιδος καὶ τοῦ οἴκου τῶν αὐτοκρατόρ-

     ρ[ω]ν δ[ωρεαῖς καὶ χρη]μάτων ἀφιρώσει τὰ νῦν φιλοτειμου-

     μένου, [συνήδομ]αι ὑμεῖν τε καὶ περὶ τἀνδρὸς [ἐμοί τ᾿ ἐ]ξ ἴσων

388 περὶ ὑμ[ῶν εἰς τὸ] ἀ[ντ]ιμηνῦσαι μαρτυρῆσαί τε [καὶ εὐ]φημίᾳ τῇ

     π[ρ]οσηκ[ούσῃ] αὐτὸν [ὑ]πὲρ ὑμῶν ἀμείψασθαι. ὅ[περ] αὐτῷ καὶ πα-

     ρ᾿ [ὑ]μῶ[ν ὀφε]ίλεσθαι νομίζω πρὸς τὸ καὶ πλε[ίου]ς εἶναι τοὺς

     ὁ[μ]οίως π[ροθ]υμουμ[έ]νους, εἰ οὗτος φαίνοι[το τ]ῆς κατὰ τὴν

(370) In the prytany of Tib. Cl. Antipater Iulianus, the month of Poseideon. Afranius Flavianus, legatus pro praetore, to the archons of the Ephesians, to the boule, to the demos, greetings. Even if it has escaped the notice of the majority, how much goodwill and devotion he has for you, it has been demonstrated in many instances that Vibius Salutaris, a most dear friend to us, who is of the most noble rank, and over and above, being of the best character, has shown himself from his attitude toward us a friend to be numbered among our closest and most indispensable. And now that he has made clear to all his extraordinary love, which from the beginning he had toward the city, considering it proper at the same time and fitting to his life and character, to adorn and reverence the religious and public realms of your greatest and most notable city, for the honor and reverence of the most manifest goddess Artemis, and the house of the Emperors, by gifts and by a dedication of money, which things now he has given munificently, I congratulate you about this man, and myself equally, on testifying in reciprocation, and on expressing appreciation, and on rewarding him in your own behalf with suitable commendation. Wherefore I think it is owed to him by you, with a view toward more being equally enthusiastic, if this man should appear to be worthy of recompense according to

392 ἀξίαν ἀμοιβῆς τυνχάν[ων.] εἴη δ' ἂν κἀμοι ἐν τοῖς μάλιστα

κεχαρισμένον καὶ ἥδιστον, εἰ, ὃν ἐξαιρέτως τῶν φίλων

τειμῶ καὶ στέργω, παρ' ὑμεῖν ὀρῴην μαρτυρίας καὶ τειμῆς

ἀξιούμενον. περὶ μέντοι γε τῆς τῶν χρημ[ά]των διατά-

396 ξεως καὶ τῶν ἀπεικονισμάτων τῆς θεοῦ καὶ τῶν εἰκόνων,

ὅπως αὐτοῖς δεήσει χρῆσθαι καὶ εἰς τὴν τίγα οἰκονομίαν

ἄνδρα τετάχθαι, αὐτόν τε τὸν ἀνατιθέν[τα] εἰσηγήσασθαι

νομίζω εὔλογον εἶναι καὶ ὑμᾶς οὔτ[ω] ψηφίσασθαι. ἐπεὶ

400 ἂν δὲ ὑπό τε αὐτοῦ τοῦ καθιερούντος καὶ ὑμῶν αὐτῶν κυρω-

θῇ τὰ δόξαντα, βούλομαι ταῦτα εἰσαεὶ μένειν ἐπὶ τῶν αὐτῶν

ἀπαραλλάκτως ὑπὸ μηδενὸς μηδεμιᾶ(ν) παρενχειρήσει λυ-

όμενα ἢ μετατιθέμενα. εἰ δέ τις πειραθείη ὁπωσοῦν ἢ συν-

404 βουλεῦσαί τι τοιοῦτον ἢ εἰσηγήσασθαι περὶ τῆς μεταθέ⟨σε⟩-

ως καὶ μεταδιοικήσεως τῶν νῦν ὑπό τε αὐτοῦ καὶ ὑφ' ὑ-

μῶν κυρωθησομένων, τοῦτον ἀνυπερθέτως βούλομαι

ε[ἰ]ς μὲν τὸ τῆς μεγίστης θεᾶς Ἀρτέμιδος ἱερὸν καταθέσ-

408 θαι προστείμου δη. β΄ μ(ύρια) πεντακισ[χί]λια, εἰς δὲ τὸν τοῦ

[κυρίου Καίσαρος φίσκον   ]

γερ[ουσία   ἄλλα δη. δισμύρια πεντακ]ισχίλια,

καθ[ὼς Ἀκουίλλιος Πρόκλος, ὁ λαμπρότατος ἀν]θύπατος,

412 καὶ π[ρότερον δι' ἧς ἀντέγραψεν πρὸς ὑμᾶς ἐ]πιστολῆς

ἐπ[εκύρωσεν καὶ ὥρισεν τὸ πρόστειμον. ἔ]ρρωσθε.

merit. And it would be especially gratifying and the sweetest of things to me, if, the man whom specially of friends I honor and love, among you should be seen as worthy of recognition and honor. About the bequest of the monies, and the type-statues of the goddess, and the images, how it will be necessary to use them, and what man will have to be assigned for each transaction, I think it is reasonable for the donor to introduce a proposal, and that you so decree it. When the right things (the resolutions) should be ratified by the dedicator himself, and by you yourselves, I wish these things to hold forever in the same terms, without any subrogation, and do not want them to be abrogated, or changed through derogation by anyone, on any pretext. If anyone should attempt in any way either to recommend such a thing, or to introduce a proposal about the changing or transferring of the things ratified now by him and you, I wish this one immediately to pay a fine of 25,000 denarii to the sanctuary of the greatest goddess Artemis, and to the [fiscus of lord Caesar] gero[usia] another 25,000 denarii, just as Aquillius Proculus, the most honored proconsul previously through the letter which he wrote to you confirmed and set the fine. Farewell.

APPENDIX I

(E) ἐπὶ πρ[υτάνεως Τιβ. Κλ. ᾿Αντιπάτ]ρου ᾿Ιουλιανοῦ,

     [μηνὸς Ποσειδεῶνος.]

416 ἔ[δοξε τῇ βουλῇ φιλοσεβάστῳ. περὶ ὧν ἐν]εφάνισαν Τι. Κλαύ.,

 [Τι. Κλ. ᾿Αλεξάνδρου υἱός, Κυρ(είνα), ᾿Ιουλιανός,] φιλόπατρις καὶ φιλο-

 [σέβαστος, ἁγνός, εὐσεβής, γραμματε]ὺς τοῦ δήμου τὸ β΄, καὶ οἱ

 σ[τρατηγοὶ τῆς πόλεως φιλοσέβ]αστοι. ὅπως ἐξῇ τοῖς χρυσο-

420 φ[οροῦσιν τῇ θεῷ φέρειν εἰς τὰς] ἐκκλησίας καὶ τοὺς ἀγῶνας

 τὰ ἀπεικ[ον]ίσματα καὶ ‹τὰς› εἰκόνας τὰ καθιερωμέν[α ὑπὸ Γαΐο]υ

 Οὐειβίου Σαλουταρίου ἐκ τοῦ προνάου τῆς ᾿Αρτέμιδος, συν-

 επιμελουμένων καὶ τῶν νεοποιῶν, συνπαραλαμβανόντων καὶ τῶν

424 ἐφήβων ἀπὸ τῆς Μαγνητικῆς πύλης καὶ συμπροπενπόντων

 μέχρι τῆς Κορησσικῆς πύλης. δεδόχθαι τῇ βουλῇ φιλοσε-

 βάστῳ, καθότι προγέγραπται, Τιβ. Κλαύ. Πρωρέσιος

 Φρητωριανός, φιλοσέβαστος, δεδογματογράφηκα. Μᾶρκος

428 Καισέλλιος Μαρκιανός, φιλοσέβαστος, δεδογματογράφηκα.

 Τιβ. Κλαύ. ᾿Ιουλιανός, φιλόπατρις, φιλοσέβαστος, ἁγνός, εὐσεβής,

430   ὁ γραμματεὺς τοῦ δήμου τὸ β΄, ἐχάραξα.

(F) ἐπὶ πρυτάνεως Τιβ. Κλ. ᾿Αντιπάτρου ᾿Ιουλιανοῦ,

432 μηνὸς Ποσειδεῶνος.

 ἔδοξε τῇ βουλῇ φιλοσεβάστῳ. περὶ ὧν ἐνεφάνισαν Τιβ.

 Κλ., Τιβ. Κλ. ᾿Αλεξάνδρου υἱ(ός), Κυρ(είνα), ᾿Ιουλιανός, φιλόπατρις

 καὶ φιλοσέβαστος, ἁγνός, εὐσεβής, γραμματεὺς τοῦ δήμου τὸ β΄,

436 καὶ οἱ στρατηγοὶ τῆς πόλεως φιλοσέβαστοι.

 ἐπεὶ οἱ χρυσοφοροῦντες τῇ θεῷ ἱερεῖς καὶ ἱερονεῖκαι ὑπέσ-

 χεντο φέρειν καὶ αὖ φέρειν τὰ ἀπεικονίσματα τὰ καθιερω-

 θέντα ὑπὸ Οὐειβίου Σαλου[τ]αρίου ᾐτήσαντό τε τόπον

440 ἐν τῷ θεάτρῳ τὴν πρώτην σ[ε]λίδα, ὅπου ἡ εἰκὼν τῆς ῾Ομονοίας,

 δεδόχθαι ἔχειν {ε} αὐτοὺς τὸν [τ]όπον, καθίζειν δὲ πρὸς τὴν εὐ-

 σέβειαν αὐτοὺς λ[ε]υχειμονοῦντας. δεδόχθαι τῇ βουλῇ

 φιλοσεβάστῳ γενέσθαι, καθότι προγέγραπται.

444 Γ. Αὐφίδιος Σιλουανός, φιλοσέβαστος, δεδογματογράφηκα.

 Λ. Μουνάτιος Βάσσος, φιλοσέβαστος, δεδογματογράφηκα.

 Νηρεὺς Θεοφίλου, φιλοσέβαστος, δεδογματογράφηκα.

(414) In the prytany of Tib. Cl. Antipater Iulianus, the month of Poseideon. It was resolved by the loyal boule. Concerning the things Tib. Cl. Iulianus, the son of Tib. Cl. Alexander, from the tribe Quirina, a patriot, loyal, pure, pious, secretary of the demos for the second time, and the loyal generals of the city have reported. That it may be permitted to the gold-bearers for the goddess to bring into the assemblies and the contests the type-statues and the images dedicated by Caius Vibius Salutaris from the pronaos of Artemis, the neopoioi sharing in the care, the ephebes sharing in receiving them from the Magnesian Gate, and in escorting the procession up to the Koressian Gate. It was resolved by the loyal boule, as written above, Tib. Cl. Proresius Phretorianus, loyal to the emperor, drafted the decree. Marcus Caesellius Marcianus, loyal to the emperor, drafted the decree. Tib. Cl. Iulianus, a patriot, loyal to the emperor, pure, pious, the secretary of the demos for the second time, had it engraved.

(431) In the prytany of Tiberius Claudius Antipater Iulianus, the month of Poseideon, it was resolved by the loyal boule. Concerning the things which Tib. Cl. Iulianus, the son of Alexander, from the tribe Quirina, a patriot and loyal, pure, pious, secretary of the demos for the second time, and the loyal generals reported: Since the priests and the sacred victors who bear gold for the goddess have promised to carry and carry back the type-statues dedicated by Vibius Salutaris and have asked as place in the theatre the first sector, where the image of Homonoia stands, let it be decreed: that they have the place and sit near the Pietas, wearing white. Let it be decreed by the loyal boule, as has been described above. C. Aufidius Bassus, loyal to the emperor, drafted the decree. L. Munatius Bassus, loyal to the emperor, drafted the decree. Nereus, son of Theophilus, loyal to the emperor, drafted the decree.

APPENDIX I

(G) Σέξτῳ 'Αττίῳ Σουβουρανῷ τὸ Β', Μάρκῳ 'Ασι-
448 νίῳ Μαρκέλλῳ ὑπάτοις πρὸ η' Καλανδῶν Μαρτίων.
     ἐπὶ πρυτάνεως Τιβ. Κλαυδίου 'Αντιπάτρου 'Ιουλιανοῦ
     μηνὸς 'Ανθεστηριῶνος Β' Σεβαστῇ.
     Γάϊος Οὐείβιος, Γ. υἱ(ός), Οὐωφεντείνα, Σαλουτάριος, φιλάρ-
452 τεμις καὶ φιλόκαισαρ, διάταξιν εἰσφέρει κατὰ τὸ προγε-
     γονὸς ψήφισμα, περὶ ὧν προσκαθιέρωκε τῇ μεγίστῃ θεᾷ 'Εφε-
     σίᾳ 'Αρτέμιδι καὶ τῇ φιλοσεβάστῳ 'Εφεσίων βουλῇ
     καὶ τῇ φιλοσεβάσ[τῳ 'Εφεσίων γερο]υσίᾳ καὶ τ[οῖς χ]ρυ-
456 σοφοροῦσι τῆς [θεοῦ 'Αρτέμιδος ἱερ]εῦσιν καὶ ἱερονείκαις πρὸ
     πόλεως κ[αὶ τοῖς αἰεὶ ἐσομένοις 'Ε]φεσίων παισὶ καὶ θεσ-
     μῳδοῖς ναρ[ῦ τῶν Σεβαστῶν ἐν 'Εφέσ]ῳ κοινοῦ τῆς 'Ασίας καὶ
     ἀκροβάταις τῆς ['Αρτέμιδος ἐπὶ] τοῖς δικαίοις καὶ προστεί-
460 μοις, ὡς ἐν τῇ πρὸ [ταύτης δι]ατάξει ἠσφάλισται, εἰκό-
     νων ἀργυρέων δύο ἐ[πι]χ[ρ]ύσων, ὥστε αὐτὰς εἶναι σὺν τοῖς
     ἀπεικονισμάτων τῆς θεοῦ ἀριθμῷ τριάκοντα καὶ μίαν,
     καὶ ἀργυρίου ἄλλων δη. χειλίων πεντακοσίων, ὥστε εἶναι
464 αὐτὰ σὺν τοῖς προκαθιερωμένοις δη. ‹β'› μυρίοις χειλίοις πέν-
     τακοσίοις. ἐφ' ᾧ εἰκὼν ἀργυρέα 'Αθηνᾶς Παμμούσου, ὁλκῆς
     σὺν τῷ ἐπαργύρῳ τῆς βάσεως αὐτῆς λειτρῶν ἑπτά, ἡμιουν-
     κίου, γραμμάτων ὀκτώ, ἡ καθιερωμένη τῇ τε 'Αρτέμιδι καὶ
468 τοῖς αἰεὶ ἐσομένοις 'Εφεσίων παισὶ, τιθῆται κατὰ πᾶσαν νό-
     μιμον ἐκκλησίαν ἐπάνω τῆς σελίδος, οὗ [ο]ἱ παῖδες καθέζ[ο]νται.
     ὁμοίως καὶ εἰκὼν ἀργυρέα Σεβασ-
     τῆς 'Ομονοίας Χρυσοφόρου, ὁλκῆς
472 σὺν τῷ ἐπαργύρῳ τῆς βάσεως αὐτῆς
     λειτρῶν ἕξ, ἡ καθιερωμένη τῇ τε 'Αρτέ-
     μιδι καὶ τοῖς ἀεὶ χρυσοφοροῦσιν ἱερεῦ-
     σιν καὶ ἱερονείκαις πρὸ πόλ[εω]ς, τίθετα[ι]
476 κατὰ πᾶσαν ἐκκλησίαν [ἐπάν]ω [τῆς] σε-
     λίδος, οὗ οἱ ἱερονεῖκαι κα[θέζ]ονται.
     ὁ δὲ προγεγρα[μ]μέν[ος σ]ταθμὸς τῶν εἰκό-
     νων καὶ βάσε[ων π]αρεστάθη Εὐμένει Εὐ-
480 μένους [τοῦ] Θεοφίλ[ο]υ, τῷ καὶ αὐτῷ στρατη-
     [γῷ τ]ῆς 'Εφεσίων πόλεως, διὰ ζυγοστά-
     του 'Ερμίου, ἱεροῦ τῆς 'Αρτέμιδος, συνπαρό[ν-]

180

(447) When Sextus Attius Suburanus for the second time and Marcus Asinius Marcellus were consuls, on the eighth day before the Kalends of March. In the prytany of Tib. Claudius Antipater Iulianus, the month of Anthesterion, on the second and Augustan day, Caius Vibius Salutaris, the son of Caius, from the tribe Oufentina, a lover of Artemis and Caesar, proposes a bequest, according to the preceding decree, about the things he previously dedicated to the greatest goddess Ephesian Artemis, and to the loyal boule of the Ephesians, and to the loyal gerousia of the Ephesians, and to the priests who bear the gold for the goddess Artemis and to the sacred victors on behalf of the city, and to whosoever shall be the paides of the Ephesians, and to the thesmodoi of the common temple of Asia of the Augusti at Ephesos, and to the acrobatai of Artemis, subject to lawsuits and fines, as in the bequest before this was secured: (namely) two silver images gold-gilded, so that together these, with the type-statues of the goddess, add up to the number of 31, and of silver, another 1,500 denarii, that these with the previously dedicated denarii add up to 21,500 denarii. On the condition that a silver image of Athena Pammousos, weight of 7 pounds, ½ ounce, 8 grammes, with the silver plating of its base, dedicated to Artemis and to whosoever shall be the paides of the Ephesians, be placed at every regular assembly above the block where the paides sit.

(470) Equally a silver image of Sebaste Homonoia Chrysophoros, weight of 6 pounds, with the silver plating of its base, dedicated to Artemis, and to whosoever the priests who bear the gold and the sacred victors on behalf of the city shall be, be placed at every assembly above the block, where the sacred victors sit. The aforementioned weight of the images and bases was furnished to Eumenes, the son of Eumenes, the grandson of Theophilus, the same man who is also a general of the city of the Ephesians, through the public weigher Hermias, sacred slave of Artemis, while Mousaios, sacred slave of Artemis, the custodian of

APPENDIX I

τος καὶ συνπαραλαμβάνοντος Μουσαίου, ἱ[εροῦ]

484   τῆς Ἀρτέμιδος, τοῦ ἐπὶ τῶν παραθημῶν.

ὑπὲρ δὲ τῶν προσκαθιερωμένων δηναρίω[ν χει-]

λίων πεντακοσίων τελέσει τόκον [Σαλου-]

τάριος δραχμιαῖον κα[θ']ἕκαστον ἐ[νιαυτὸν]

488   τὰ γεινόμενα δηνά[ρ]ια ρλε΄, [ἀφ' ὧν δώσει]

τῷ γραμματεῖ τῆς Ἐφεσίων βου[λῆς δη. νε΄,]

ὅπως κλῆρον ἐπιτελῇ ἐκ τῶν [βουλευτῶν τῇ ε΄]

ἱσταμένου τοῦ Θαργηλιῶν[ος εἰς ὀνόματα]

492   ε΄. οὗτοί τε οἱ λαχόντες θυσ[ίαν θύσουσι]

τῇ Ἀρτέμιδι τῇ ἕκτῃ το[ῦ μηνός, τῇ γενεσίῳ]

τῆς θεοῦ, ἀγοράζο[ν]τες [δη. εἴκοσι]

ἑπτὰ ἡμίσους, καὶ [τ]ὰ [λοιπὰ δη κζ΄ ἀσ. θ΄]

496   δαπανήσουσιν [ἐν τῷ ἱερῷ τῆς Ἀρτέμι-]

497   δοσ εἰς τὴν ο[   ]

500a [   ]γ[.]σο[   ]

500b [ὁμοίως δώσει ἀπὸ τοῦ πρ]ογεγραμ[μένου τόκου]

500c [τοῖς χρυσοφοροῦσι καὶ ἱ]ερ[ο]νείκ[αις πρὸ πόλεως]

500d [ση. ς΄ ἀσ. ιγ΄ ἥμισυ, ὅπως κλῆρον ἐπιτελῶσι κτλ.]

----

519   [ὁμοίως δώσει ἀπὸ τοῦ προγεγραμμένου τόκου]

520   τ[οῖς παιδωνόμοις δη. ιε΄ ἀσ. δεκατρία ἥμισυ,]

ὅπ[ως ἐπιτελῶσι κλῆρον ἐκ τῶν παίδων πάν-]

τ[ων   ]

[   ]

524   [τῇ γενεσίῳ τῆς θεοῦ ἡμέρᾳ εἰς ὀνόματα]

ἑξήκον[τα τρία. οὗτοί τε οἱ λαχόντες εὔξονται]

ἐν τῷ ἱερῷ τῆς Ἀρτ[έμιδος   γει-]

νομένων κατὰ ἀν[.]

528   ἐὰν δέ τινες τῶν λαχόντων [ἀνδρων ἢ παίδων ἢ]

τὰς θυσίας μὴ θύσωσιν ἢ μὴ εὔ[ξωνται ἐν τῷ]

ἱερῷ, ὡς διατέτακται, ἀποδότω[σαν εἰς προσ-]

κόσμημα τῆς Ἀρτέμιδος δη. ε΄.

532   ὁμοίως δώσει ἀπὸ τοῦ προγεγραμμένου [τόκου]

καὶ τοῖς θεσμῳδοῖς εἰς διανομὴν δη. ζ΄,

deposits, was present, and participated in receiving it. Concerning the additionally dedicated 1,500 denarii, Salutaris will pay the interest at a rate of 9 per cent every year, the sum of 135 denarii, from which he will give to the secretary of the boule of the Ephesians 55 denarii, that he may carry out a lottery from the boule members on the fifth day of Thargelion to five named individuals. Those who win the lottery will make a sacrifice to Artemis on the sixth of the month, on the birthday of the goddess, buying [ ] 27½ denarii, and the remaining 27 denarii and 9 asses they will spend in the sanctuary of Artemis for the [21 lines missing]

(500b) Equally he will give from the aforementioned interest to the ones who bear the gold and the sacred victors on behalf of the city 6 denarii 13½ asses, that they may complete a lottery. . . . . .

(519) Equally he will give from the aforementioned interest to the paidonomoi 15 denarii 13½ asses that they may complete a lottery from all the paides [ ]

[ ]

(524) on the birthday of the goddess, to 63 named individuals. Those who win the lottery will pray in the temple of Art[emis] existing according [ ]

(528) If any of the winning men or paides either do not make sacrifices, or do not pray in the sanctuary, as has been ordered, let them pay for the further adornment of Artemis 5 denarii.

ὥστε λαμβάνειν αὐτοὺς ἐν τῷ ἱερῷ τῆς Ἀρτέμιδος τῇ γενεσίῳ τῆς θεοῦ ἀνὰ ἀσσάρια θ΄.

536 ὁμοίως δώσει ἀπὸ τοῦ προγεγραμμένου τόκου
καὶ τοῖς ἀκροβάταις τῆς θεοῦ εἰς διανομὴν
δη. ιε΄ ὥστε λαμβάνειν αὐτοὺς τῇ γενεσίῳ
τῆς θεοῦ ἀνὰ ἀσσάρια δεκατρία ἥμισυ.

540 πρὸς δὲ τὸ μένειν τὰ ἀπεικονίσματα πάντα
καθαρὰ ἐξέστω, ὁσάκις ἂν ἐνδέχηται,
ἐκμάσσεσθαι γῇ ἀργυρωματικῇ ὑπὸ τοῦ
αἰεὶ ἐσομένου ἐπὶ τῶν παραθηκῶν, παρόν-

544 των δύο νεοποιῶν καὶ σκηπτούχου,
ἑτέρᾳ δὲ ὕλῃ μηδεμιᾷ ἐκμάσσεσθαι. καὶ
τὰ λοιπὰ δη. ὀκτὼ δοθήσεται καθ᾽ ἕκαστον
ἐνιαυτὸν τῷ ἐπὶ τῶν παραθηκῶν εἰς τὴν

548 ἐπιμέλειαν τῶν ἀπεικονισμάτων καὶ τὸν
ἀγορασμὸν τῆς ἀργυρωματικῆς γῆς.
ὑπέσχετο δὲ Σαλουτάριος δώσειν καὶ δη.
ἑκατὸν τριάκοντα πέντε, ὥστε ἄρξασθαι

552 τὴν φιλοτιμίαν αὐτοῦ τῷ ἐνεστῶτι ἔτει
τῇ γενεσίῳ τῆς θεοῦ ἡμέρᾳ.
τὰς δὲ προγεγραμμένας εἰκόνας καὶ τὰς
προκαθιερωμένας ἐν τῇ πρὸ ταύτης δια-

556 τάξει καὶ τὰ ἀπεικονίσματα πάντα τῆς θεοῦ
φερέτωσαν ἐκ τοῦ προνάου κατὰ πᾶσαν ἐκκλησίαν εἰς τὸ θέατρον καὶ τοὺς γυμνικοὺς ἀγῶνας, καὶ εἴ τινες ἕτεραι ὑπὸ τῆς βουλῆς καὶ τοῦ

560 δήμου ὁρισθήσονται ἡμέραι, ἐκ τῶν νεοποιῶν δύο καὶ οἱ ἱερονεῖκαι καὶ σκηπτοῦχος καὶ
φύλακοι καὶ πάλιν ἀποφερέτωσαν εἰς τὸ
ἱερὸν καὶ [κατ]ατιθέσθωσαν συνπαραλαμβα-

564 νόντων καὶ τῶν ἐφήβων ἀπὸ τῆς Μαγνητικῆς πύλης καὶ μετὰ τὰς ἐκκλησίας
συνπροπενπόντων ἕως τῆς Κορησσικῆ[ς]
πύλης, καθὼς καὶ ἐν τοῖς προγεγονόσι

568 ψηφίσμασι ἡ βουλὴ καὶ ὁ δῆμος ὥρισ[α]ν.

(532) Equally he will give from the aforementioned interest to the thesmodoi for distribution 7 denarii, that they may receive in the temple of Artemis on the birthday of the goddess 9 asses apiece.

(536) Equally he will give from the aforementioned interest to the acrobatai of the goddess for distribution 15 denarii, that they may receive on the birthday of the goddess 13½ asses apiece. In order that the type-statues may all remain clean, let it be permitted, that as often as may be approved, they be rubbed with argyromatic earth, in the presence of two neopoioi, and a beadle, by whoever happens to be custodian of deposits, but by no other material to be wiped clean.

And the remaining 8 denarii will be given each year to the custodian of the deposits, for the care of the type-statues, and the purchase of argyromatic earth.

(550) Salutaris promised to give 135 denarii, to begin his munificence in the current year on the birthday of the goddess. Let two of the neopoioi, and the sacred victors, and a beadle, and guards carry the aforementioned images, and those things previously dedicated in the bequest before this, and all the type-statues of the goddess, from the pronaos at every assembly into the theatre and the gymnastic contests, and if any other days be determined by the boule and the demos, and carry them back into the sanctuary, and deposit them, the ephebes receiving them from the Magnesian Gate, and after the assemblies escorting the procession up to the Koressian Gate, just as in the pre-existing decrees the boule and the demos determined.

Appendix II

ANALOGOUS FOUNDATIONS

No foundation portfolio of the Hellenistic period or principate from Asia Minor concerned with the creation or revision of a procession, or with distributions of cash to civic bodies at the birthday of a deity, emperor, founder, or relation, or both (the main activities endowed by Salutaris), equals the 568 lines, the physical size (208–430 cm in height, 494 cm in breadth), the centrality of visual display (theatre and Artemision), or details of legal process related, of the Salutaris foundation within the city.

For the closest parallels see the foundation of Hermias (*Ilion*, 52), during the second century BC, in which the procession which formed part of the Ilion games was described at lines 21–32 in an inscription of 32 lines, with very little detail about the legal process involved in the foundation, except that the foundation was proposed to the boule and demos. The inscription is 77 cm high, 66 cm broad, and was found in the cemetery of Halileli and Çiplak.

See next, the foundation of P. Aelius Menekrates, from Almoura during the post-Hadrianic period, which describes how Menekrates (who is honored by the inscription) offered to the priesthood, and dedicated a basket, to be carried around in the kalathos processions which preceded the celebrations of the mysteries of Demeter, and also a silver standard, which was to be carried ahead of the procession which took place before the celebration of the mysteries of Mēn. We also read about men who were assigned by lot to the procession, and who were to be entertained by Menekrates in his house (lines 16–18). This foundation, unlike the Salutaris foundation, involved two pre-existing processions, which the founder added objects to, and earmarked revenues for incense offerings, and the subsequent banquet of those who participated in the kalathos procession, and the village archons. We are not told who accepted the dedication of the workshops in front of Menekrates' house which provided these revenues, or what the legal steps of acceptance were, only that it happened while L. Verius Bassus was archon of the village (of Almoura), along with his fellow archons. The inscription is 25 lines long, and its size is not noted by Condoléon (*Revue des Études Greques*, V (1892) 341–2) or Homolle (*BCH*, 18 (1894) 539). Where the inscription stood in the village also is unknown. For the definitive publication, see Pleket (1970) 61–74.

See also the foundation of C. Iulius Demosthenes of Oinoanda under Hadrian, which set up a penteteric agonistic festival, for which Demosthenes provided 4,450 denarii, including 1,900 denarii for prizes at the competitions. He also stipulated that the agonothete, the civic priest and priestess of the emperors, the priest of Zeus, the three panegyriarchs, the secretary of the council, the five prytaneis, the two market supervisors, the two gymnasiarchs, the four treasurers, the two paraphylakes, the ephebarch, the paidonomoi, the supervisor of the public buildings, the villages, and other cities should process through the city and sacrifice specified numbers of bulls on the days of the festival. The record of the foundation is 117 (double) lines long, 187 cm high, 105 cm broad, and the portfolio of five documents, which perhaps did not include certain legal proceedings, such as Demosthenes' declaration of the intention also to donate a crown and an altar (see the review of Wörrle in *JRS* (1990) by S. Mitchell) was placed in the stoa in front of the food market next to the statue of Demosthenes. See Wörrle (1988) 4–17.

For distributions timed to coincide with birthdays, see Laum, II (1914) 130, the foundation of T. Aelius Alkibiades from Nysa during the Antonine period, in which distributions were organized, to be made every year on the birthday of the god Hadrian. We are told very little about the legal process behind the foundation. In *BCH*, IX (1885) 124–7 the inscription is 77 lines long. We are not told how large the inscription is, or where it was originally set up.

Next, see Laum, II (1914) no. 81, the foundation of Publius Aelius Aelianus from Thyateira at the end of the second or beginning of the third century AD, in which 6,500 denarii was left to the boule, and municipal officials, for distributions each year on the birthday of Aelius' son. The inscription provides little information about the legal process of making the foundation. In

J. Keil and A. v. Premerstein, *Bericht über eine zweite Reise in Lydien* (Wien 1911) no. 40 the inscription, which was found in Meder, is 13 lines long, and .58 cm high, .78 cm broad. Where the inscription stood in Thyateira is not known.

Also, see Laum, II (1914) no. 83, the foundation of Cornelia from Philadelphia, in which a piece of land was set aside so that members of the boule would take a distribution on the birthday of her brother. The inscription tells us little about the legal process behind the foundation, and its size is 108.5 cm high, 57–62 cm broad in J. Keil and A.v. Premerstein, *Bericht über eine Reise in Lydien und der sudlichen Aiolis* (Wien 1906) 32. The position of the inscription in Philadelphia is unknown.

Also from Philadelphia, see Laum, II (1914) no. 85, the foundation of Diogenes, in which 2,500 denarii was dedicated to the boule, and another 1,500 to the sunhedrion of the elders, the interest to be distributed on Diogenes' birthday. No background about the legal proceedings is given. In *CIG*, II 3417, the inscription is 23 lines long. No size or original position in the city is reported.

Finally, from Tralleis at the beginning of the third century AD, the foundation of M. Aurelius Euarestos, in which 3,333 denarii was dedicated for distributions to the Claudian Boule on the founder's birthday, offers little information about legal proceedings. In *Tralleis*, 66, the inscription is 13 lines long. The size is not reported, nor the original setting.

Thus, in cases of analogous foundations from the period, only the Demosthenes foundation provides a strong parallel to the Salutaris foundation in terms of content, publication of almost the entire legal process, length and size of inscription, and centrality of position in the city. In the other cases, we perhaps should not expect to find too much detail about the legal process behind foundations which are reported in the context of honorary inscriptions.

Appendix III

THE FOUNDATION OF
DEMOSTHENES OF OINOANDA

The festival foundation of C. Iulius Demosthenes from Oinoanda, now the subject of a careful and learned study by M. Wörrle (1988), provides an interesting parallel to the Salutaris foundation, although the superficial similarities between the two foundations are far outweighed by the substantive differences. It is true that both Demosthenes (Tribe Fabia, Wörrle text, line 7), and Salutaris (Oufentina, line 139 restored from *IE*, 28.12) were Roman citizens, both had made previous benefactions to their cities (Demosthenes, lines 10–11; Salutaris, lines 19–22), both ultimately wanted to use revenues generated from land to finance their foundations (Demosthenes, line 15; Salutaris, lines 305–8), and both had their foundations confirmed by the Roman government (Demosthenes' by the emperor Hadrian himself, lines 1–5; Salutaris' by the proconsul Proculus, lines 333–69, and the legate Flavianus, 370–413).

However, the foundation of Demosthenes comes from a generation after Salutaris' (*c.* AD 124/25, for the dating see Wörrle, 33–43, compared to AD 104), and, obviously, from a much smaller city than Ephesos. Salutaris' inscription was also much larger, as it appeared on the marble wall of the theatre (208–430 cm high and 494 cm wide) than the Demosthenes inscription (187 cm high and 105 cm wide), set up on the stoa in front of the market, where, at 117 lines it could have been consulted, or even read on a regular basis. The costs of the two foundations were also unequal: 4,450 denarii (lines 20f.), plus a golden crown and a silver altar (lines 52–3) in the case of Demosthenes' foundation, and 21,500 denarii (lines 464–5), plus 127 pounds, ½ ounce, 8 grammes of precious metal in Salutaris' case. This disproportion is also reflected in the stipulated fines for tampering with the foundations: 2,500 to Apollo, and 5,000 to the fiscus for Demosthenes (lines 36–7), and 25,000 to Artemis, and 25,000 to the fiscus for Salutaris (lines 108, 116, 321–5). By no set of objective criteria could the Salutaris foundation be called 'Vergleichbar umfangreich' ('comparably extensive') (Wörrle, 20) to the Demosthenes foundation. The Salutaris foundation is simply larger, and affected thousands of people directly, throughout the year, in the most important city of perhaps the richest province in the Roman empire.

More important, however, than these differences of scale, is the fact that the purposes of the two foundations were utterly different. Salutaris organized various lotteries and distributions in the city, timed to coincide with, but not replace, the celebration of the mysteries of Artemis, which Strabo (*Geography,* 14.1.20) does indeed call a general festival, and also a procession of statues through the streets of the city throughout the year. Demosthenes' foundation explicitly set up a general festival (line 12) called the Demostheneia. Therefore, if comparisons are to be made, they should be made between Demosthenes' general festival, and the other general festival we do know about, the celebration of the mysteries of Artemis at Ephesos.

Finally, a point about the festival of Demosthenes may still bear further investigation. If the structure of the nine competitions and prizes at the festival as set out originally on 25 July AD 124 was based almost purely upon Hellenistic precedents (as Wörrle claims, pp. 234–6), can the later additions to the celebration, (which were enumerated only in the 'preliminary proposal' of 5 July AD 125, including the prominent, but in no way dominant role the civic priest of the emperors, and the priestess of the emperors, and the imperial image of Hadrian on the crown worn by the agonothete, seems to have played in the procession through the theatre during the days of the festival, which began on Augustus' day in the month of Artemeisios every fourth year), be said to exist side by side in 'spannungsloser Selbsverständlichkeit' (p. 258)? If the older framework of the festival defined where, when, and what new elements were relevant to the celebration, can we really believe that Greek tradition and the imperial cult existed side by side in a 'tension-free relationship' at Oinoanda? Were not choices about how to accommodate the older and newer traditions which comprised the festival made at every stage of planning of the festival, in consultation with the civic groups and villages affected, and can we not assess those choices on a hierarchical basis?

SELECT MODERN
BIBLIOGRAPHY

This bibliography includes only those articles and books which have been the most important for this interpretation of the Salutaris foundation. It is not intended to comprise a comprehensive bibliography for Roman Ephesos. For those interested in such a comprehensive bibliography up to 1987, see Oster (1987).

Abbott, F.F., and Johnson, A.C., *Municipal Administration in the Roman Empire* (Princeton 1926).
Alzinger, W., *Die Stadt des siebenten Weltwunders* (Wien 1962).
Alzinger, W., *Augusteische Architektur in Ephesos* (Wien 1974).
Alzinger, W. (ed.), *Pro Arte Antiqua: Festschrift für Hedwig Kenner*, I and II (Wien–Berlin 1982–5).
Atkinson, K., 'The Constitutio of Vedius Pollio and its Analogies', *Revue Internationale des Droits de l'Antiquité*, 3,9 (1962) 261–89.
Baines, J., 'Literacy, Social Organization, and the Archaeological Record: the Case of Early Egypt', in Gledhill, J., Bender, B., and Larsen, M. (eds.), *State and Society* (London 1988) 192–214.
Bammer, A., *Die Architektur des jüngeren Artemision von Ephesos* (Wiesbaden 1972).
Bammer, A., *Das Heiligtum der Artemis von Ephesos* (Graz 1984).
Bammer, A., *Ephesos* (Graz 1988).
Barrett, J. 'Fields of Discourse, Reconstituting a Social Archaeology', *Critique of Anthropology*, 7 (1987/8) 5–16.
Ben-David, J., and Clark, T. (eds.), *Culture and its Creators: Essays in Honor of Edward Shils* (Chicago 1977).
Berchem, D., 'La Gérousie d'ephèse', *Museum Helveticum*, 37 (1980) 25–40.
Berger, P., *The Sacred Canopy* (New York 1969).
Blümel, W., *Die Inschriften von Iasos*, I and II (Bonn 1985).
Bowie, E., 'Greeks and their Past during the Second Sophistic', *Past and Present*, 46 (1970) 3–41 and in Finley, M.I. (ed.), *Studies in Ancient Society* (London 1974) 166–209.
Braund, D. (ed.), *The Administration of the Roman Empire 241 BC – AD 193* (Exeter 1988).

Brunt, P., *Roman Imperial Themes* (Oxford 1990).

Burkert, W., *Greek Religion* (Cambridge 1985).

Burton, G.P., 'Proconsuls, Assizes and the Administration of Justice under the Empire', *JRS*, 65 (1975) 92–106.

Clanchy, M., *From Memory to Written Record: England 1066–1307* (Cambridge 1979).

Coulton, J.J., 'Opramoas and the Anonymous Benefactor', *JHS*, 107 (1987) 171–8.

Darnton, R., *The Great Cat Massacre and Other Episodes in French Cultural History* (New York 1984).

Davis, N., 'The Sacred and the Body Social in Sixteenth–Century Lyon', *Past and Present*, 90 (1981) 40–70.

Devijver, H., *The Equestrian Officers of the Roman Imperial Army* (Amsterdam 1989).

Driscoll, S., 'Power and Authority in Early Historic Scotland: Pictish Symbol Stones and Other Documents', in Gledhill, J., Bender, B., and Larsen, M. (eds.), *State and Society* (London 1988) 215–33.

Eck, W., *Senatoren von Vespasian bis Hadrian* (Munich 1970).

Foss, C., *Ephesus after Antiquity: A Late Antique, Byzantine, and Turkish City* (Cambridge 1979).

Fossel-Peschl, E., *Die Basilika am Staatsmarkt in Ephesos* (Graz 1982).

Frisch, P., *Die Inschriften von Ilion* (Bonn 1975).

Gauthier, P., *Les Cités grecques et leurs bienfaiteurs (IVe–Ier siècle avant J.–C.): contribution à l'histoire des institutions* (Paris 1985).

Geertz, C., *The Interpretation of Cultures* (New York 1973).

Gibson, M., 'The Archaeological Uses of Inscribed Documents', *Iraq*, 34 (1972) 113–23.

Gordon, R.L., 'The Real and the Imaginary: Production and Religion in the Graeco–Roman World', *Art History*, 2 (1979) 5–34.

Graillot, H., *Le Culte de Cybèle* (Paris 1912).

Habicht, C., 'Zwei Römische Senatoren aus Kleinasien', *ZPE*, 13 (1974) 1–6.

Habicht, C., 'New Evidence on the Province of Asia', *JRS*, 65 (1975) 64–91.

Haenchen, E., *The Acts of the Apostles* (Philadelphia 1971).

Halfmann, H., *Die Senatoren aus dem östlichen Teil des Imperium Romanum bis zum Ende des 2. Jahrhunderts n. Chr.* (Göttingen 1979).

Halfmann, H., 'Die Senatoren aus den kleinasiatischen Provinzen des römischen Reiches von 1. bis 3. Jahrhundert', in *Epigrafia e ordine senatorio*, II (Roma 1982) 603–49.

Head, B.V., *Catalogue of Greek Coins in the British Museum* (London 1964 edition).

Herrmann, P., 'Kaiserliche Garantie für Private Stiftungen', *Studien zur Antike Sozialgeschichte* (1980) 339–56.

Hicks, E.L., *Ancient Greek Inscriptions in the British Museum*, III, 2 (Oxford 1890).

Hueber, F., 'Der Embolos, ein urbanes Zentrum von Ephesos', *Antike Welt*, 15.4 (1984) 1–23.

Ihnken, T., *Die Inschriften von Magnesia am Sipylos* (Bonn 1978).

Jones, C.P., 'A Deed of Foundation from the Territory of Ephesos', *JRS*, 73 (1983) 116–25.

Kallet-Marx, R., 'Asconius 14–15 Clark and the Date of Q. Mucius Scaevola's Command in Asia', *Classical Philology*, 84 (1989) 305–12.

Kandler, M., Karwiese, S., and Pillinger, R., (eds.), *Lebendige Altertumswissenschaft. Festgabe zur Vollendung des 70. Lebensjahres von Hermann Vetters dargebracht von Freunden, Schülern und Kollegen* (Wien 1985).

Karwiese, S., *Die Marienkirche in Ephesos* (Wien 1989).

Kearsley, R., 'The Archiereiai of Asia and the Relationship of the Asiarch and the Archiereus of Asia', *GRBS*, 27 (1986) 183–92.

Keil, J., *Ephesos: ein Führer durch die Ruinenstätte und ihre Geschichte* (Wien 1955).

Knibbe, D., 'Ursprung, Begriff und Wesen der ephesischen Kureten', *FiE*, IX/1/1 (1981) 70–92.

Kraay, C., *Archaic and Classical Greek Coins* (Berkeley 1979).

Laum, B., *Stiftungen in der griechischen und römischen Antike*, I and II (Leipzig 1914).

Lefkowitz, M., and Fant, M., *Women's Life in Greece and Rome* (Baltimore 1985).

Lévi-Strauss, C., *Tristes tropiques* (Paris 1955).

Lewis, B., *History – Remembered, Recovered, Invented* (Princeton 1975) 3–41.

Macready, S., and Thompson, F.H. (eds.), *Roman Architecture in the Greek World* (London 1987).

Magie, D., *Roman Rule in Asia Minor*, I and II (Princeton 1950).

Marshall, F.H., *Ancient Greek Inscriptions in the British Museum*, IV (Oxford 1916) 481.

Melville Jones, J., 'Denarii, Asses and Assaria in the Early Roman Empire', *Bulletin of the Institute of Classical Studies*, 18 (1971) 99–105.

Merkelbach, R., 'Die ephesischen Monate in der Kaiserzeit', *ZPE*, 36 (1979) 157–62.

Merkelbach, R., 'Der Kult der Hestia im Prytaneion der griechischen Städte', *ZPE*, 37 (1980) 77–92.

Millar, F., *The Emperor in the Roman World* (London 1977).

Millar, F., 'Epigraphy', in Crawford, M. (ed.), *Sources for Ancient History* (Cambridge 1983) 80–136.

Millar, F., '"Senatorial" Provinces: An Institutionalized Ghost', *Ancient World*, 20 (1989) 93–7.

Mollat, M., *The Poor in the Middle Ages* (New Haven 1986) 87–145; trans. by A. Goldhammer.

Muir, E., *Civic Ritual in Renaissance Venice* (Princeton 1981).

Norberg, K., *Rich and Poor in Grenoble, 1600–1814* (Berkeley 1985) 81–168.

Oberleitner, W., *Funde aus Ephesos und Samothrake* (Wien 1978).

Oliver, J., *The Sacred Gerusia* (Baltimore 1941).

Oliver, J., *The Ruling Power: A Study of the Roman Empire in the Second Century After Christ Through the Roman Oration of Aelius Aristides* (Philadelphia 1953).

Önen, Ü., *Ephesus Ruins and Museum* (Izmir 1983).

Oster, R., 'The Ephesian Artemis as an Opponent of Early Christianity', *Jahrbuch für Antike and Christentum*, 19 (1976) 24–44.

Oster, R., *A Bibliography of Ancient Ephesus* (Metuchen 1987).

Pelling, C., *Plutarch: Life of Antony* (Cambridge 1988).

Picard, C., *Éphèse et Claros* (Paris 1922).

Pleket, H., 'Nine Greek Inscriptions from the Cayster–valley in Lydia: A Republication', *Talanta*, II (1970) 55–82.

Poljakov, F., *Die Inschriften von Tralleis und Nysa*, I (Bonn 1989).

Price, S., *Rituals and Power: The Roman Imperial Cult in Asia Minor* (Cambridge 1985).

Rice, E., *The Grand Procession of Ptolemy Philadelphus* (Oxford 1983).

Robert, L., *Hellenica*, I (Paris 1940).

Robert, L., *Opera Minora Selecta*, II (Amsterdam 1969).

Rogers, G.M., 'Demetrios of Ephesos: Silversmith and Neopoios?' *Belleten* (1987) 877–82.

Rossner, M., 'Asiarchen und Archiereis Asias', *Studii Clasice*, XVI (1974) 101–42.

Şahin, S., Schwertheim, E., and Wagner, J. (eds.), *Studien zur Religion und Kultur Kleinasiens. Festschrift für Friedrich Karl Dörner zum 65. Geburtstag am 28. Februar 1976*, I and II (Leiden 1978).

Scott, K., 'The Significance of Statues in Precious Metals in Emperor Worship', *TAPA*, 62 (1931) 101–23.

Sherwin-White, A., *Roman Foreign Policy in the East* (London 1984).

Talbert, R., *The Senate of Imperial Rome* (Princeton 1984).

Tilley, C., 'Interpreting Material Culture', in Hodder, I. (ed.), *The Meanings of Things* (London 1989) 185–94.

Trexler, R., 'Ritual in Florence: Adolescence and Salvation in the Renaissance', in *The Pursuit of Holiness in Late Medieval and Renaissance Religion*, ed. Trinkaus, C., and Oberman, H. (Leiden 1974) 200–64.

Trexler, R., 'Ritual Behavior in Renaissance Florence: The Setting', *Medievalia et Humanistica*, 34 (1983) 125–44.

Vermeule, C., *Roman Imperial Art in Greece and Asia Minor* (Cambridge 1968).

Veyne, P., *Bread and Circuses* (London 1990).

Ward-Perkins, J.B., *Roman Imperial Architecture* (London 1983).

Weber, E., and Dobesch, G. (eds.), *Römische Geschichte, Altertumskunde und Epigraphik. Festschrift für A. Betz* (Wien 1985).

Weber, M., *Economy and Society* (Berkeley 1978).

Whitehorne, J.E.G., 'Golden Statues in Greek and Latin Literature', *Greece and Rome*, 22, 2 (1975) 109–19.

Wood, J.T., *Discoveries at Ephesus* (London 1877).

Wörrle, M., *Stadt und Fest im kaiserzeitlichen Kleinasien* (Munich 1988).

Zanker, P., *The Power of Images in the Age of Augustus* (Michigan 1988)

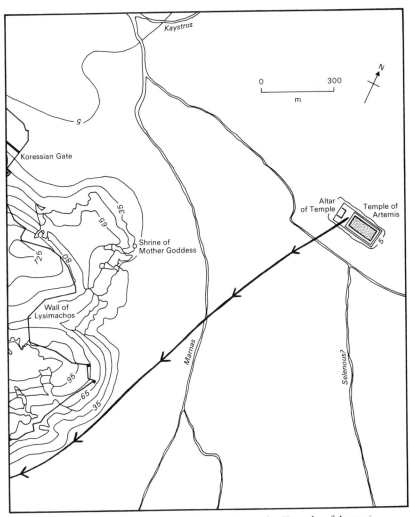

1 The route of the Procession of Statues from the Temple of Artemis across the Selenous and the Marnas toward the Magnesian Gate.

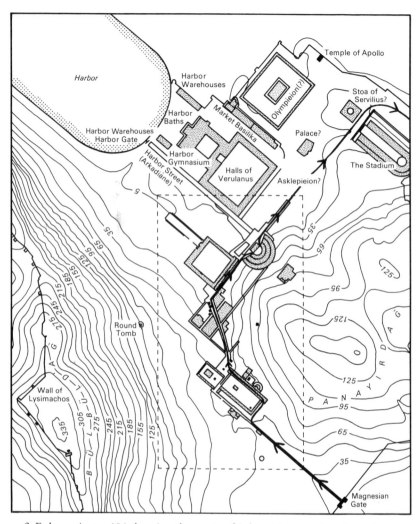

2 Ephesos in AD 104 showing the route of Salutaris' procession from the
Magnesian Gate to the Stadium, with architectural details of the
Harbor area.

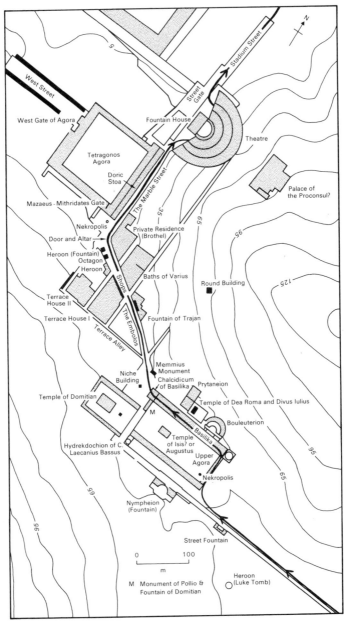

West Street

West Gate of Agora

Fountain House

Stadium Street

Street Gate

Theatre

Tetragonos Agora

Doric Stoa

Palace of the Proconsul?

Mazaeus - Mithridates Gate

The Marble Street

Nekropolis

Private Residence (Brothel)

Door and Altar

Heroon (Fountain) Octagon Heroon

Shops

Baths of Varius

Round Building

Terrace House II

Terrace House I

Terrace Alley

The Embolos

Fountain of Trajan

Memmius Monument

Niche Building

Chalcidicum of Basilika

Prytaneion

Temple of Domitian

Temple of Dea Roma and Divus Iulius

M

Basilika

Bouleuterion

Hydrekdochion of C. Laecanius Bassus

Temple of Isis? or Augustus

Upper Agora

Nekropolis

Nympheion (Fountain)

Street Fountain

0   100

m

M Monument of Pollio & Fountain of Domitian

Heroon (Luke Tomb)

3 Detailed architectural plan of the Upper and Lower city of Ephesos in AD 104.

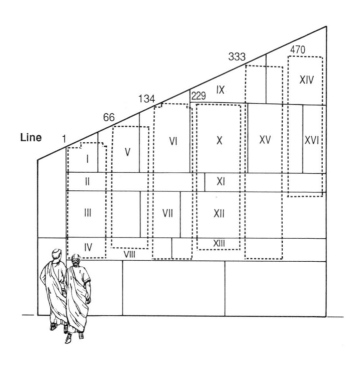

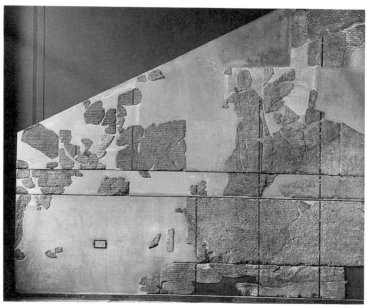

5a (bottom of opposite page) and b (above) The text of the inscription (by permission of the British Museum).

4 (top of opposite page) Two citizens of Ephesos (right figure, 165 cm or 5 feet 5 inches tall) in front of a diagram of the Salutaris foundation as adapted from the drawing in *IE*, Ia (Bonn 1979) 169.

6 The Temple of Artemis with the Basilika of John and the Mosque of Isa Bey on the Citadel of Ayasoluk in the background.

7 The Basilika of the Upper Agora, dedicated between AD 4 and 14.

8 The view down the Embolos toward the Library of Celsus.

9 The Fountain of Trajan on the northern side of the Embolos, dedicated by Aristio and Laterane between AD 102 and 104.

10 The view of the 'Marble Street', along the Doric Gallery, toward the Theatre.

11 The Theatre and the Arkadiane from above, on Panayir Dağ.

INDEX

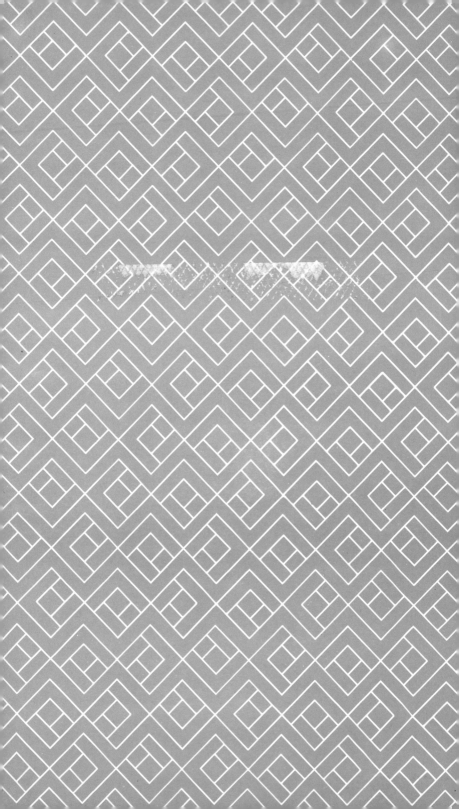